Austin Thomas

Two Fifteenth-century Cookery-Books

Austin Thomas

Two Fifteenth-century Cookery-Books

ISBN/EAN: 9783744789523

Printed in Europe, USA, Canada, Australia, Japan

Cover: Foto ©Andreas Hilbeck / pixelio.de

More available books at **www.hansebooks.com**

Two
Fifteenth-Century Cookery-Books.

HARLEIAN MS. 279 (ab. 1430), & HARL. MS. 4016 (ab. 1450),

WITH

EXTRACTS FROM ASHMOLE MS. 1429,
LAUD MS. 553, & DOUCE MS. 55.

EDITED BY
THOMAS AUSTIN.

LONDON:
PUBLISHED FOR THE EARLY ENGLISH TEXT SOCIETY
BY N. TRÜBNER & CO., 57 AND 59 LUDGATE HILL, E.C.

1888.

FOREWORDS.

The Ancient Cookeries edited in this volume have been copied from Harleian MSS. 279 and 4016, in the British Museum. The first MS. was copied, and partly prepared for the press, by the late Mr. Faulke Watling, of the University of Oxford, but his untimely death prevented his seeing it through the Press. This MS. is divided into three Parts, the first, headed *Kalendare de Potages dyuers*, containing 153 recipes: the second Part, *Kalendare de Leche Metys*, has 64 recipes, and the third Part, *Dyuerse bake metis*, 41 recipes. This MS., besides the Cookery, contains the Bills of Fare of several Banquets which are noticed more fully below. The date of this MS. is about 1430 or 1440, and has been given a little too early on pages 1 and 5. This has been collated with Ashmole MS. 1439, in the Bodleian, noted as A. in the text. For the second MS. it was originally intended to publish Douce MS. 55, in the Bodleian Library, but this was found imperfect, and was replaced by Harleian MS. 4016. They are similar books, and contain the same recipes in nearly the same words, the latter having a few that are not in the former, and *rice versâ*. The Harleian Cookery has 182 Recipes, while the Douce Cookery has 184. The two have been collated, and are of about the same date, *c.* 1450. Two Banquets are prefixed to this MS., which are also more fully noticed below. Several of the recipes of the Douce MS. are appended at page 115.

Some recipes for sauces, taken from Ashmole MS. 1439, are given at page 108. This MS. is about the same date as Harleian MS. 279, and has the same Feasts added, though some of the leaves are missing. These recipes are followed by others taken from two odd leaves in Laud MS. 553, in the Bodleian Library; see page 112.

The first English Cookery Book seems to be that of Neckam, in the twelfth century, but the *Forme of Cury* is the oldest practical work. This was compiled by the Chief Master Cooks of Richard II., and contains 196 recipes. The MS. that we possess was presented to Queen Elizabeth by Lord Stafford, and afterwards belonged to the Earl of Oxford, being purchased at his sale; it is now in the British Museum. This volume, with the Cookeries in WARNER, *Antiquitates Culinariæ* (1791), the Cookery published by MRS. NAPIER in 1882, known as the *Noble Boke of Cookry*, and *Liber Cure Cocorum*, have been used for purposes of reference, and elucidation of the recipes in the following MSS. The Cookery edited by Mrs. Napier had however, though then unknown, been previously edited by Pynson, as early as 1500, and again by John Byddell in 1650.

Much of the scientific Cookery was of course French, and, as will be seen in the following Recipes, the French titles got singularly perverted, and in some cases are extremely hard to recognise. For instance, who at first sight would recognise *Lait* under *Let*, *Froide* as *Fryit*, or *Sauce* in *Sauke*? Again *Herbelettes* becomes *Arbolettys*, and *Aigredoux* or *Aigredouce*, *Egredounrye*. The earliest Cookery Books that may be called English only date from the latter half of the seventeenth century.

Many of the Recipes that are given here would astonish a modern Cook. Our forefathers, possibly from having stronger stomachs, fortified by outdoor life, evidently liked their dishes strongly seasoned and piquant, as the Cinnamon Soup on p. 59 shows. Pepper, Ginger, Cloves, Garlic, Cinnamon, Galingale, Vinegar, Verjuice, and Wine, appear constantly in dishes where we should little expect them; and even Ale was frequently used in Cookery. Wine is used in the recipe for *Roast Partridge*, on p. 78, and also, as seems more natural to us, in the *Partridge Stews* on pages 9 and 78: it is also used for *Brawn in Poirrade* on p. 71. Ale is introduced in the *Bowres* on p. 8, in the *Sops Chamberlain* on p. 11, and in the *Mortrews de Chair* on p. 71, and is even used in the *Charlette* on p. 17, though Milk is also one of the ingredients: both Ale and Wine appear in the *Maumenny Royal*, on p. 22. Ale is also used with the *Tench in Bruet*

on p. 23, in the *Whelks* and *Oysters in Bruet*, on the same page, and
in fact seems to be a characteristic of the *Bruets*, as most of these
dishes have it as an ingredient. Ale was also mingled with the
water in which the fish was boiled : note the *Boiled Pike* on page
101, the *Plaice* on page 103, and the *Barbel*, p. 104. *Stale* Ale is
used for the *Oil Sops* on page 12, possibly in place of Vinegar.
Vinegar is used in the *Brawn* on pages 11 and 12, in the *Numbles of*
Venison on pages 10 and 70, and in the *Venison in broth* on p. 70 :
Vinegar or Verjuice is added to the *Stewed Mutton* on page 72,
Verjuice to the *Meat Custard* or *Pie*, on p. 74, and to the *Tripe* on
pages 7 and 18. Here our ancestors shewed their wisdom, as the
acid served as a corrective to the richness of the dishes. Sugar on
the other hand is also used with Brawn, see the *Blaunche Brawn* on
p. 34, and the *Fried Brawn* on p. 43, and was quite lately taken with
it at St. John's College, Oxford.

Almond milk was also a constant ingredient of the dishes : see the
Brawn in Comfit on page 71, and the *Sturmye* on page 26 : it was
also used with fish, as in the *Viande de Cyprus in Lent*, on page 28.
Both Sugar and Salt are used in the *Quinade* on page 27, and in the
Mortrews of Pork on page 28. Marrow was then much more used
than at present : note the 300 marrowbones on page 67.

Meats that we do not eat at the present day, or eat but seldom,
also appear in the Banquets of our ancestors, as Whale, Porpoise,
Seal, Swan, Crane, Heron, and Peacock ; while even the fishy Gull
was eaten. One would imagine that Sturgeon was then more
plentiful, to judge by the recipes for its cookery. Stockfish[1] was
of course much more in vogue, from the difficulty of obtaining
fresh fish. We may suppose that the Pudding of Capon Neck on
page 41, and the Pudding of Swan Neck on page 61, were dainties.
It would appear, from page 67, that Oxen were salted whole,
while, to descend to the other end of the scale, small birds were
eaten, as they still are in France (see the recipe on page 9, and
the Royal Banquet on page 58). Our flaming Christmas Pudding
is recalled by the *Viande Ardente* in the Banquet on page 61.

[1] See Glossary.

Some of the designs, or *Subtleties*, exposed on the Tables, as ornament, were of rather an ambitious character ; far more so than most of those mentioned on pages 57, 58, etc. These were devices in sugar and paste, and apparently in jelly, and were, at any rate at times, made to be eaten. Those displayed at the Enthronement of Abp. Warham in 1505, must have been of considerable size, as their description shews. They represented silvan and hunting scenes, and one displayed the interior of an Abbey Church with its various altars. In other cases such devices as a ship, fully armed with her ordnance, with the Barons of the Cinque Ports on board, or buildings with vanes and towers are exhibited. A great Custard, planted, is displayed in a banquet given by Leland in his *Collectanea*. The dishes were also gilt at times, for purpose of display, as a Leche Lombard in the same volume; a Peacock also is mentioned with a gilt nib. The Subtleties mentioned in this volume are of a much more modest character, representing simply an *Agnus Dei*, an *Eagle*, a *Doctor of Law*, etc. ; though those at the Stalling of John Stafford, on page 68, are more complicated. They seem both to have preceded the various courses, and also to have closed them, the first being called *Warners*, as giving warning of the entry of a fresh service.

We will now turn to the Banquets, whose Bills of Fare the Cookeries give us. The first of them [p. 57], both in place and importance, is that given at the Coronation of Henry the Fourth, and it has especial interest in the fact that a description of it is in the Chronicles of Froissart. Henry succeeded the dethroned Richard II. in 1399, as Froissart says, with the approval of the People of England ; Richard having previously personally surrendered his Crown to him. Stow says that Henry was chosen at Westminster Hall, at a Parliament there. The Archbishop of Canterbury, Thomas Arundel, having first preached a Latin sermon, on the text, *Habuit Jacob benedictionem à patre suo*, a Doctor of Law stood up, and read an Instrument which averred that Richard by his own confession was unworthy to reign, and would resign the Crown to a competent person. This having been read, the Archbishop advised

them to proceed to the election of a new king, and on a vote being
taken, the whole assembly was in Henry's favour; Richard not
having four votes for him. Henry then accepted the Crown, but
Stow says that he acquired the throne more by force than by lawful
succession or election.

Henry left the Tower of London, where he was then residing, on
Sunday the 12th of October, 1399, having previously made forty-six
new Knights of the Bath: he was dressed in a jacket after the
German mode. He went to Westminster to sleep, and at night
bathed, after the fashion of chivalry; next morning, Monday the
13th, and St. Edward's day, he confessed himself and heard three
Masses, preparatory to his Coronation. The Prelates and Clergy
then came in procession from the Abbey, and escorted him thither,
the return procession entering the sacred place at about nine o'clock
in the morning. The Lord Mayor with chosen Citizens of London,
were in the Procession, clothed alike in red. Cloth was laid down
for the king's passage, and the Abbey was also laid with cloth.
Henry was under a Canopy of blue silk, according to Froissart,
but Holinshed makes it of Cloth of Gold, with a golden bell jingling
at each corner; the Canopy was borne, says Holinshed, by sixteen
Barons of the Cinque Ports, four to each Staff, though Froissart
again differs, noting that it was borne by only four Burgesses, Dover
ones. Holinshed is more likely right. We may suppose that these
were the actual bearers of the Canopy: Stow, however, tells us that
there were four other, apparently honorary bearers—the Dukes of
York, Surrey, Aumarle, and the Earl of Gloucester. The Burgesses
had as fees Canopy, bells, and staves.

Preparatory to the Coronation and Banquet, Officials had been
appointed on October 4th. The Earl of Northumberland was High
Constable, and as holding the Isle of Man, bore on the king's left at
the Coronation a naked sword, called Lancaster's Sword, with which
Henry was girt when crowned; the Earl of Somerset carried a
sword before the king, and Thomas Beauchamp, Earl of Warwick,
bore a third sword, by inherited right, and was also Pantler: the

Earl of Westmoreland was Marshal. Sir Thomas Erpingham was
Lord Chamberlain, and furnished the monarch with water for his
hands, both before and after the Banquet, having as fee the Basin,
Ewer, Towels, etc. The Earl of Somerset was Carver, in right of
his Earldom of Lincoln, and Sir Wm. Argentine, by reason of his
tenure of the Manor of Wilmundale, or Wymondley, Herts, served
the king with the first cup of drink at dinner, and received the
silver-gilt Cup as his fee. Thomas, Earl of Arundel, was chief
Butler, and had the royal goblet as gift; Citizens of London,
chosen by the City, served in the Hall as attendants while Henry
banqueted. Lord Latimer was Almoner for the day, the silver
money being in a fine linen cloth; whilst William le Venour had
the honour of making wafers for the king: Edmond Chambers was
larderer, and Lord Grey of Ruthyn was Naperer (see post).

Henry took his seat on a throne that stood on a scaffold covered
with crimson cloth, and was then proclaimed king from the four
corners of it by the Archbishop of Canterbury, who asked the consent
of the people: his words were greeted with shouts of "Aye!"
Henry was then stripped naked to his shirt previous to anointing,
and was anointed in six places, as Froissart says, the head, breast,
shoulders, back, and hands: he was afterwards dressed in deacon's
clothes, with shoes of crimson velvet, and wore spurs without rowels.
The Sword of Justice was next drawn and blessed, and given to the
King, who returned it to the scabbard: it was then girt about him
by the Prelate, by whom the Crown of St. Edward was also placed
on his head. Lord Furnivall, as holding the Manor of Farnham,
gave the King his right-hand glove, and supported his arm while he
held the sceptre. Henry quitted the Abbey when Mass was over
and returned to Westminster Hall, where the Banquet was given.

At the Banquet the King sat at the first table, and at the Royal
board were the two Archbishops and seventeen Bishops: at the
bottom of the table was the Earl of Westmoreland with the Sceptre.
The King was served by the Prince of Wales, who carried the Sword
of Mercy, and on the opposite side by the Constable, bearing the

Sword of Justice. At the second table sat the five great Peers of England, probably the Dukes of Lancaster, York, Aumarle, Surrey,[1] and Exeter : at the third table were the principal Citizens of London, apparently the Lord Mayor and Aldermen, whose table was at the left of the Royal table. The Barons of the Cinque Ports sat at a table on the right of the King : at another table sat the newly-created Knights ; while all Knights and Squires of Honour sat at a sixth.

When the Feast was half over, the Champion, Sir Thos. Dymock, entered the Hall in full armour, mounted on a horse barded with crimson housings. He was equipped for Wager of Battle, and pre-ceded by another Knight, bearing his lance, and himself carried a drawn sword, and had by his side a naked dagger. The Champion presented a paper to the King, which affirmed that he was ready to offer combat to any Knight or Gentleman who dared maintain that Henry was not a lawful sovereign. By the King's orders Heralds proclaimed this Challenge in six different parts of the Hall and City, without gainsaying. The Champion received as his fee one of the best horses in the Royal Stable, with saddle and trappings, and one of the best suits of armour. When Henry had dined, and partaken of wine and spices, he withdrew to his private apartments, whither the Lord Mayor brought him a Cup of gold filled with wine, taking it again as his fee, together with a second cup that had contained water to allay the wine.

Next follows, on page 58, the Banquet given at the King's second marriage, in 1404. Henry, when Earl of Derby, had married Mary, the younger daughter and coheiress of Humphrey de Bohun, Earl of Hereford and Northampton, who died in 1394. His second wife, in whose honour the feast was given, was Joan of Navarre, widow of John de Montfort, Duke of Brittany. She landed a few days previously at Falmouth, and was married in Winchester Cathedral on the 7th of February : the Banquet was possibly in the Hall of

---

[1] Thomas Holand, Duke of Surrey, is said to have been deprived of his Dukedom on Oct. 6th 1399, and was soon afterwards beheaded. Stow however writes as above.

the Castle, which still remains. She was crowned at Westminster on the 28th of the same month, and survived her husband.

Fabyan's Chronicle gives an account of the Feast at the Coronation of the Queen of Henry V., which took place on Feb. 24th, 1420, being St. Matthew's Day; for which reason the Bill of Fare was entirely Fish, with the exception of Brawn with Mustard in the first Course. The Queen, at table, had the Archbishop of Canterbury on her right, and Henry Cardinal of Winchester on her left. The Duke of Gloucester had charge of the Banquet, and stood bareheaded before the Queen, while Sir Richard Neville was Carver. The brother of the Earl of Suffolk was cup-bearer, Sir John Stewart, Sewer, and Lord Clifford, Panterer; and Lord Grey of Ruthyn was again Naperer. The Barons of the Cinque Ports were at the head of the table on the right of the Queen, towards St. Stephen's Chapel, and the Bowchiers of the Chancery (? the Proctors) were below them at the same table: at a table on the Queen's left sat the Lord Mayor and Aldermen of London. The Bishops were at the head of the table next to that at which the Barons of the Cinque Ports sat, and the Ladies had a table next to the Lord Mayor's table. The Feast, as usual, was of three Courses, which were of the same character. Whale was served in the first Course: in the second was a *Leche damask* with the king's motto flourished on it, which was *Une sanz plus;* meaning of course the Queen. In the third Course was Porpoise, and in this Course was a subtlety of a Tiger looking into a Mirror, with a man on horseback fully armed, grasping a Tiger's whelp.

Henry the Sixth's Coronation Feast is also mentioned in Fabyan: like the others, it was in Westminster Hall, and was also of three Courses. In the first Course was a *Viande royale* planted with lozenges of gold, and a *Custard Royal* with a leopard of gold sitting thereon. There was a *Peacock enhackled* in the second Course: in the third was a *Baked meat* like a shield, quartered red and white, and set with gilt lozenges and Borage flowers. There was a subtlety both before and after this Course, the last one representing the

Virgin and Child, with St. George and St. Denis kneeling on either side, and presenting to the Queen a figure of Henry with the following ballad in his hand :—

> " O blessyd Lady, Cristes moder dere,
> " And thou, seynt George ! that called art her knyght ;
> " Holy seynt Denys, O marter most entere,
> " The sixt Henry here present in your syght,
> " Shedyth,[1] of your grace, on him your heuenly lyght :
> " His tender youth with vertue doth[1] auaunce,
> " Borne by discent, and by tytle of ryght,
> " Iustly to reygne in Englande and in Fraunce."

It is uncertain who the Lord de la Grey was, whose Banquet follows [p. 59] : if, however, the feasts are given in chronological order, the date can be assigned within a given period. Holinshed mentions a Lord Reginald Grey of Ruthyn that was Naperer[2] at Henry the Fourth's Coronation, on account of a manor that he held, and who bore the great spurs before Henry IV., by right of inheritance from the Earl of Pembroke. He is also mentioned above, on the previous page, and may be the person in question.

Next follows [p. 60] the Feast of Richard Fleming, Bishop of Lincoln from 1420 to 1431 : he was Canon of York when preferred to the Bishopric. As Bishop he exhumed and burnt the bones of Wycliffe, in accordance with the sentence of the Council of Constance, in 1425. A dinner of John Chandler, Bishop of Salisbury from 1417 to 1426, follows the above [p. 60], and was given at his entrance on the episcopate.

Then follows [p. 61] an Entertainment given on the 4th of December, 1424, on the occasion of the funeral of Nicholas Bubwith, Bishop of Bath and Wells. He was originally Bishop of London, for only a short time, and was transferred to Salisbury in 1407, and in the same year shifted to Bath and Wells. He was present at the Council of Constance. He built the north tower and a chantry in the Cathedral of Wells, he also founded an almshouse at Wells.

---

[1] Imperatives : *make advance*, in second case.   [2] He provided the table-linen.

It will be noticed with regard to this Dinner, that a separate fare of Fish was provided for the Clergy, doubtless on account of the melancholy occasion.

On page 62 is a festival given by John Stafford, Bishop of Bath and Wells, on the occasion of induction into his Episcopate, September 16th, 1425. He was born at Hook in the parish of Abbotsbury, Dorset, close to the Chesil Bank, and was descended from a collateral branch of the Stafford family. His father was Sir Humphrey Stafford, Sheriff of Somerset and Dorset, and his mother was Elizabeth Dyrham, relict of Sir John Maltravers. He was educated at Oxford, and first practised in the Ecclesiastical Courts, afterwards entering holy orders. He became Archdeacon of Salisbury in 1419, and was made Chancellor of England, according to Stow about the 12th of Henry VI., 1434, according to Hook in 1421. In 1422 he was Dean of St. Martin's Le Grand at Charing Cross: he was also Keeper of the Privy Seal, and Lord High Treasurer to Henry VI. He got the Bishopric of Bath and Wells, as stated above, in 1425, and in 1443 was translated to the Archbishopric of Canterbury, on the nomination of Pope Eugenius IV., to whom he had been recommended by Chichele, his predecessor. The Banquet that he gave on being made Archbishop is at page 68, and he gave quite a different Bill of Fare on that occasion. He officiated at the marriage of Henry VI. with Margaret of Anjou in 1445, and also crowned that Queen. He was a Statesman, and was instrumental in the dispersion of Jack Cade's forces: curiously enough he also engaged in trade. He died at Maidstone, May 25th, 1452, and was buried at Canterbury in the Martyrdom.

The last Feast in Harleian MS. 279 [p. 63], is one given at the wedding of the Earl of Devonshire, and is without date. Concerning the Earl in question, Mr. Cokayne, Norroy King at Arms, has been kind enough to supply the following note, through Dr. Furnivall :—

"Hugh Courtenay, Earl of Devon (or Devonshire), was born 1389, being aged 30 when he succeeded his father in that Earldom in 1419. His marriage, with Anne Talbot, was before 1414, and before he became an Earl. He died 1422.

"His son is probably the Earl you want, viz. Thomas Courtenay, Earl of Devon, born 1414 (being aged 8 in 1422), who became Earl on his father's death in 1422. He married Lady Margaret Beaufort, second daughter of John, Earl of Somerset, probably about 1431, when he would be but 17, but certainly before 1432, when their son Thomas, (aged 26 at his father's death in 1458,) was born. Lady Margaret's eldest brother was born 1401, and her eldest sister Joan, Queen of Scotland, was married in 1423, so that she probably was quite as old as, if not older than her husband."

The remaining Festival [p. 67] is that given to Richard the Second by the Bishop of Durham, at Durham House, London, on the 23rd of September, 1387. The Bishop that feasted the King was John Forham, or Fordham, who held the Bishopric from 1381 to 1388, having previously occupied the See of Ely. He was one of Richard's evil counsellers, and held the Office of Lord High Treasurer, but was discharged of it in 1386. He was among the Lords that rebelled against the King in 1388, but was not imprisoned, though in that year he was deprived of his See, and permitted to retire to his old Bishopric, which was of far less dignity.

The Editor must add, that he has to thank Dr. Furnivall for most kindly collating the text with that of both the MSS., and he has also to thank him for some hints and information. He has, besides, to thank the Rev. A. L. Mayhew for criticizing the glossary, and for furnishing him with some old French derivations, etc.

Oxford, *Nov.* 1888.

The Ashmole MS. gives, by collation, the following variations and additions, but a sheet or two of it is missing in the third part.

Pt. I, No. vi, line 3, " sette," not *sethe*, also in viij, p. 7, line 3.

xii, p. 8, line 1, A. adds, after " þer-to," " temper hit with alle : take raysons of corance clene wasshid : put þem þer-to."

xiiij, line 5, A. reads " styue," *i.e.* stew, not *stere* : rightly.

xxiiij, Title, A. " Brawne gruelle "; line 2, " pricke it."

xxxiij, line 5, after *Salt* is added " then cut fair brewis, and dresse theym yn disshes, & cast þe lire theron."

xxxv, page 13, line 1, " leche them in faire gobettis, and pike out the core, and cast."

xlv, line 4, " stue," altered from " streyne," for *stere*.

xlviij, line 2, after *Roysouns*, A. adds " þerto, raisons "; rightly.

lij, line 6, A. reads " sode in, and stepe þer-on," making sense.

lxvij, instead of [*mynce*], A. has " larde," *i.e.* " cut in thin slices."

lxxx, after *clene*, A. adds, " and sethe þem."

lxxxiiij, line 6, " cleue," before *nout*; making sense.

lxxxvij, line 7, after *is*, " & confeccions or chare de quynce a good quantite," inserted.

Cix, lines 1, 2, " and lete wexe al white," not " an make hem alle þe whyte."

Cx, after *Stokkefysshe* A. adds, " or of freishe mylwel or codling," and reads " of Plays."

Cxlv, line 6, " fro þe holys," rightly.

Cliiij, line 3, A. omits *sugre*, (the " white " means White of egg,) and in line 11 reads " a-boue " in place of " aneward."

Pt. II, viij, last line on p. 35, " and " after *Pepir*, making sense.

x, A. reads at line 6, *an lat it* " clene ouer-renue."

xij, page 37, A. adds " þe Ius," after *wrynge*, and has no " þe " before *grene*.

xiiij, page 37, " þanne take braw[n] y-broylyd and cast þer-to," added after " þer-to," in line 2.

xvij, page 37, last line, A. reads, " and so ley hit colde in þe dysshe, and þat but a litil, þat vnnethe þe bottumys be holnyd."

xxiij, page 39, line 1, the second *salt* is not in A.

xxvij, page 39, A. reads " al aboute loke þat " *it be ransched* ; " and lete hit be wel sodyn," later.

xxviij, page 40, after *Eyroun*, "and rawe creme or swete mylke," added.

xxix, page 40, after *Gredelle* A. adds, "til hit be broune."

xxxvij, p. 41, A. adds "fete," after *Piggys*, which is required; and reads "and moche sauge."

xxxix, last line on page 41, A. reads "& do þer-to a lytil pouder Canelle;"

xliv, page 42, last line, after *panne*, A. adds between lines, "& let frie y-nogh."

l, page 44, last line but two, A. adds "& let hete a litel," between lines, after "þer-on," and in next line adds, "and leche it, or els al hole," after *vp*.

lx, page 46, line eight, A. reads "white" before "Sug*re*," not "w*ith*-al."

Pt. III, xvj, page 50, last line, A. adds, "but lete þe cofyns," before *bake*; making sense.

xxij, page 51, no blank.

xxiij, page 52, A. adds after *cofyn*, line 8, "then caste in the sew rounde a-boute vppon hym yn þe cofyne," and makes sense.

The Editor did not discover the Ashmole MS. till much of the first Cookery was in print, and consequently was unable to make full use of it for purpose of collation. The reader will kindly correct the following Errata.

p. 15, note 4, read *Lozenges* in place of "long thin strips."

p. 17, last line, dele comma after *Almaunden.*

p. 19, l. 4, put comma after *mylke.*

p. 21, l. 14, read *slake Water;* 4th line from bottom, read "þif it [cleue] nowt," with A.

p. 27, l. 17, read, "or hony caste þer-to;" with no semicolon after *hony.*

p. 31, 4th line from bottom, read *þrifti.*

p. 48, l. 5, read "hele þin cofyns."

p. 49, l. 7, read "or a bore, or of a Bere:" l. 8, put semicolon after "Eyroun;" and dele the semicolon after *tyne,* reading *cyue* in place of that word, and also in place of the *tyne* in the line above.

p. 50, l. 20, read "for defaute," and before bottom line add, "but lete þe cofyns," with A.

p. 57, Heading 6, read "ad Episcopatum Bathonensem et Wellensem."

FIFTEENTH CENTURY COOKERY BOOK. I.

HARLEIAN MS. 279, ab. 1420 A.D.

---

[1] Incipit li Kalendare de Potages dyuers.

[1] leaf 1.

1

[1] *leaf 2.*   [2] *leaf 2 bk.*   [3] *leaf 3.*

[2] Hic incipit Kalendare de Leche Metys.

Here begynnyth dyuerse bake metis.

[1] *leaf* 5.

FIFTEENTH CENTURY COOKERY BOOK. I.

Ab. 1420 A.D.

---

¹POTAGE DYVERS.

.j. **Lange Wortys de chare.**—Take beeff and merybonys, and boyle yt in fayre water; þan take fayre wortys and wassche hem clene in water, and parboyle hem in clene water; þan take hem vp of þe water after þe fyrst boylyng, an cut þe leuys a-to or a-þre, and caste hem in-to þe beff, and boyle to gederys: þan take a lof of whyte brede and grate yt, an caste it on þe pot, an safron & salt, & let it boyle y-now, and serue forth.

.ij. **Lange Wortes de pesoun.**—Take grene pesyn, an washe hem clene an caste hem on a potte, an boyle hem tyl þey breste, an þanne take hem vppe of þe potte, an put hem with brothe yn a-noþer potte, and lete hem kele; þan draw hem þorw a straynowre in-to a fayre potte, an þan take oynonys, and screde hem in to or þre, an take hole wortys and boyle hem in fayre water: and take hem vppe, an ley hem on a fayre bord, an cytte on .iij. or iiij., an ley hem to þe oynonys in þe potte, to þe drawyd pesyn; an let hem boyle tyl þey ben tendyr; an þanne tak fayre oyle and frye hem, or ellys sum fresche broþe of sum maner fresche fysshe, an caste þer-to, an Safron, an salt a quantyte, and serue it forth.

.iij. **Joutes.**—Take Borage, Vyolet, Malwys, Percely, Yong Wortys, Bete, Auence, Longebeff, wyth Orage an oþer, pyke hem clene, and caste hem on a vessel, and boyle hem a goode whyle; þan take hem and presse hem on a fayre bord, an hew hem ryght smal, an put whyte brede þer-to, an grynd wyth-al; an þan caste hem in-to a fayre potte, an gode fresche brothe y-now þer-to þorw a straynowr, [& caste] þer-to .ij. or .iij. Marybonys, or ellys fayre fresche brothe of beff, and let hem sethe to-gederys a whyle:

an þan caste þer-to Safron, and let hem sethe to-gederys a whyle, an þan caste þer-to safron and salt; and serue it forth in a dysshe, an bakon y-boylyd in a-noþer dysshe, as men scruyth furmenty wyth venyson.

[1].iiij. **Caboges.**—Take fayre caboges, an cutte hem, an pike hem clene and clene wasshe hem, an parboyle hem in fayre water, an þanne presse hem on a fayre bord; an þan choppe hem, and caste hem in a faire pot with goode freysshe broth, an wyth mery-bonys, and let it boyle: þanne grate fayre brede and caste þer-to, an caste þer-to Safron an salt; or ellys take gode grwel y-mad of freys flesshe, y-draw þorw a straynour, and caste þer-to. An whan þou seruyst yt inne, knocke owt þe marw of þe bonys, an ley þe marwe .ij. gobettys or .iij. in a dysshe, as þe semyth best, & serue forth.

.v. **Whyte wortes.**—Take of þe erbys lyke as þou dede for jouutes, and sethe hem [in] water tyl þey ben neysshe; þanne take hem vp, an bryse hem fayre on a bord, as drye as þow may; þan choppe hem smale, an caste hem on a potte, an ley hem with flowre of Rye; take mylke of almaundys, an cast þer-to, & hony, nowt to moche, þat it be nowt to swete, an safron & salt; an serue it forth ynne, ryȝth for a good potage.

.vj. **Beef y-Stywyd.**—Take fayre beef of þe rybbys of þe fore quarterys, an smyte in fayre pecys, an wasche þe beef in-to a fayre potte; þan take þe water þat þe beef was soþin yn, an strayne it þorw a straynowr, an sethe þe same water and beef in a potte, an let hem boyle to-gederys; þan take canel, clowes, maces, graynys of parise, quibibes, and oynons y-mynced, perceli, an sawge, an caste þer-to, an let hem boyle to-gederys; an þan take a lof of brede, an stepe it with brothe an venegre, an þan draw it þorw a straynoure, and let it be stylle; an whan it is nere y-now, caste þe lycour þer-to, but nowt to moche, an þan let boyle onys, an cast safroun þer-to a quantyte; þan take salt an venegre, and cast þer-to, an loke þat it be poynaunt y-now, & serue forth.

.vij. **Gruelle a-forsydde.**—Take otemele, an grynd it smal, an sethe it [2]wyl, an porke þer-ynne, an pulle of þe swerde [3] an pyke owt þe bonys, an þan hewe it, an grynd it smal in a morter; þan neme þin [4] grwel an do þer-to, þan strayne it þorw a straynour, an put it in a potte an sethe it a lytel, an salt it euene[5]; an colour it wyth safroun, an serue forth rennyng.

.viij. **Venyson with Furmenty.**—Take whete an pyke it clene, and do it in a morter, an caste a lytel water þer-on; an stampe with a pestel tyl it

[1] lf. 6 back.   [2] leaf 7 (wyl = well).   [3] sward, rind, skin.   [4] thine.   [5] equally.

hole¹; þan fan owt þe holys,² an put it in a potte, an let sethe tyl it breke ;
fan set yt dounn, an sone after set it ouer þe fyre, an stere it wyl ; an whan
þow hast sothyn it wyl, put þer-inne swete mylke, an seþe it y-fere, an stere
it wyl ; and whan it is y-now, coloure it wyth safron, an salt it euene, and
dresse it forth, & þin venyson in a-nother dyshe with fayre hot water.

.ix. **Trype de Motoun.**—Take þe pownche of a chepe, and make it clene,
an caste it on a pot of boylyng water, an skyme it clene, an gader þe grece
al a-way, an lat it boyle tyl it be tender ; þan ley it on a fayre bord, an
kyt it in smale pecys of the³ peny brede, an caste it on an erþen pot with
strong brothe of bef or of moton ; þanne take leuys of þe percely an hew
hem þer-to, an let hem boyle to-gederys tyl þey byn tender, þan take
powder of gyngere, and verious, þan take [Safroun]⁴ an salt, and caste
þer-to, an let boyle to-gederys, an serue in.

.x. **Wardonys in syryp.**—Take wardonys, an caste on a potte, and boyle
hem till þey ben tender ; þan take hem vp and pare hem, an kytte hem in
to⁵ pecys ; take y-now of powder of canel, a good quantyte, an caste it on
red wyne, an draw it þorw a straynour ; caste sugre þer-to, an put it [in] an
erþen pot, an let it boyle : an þanne caste þe perys þer-to, an let boyle to-
gederys, an whan þey haue boyle a whyle, take pouder of gyngere an caste þer-
to, an a lytil venegre, an a lytil safron ; an loke þat it be poynaunt an dowcet.

⁶.xj. **Froyde almoundys.**—Take blake sugre, an cold water, an do hem
to⁷ in a fayre potte, an let hem boyle to-gedere, an salt it an skeme it clene,
an let it kele ; þan take almaundys, an blawnche hem clene, an stampe
hem, an draw hem, with þe sugre water thikke y-now, in-to a fayre vessel :
an [yf] þe mylke be noȝt swete y-now, take whyte sugre an caste þer-to.

.xij. **Fride Creme of Almaundys.**—Take almaundys, an stampe hem, an
draw it vp wyth a fyne thykke mylke, y-temperyd wyth clene water ; throw
hem on, an sette hem in þe fyre, an let boyle onys : þan tak hem a-down,
an caste salt þer-on, an let hem reste a forlongwey⁸ or to, an caste a lytyl
sugre þer-to ; an þan caste it on a fayre lynen clothe, fayre y-wasche an
drye, an caste it al a-brode on þe clothe with a fayre ladel : an let þe clothe
ben holdyn a-brode, an late all þe water vnder-nethe þe clothe be had a-way,
an þanne gadere alle þe kreme in þe clothe, an let hongy on an pyn, an let
þe water droppe owt to⁷ or .iij. owrys ; þan take it of þe pyn, an put it on a
bolle of tre, and caste whyte sugre y-now þer-to, an a lytil salt ; and ȝif it

---

¹ Hull, lose the husks.   ² Hulls ; husks.   ³ MS. *they.*   ⁴ Added from A.
⁵ ? = ' in two pieces.'   ⁶ lf. 7 bk.   ⁷ two.   ⁸ Other MS. *forlange.*

wexe þikke, take swete wyn an put þer-to þat it be noȝt sene: and whan it is I-dressid in the maner of mortrewys, take red anys in comfyte, or þe leuys of borage, an sette hem on þe dysshe, an serue forth.

.xiij. Creme Boylede.—Take creme or mylke, & [1] brede of paynemayn, or ellys of tendyr brede, an breke it on þe creme, or ell*es* in þe mylke, an set it on þe fyre tyl it be warme hot; and þorw a straynour þrowe it, and put it in-to a fayre potte, an sette it on þe fyre, an stere euermore: an whan it is almost y-boylyd, take fayre ȝolkys of eyron, an draw hem þorw a straynowr, an caste hem þer-to, and let hem stonde ouer the fyre tyl it boyle almost, an till [2] it be skylfully [3] þikke; þan [4]caste a ladel-ful, or more or lasse, of boter þer-to, an a good quantite of whyte sugre, and a litel salt, an þan dresse it on a dysshe in maner of mortrewys.

.xiiij. Quystis Scune.—Take a pece of beef or of mutou*n*, and wyne and fayre water, and caste in-to a potte, an late hem boyle, an skeme it wyl an clene; þan take quys*tes*, an stoppe hem wyth-in wyth hole pepyr, and marwe, an þan caste hem in-to þe potte, an ceuere wyl þe potte, an let hem stere ryȝth wyl to-gederys; an þan take powder gyngere, an a lytel verious an salt, and caste þer-to, an þanne serue hem forth in a fayre dysshe, a quyste or to in a dysshe, in þe mauer of a potage: an whan þowe shalt serue hem forth, take a lytil of þe broth, an put ou dysshe wyth quystys, an serue forth.

.xv. Bowres.—Take Pypis, Hertys, Nerys, Myltys, an Rybbys of the Swyne; or ellys take Mawlard, or Gees, an chop hem smal, and thanne parboyle hem in fayre water; an þan take it vp, an pyke it clene in-to a fayre potte, an caste þer-to ale y-now, & sawge an salt, and þan boyle it ryȝth wel; and þanne serue it forthe for a goode potage.

.xvj. Fylettys en Galentyne.—Take fayre porke, þe fore quarter, an take of þe skyne; an put þe porke on a fayre spete, an rost it half y-now; þan take it of, an smyte it in fayre pecys, & caste it on a fayre potte; þan take oynonys, and schrede hem, an pele hem (an pyle hem nowt to smale), an frye in a panne of fayre grece; þan caste hem in þe potte to þe porke; þan take gode broth of moton or of beef, an caste þer-to, an þan caste þer-to pouder pepyr, cauel, clowys, an macys, an let hem boyle wyl to-gederys; þan tak fayre brede, an vynegre, an stepe þe brede w*ith* þe same brothe, an strayne it on blode, with ale, or ellys sawnderys, and [5]salt, an lat hym boyle y-now, an serue it forth.

---

[1] MS *or.*   [2] MS. *þow.*   [3] reasonably.   [4] leaf **8.**   [5] leaf 8 bk.

.xvij. Garbage.—Take fayre garbagys of chykonys, as þe hed, þe fete, þe lyuerys, an þe gysowrys; washe hem clene, an caste hem in a fayre potte, an caste þer-to freysshe brothe of Beef or ellys of moton, an let it boyle; an a-lye it wyth brede, an ley on Pepir an Safroun, Maces, Clowys, an a lytil verious an salt, an serue forth in the maner as a Sewe.

.xviij. Pertrich stewyde.—Take fayre mary,[1] brothe of Beef or of Motoun, an whan it is wyl sothyn, take þe brothe owt of þe potte, an strayne it thorw a straynour, an put it on an erþen potte; þan take a gode quantyte of wyne, as þow it were half, an put þer-to; þan take þe pertryche, an stuffe hym wyth hole pepir, an merw,[2] an than sewe þe ventys of þe pertriche, an take clowys an maces, & hole pepir, an caste it in-to þe potte, an let it boyle to-goderys; an whan þe pertryche is boylid y-now, take þe potte of þe fyre, an whan thou schalt serue hym forth, caste in-to þe potte powder gyngere, salt, safron, an serue forth.

.xix. Smale Byrdys y-stwyde.—Take smale byrdys, an pulle hem an drawe hem clene, an washe hem fayre, an schoppe of þe leggys, and frye hem in a panne of freysshe grece ryȝt wyl; þan ley hem on a fayre lynen clothe, an lette þe grece renne owt; þan take oynonys, an mynce hem smale, an frye hem on fayre freysshe grece, an caste hem on an erþen potte; þan take a gode porcyon of canel, an wyne, an draw þorw a straynoure, an caste in-to þe potte with þe oynonys; þan caste þe bryddys þer-to, an clowys, an maces, an a lytil quantyte of powder pepir þer-to, an lete hem boyle to-goderys y-now; þan caste þer-to whyte sugre, an powder gyngere, salt, safron, an serue it forth.

.xx. Papyns.—Take fayre Mylke an Flowre, an drawe it þorw a [3]straynoure, an set it ouer þe fyre, an let it boyle a-whyle; þan take it owt an let it kele; þan take ȝolkys of eyroun y-draw þorwe a straynour, an caste þer-to; þan take sugre a gode quantyte, and caste þer-to, an a lytil salt, an sette it on þe fyre tyl it be sum-what þikke, but let it nowt boyle fullyche, an stere it wyl, an putte it on a dysshe alle a-brode, and serue forth rennyng.

.xxj. Blandissorye.—Take almaundys, an blawnche hem, an grynde hem in a morter, an tempere hem with freysshe broþe of capoun or of beef, an swete wyne; an ȝif it be lente or fyssday, take brothe of þe freysshe fysshe, an swete wyne, an boyle hem to-goderys a goode whyle; þenne take it up, an caste it on a fayre lynen cloþe þat is clene an drye, an draw under þe

---

[1] Marrow. No. 28, in Douce MS., has myȝty brothe.　[2] Marrow.　[3] lf. 9.

cloþe, wyth a ladel, alle þe water þat þow may fynde, ryth as þow makyst cold creme; þanne take owt of the potte, an caste it in-to a fayre potte, an let it boyle ; an þanne take brawn of Capoun, an tese it smal an bray it [in] a morter : or ellys on a fyssday take Pyke or Elys, Codlyng or Haddok, an temper it wyth almaun mylke, an caste Sugre y-now þer-to ; An þan caste hem in-to þe potte and lete hem boyle to-goderys a goode whyle : þenne take it owt of þe potte alle hote, an dresse it in a dysshe, as meni[1] don cold creme, an sette þer-on Red Anys in comfyte, or ellys Allemaundys blaunchid, an þanne serue it forth for a goode potage.

.**xxij. Venyson in Broth.**—Take Rybbys of Venysoun, and wasshe hem clene in fayre water, an strayne þe same water þorw a straynoure in-to a potte, an caste þer-to Venysoun, also Percely, Sawge, powder Pepyr, Clowys, Maces, Vynegre, and a lytyl Red wyne caste þere-to ; an þanne latte it boyle tyl it be y-now, & serue forth.

.**xxiij. Nomblys of þe venyson.**—Take þe Nombles of Venysoun, an cutte hem smal whyle þey ben raw ; þan take Freysshe broþe, Watere, an Wyne, of eche a quantyte, an powder Pepir an Canel, and let hem [2]boyle to-goderys tyl it be almost y-now ; An þenne caste powder Gyngere, an a lytil venegre an Salt, an sesyn it vp, an þanne serue it forth in þe maner of a gode potage.

.**xxiiij. Drawyn grwel.**—Take fayre water an lene Bef, an let hem boyle ; an whan þe beef hath y-boylid, take it vp an pyke it, an lete it blede in-to[3] a vessel, an þenne caste þe blode an þe Fleysshe in-to a potte ; an þanne caste þer-to Otemele, Percely, & Sawge, an make þer-of an gode grwele ; þen draw it þorw a straynowre, an putte it on a fayre potte, an let it boyle ; þanne caste þer-to Salt ; An ȝif it be nowt brown y-now, take a litil blode an caste þer-to or it be y-draw, an make it broun y-now, an serue it forth.

.**xxv. Balloke Brothe.**—Take Elys and fle hem, an kytte hem in gobowns, an caste hem in-to a fayre potte wyth fayre water ; þan take Percely and Oynonys, an schrede hem to-goderys nowt to smal ; take Clowes, Maces, an powder Pepyr, an caste þer-to a gode porcyon of wyne ; þen take ȝest of New ale an caste þer-to, an let boyle : an when þe Elys byn wyl y-boylid, take fayre stokfysshe, an do a-way þe skyn, an caste þer-to, an let boyle a whyle ; þen take Safroun and Salt, an a lytil Venegre, an caste þer-to, an serue forth.

.**xxvj. Coleys.**—Take a gode Capoun an boyle hem tendere, an pyke a-way

<hr>

[1] MS. *men*.   [2] lf. 9 bk.   [3] MS. *blede in-to*, repeated.

clene þe bonys an þe Skyn, an bray hym in a morter, an tempere hym wyth
þe same brothe, an strayne hym þorw a straynoure; þenne take þe brawn an
þe fleysshe, an a lytil whyte brede, an bray hem alle to-gederys in a morter;
þen take þe lycowr of þe bonys, an þe skyn, an þe brothe þat þe Capoun was
sothyn ynne, an with al tempere it, but nowt to þicke; þen put it in a potte,
an let it be al hote, but let it boyle for no þing; an caste þer-to a litil powder
of Gyngere, Sugre an Salt.   An ȝif it be on a fyssheday, take Haddok,
Pyke, Tenche, Reȝge, Codlynd, an pyke a-way þe bonys 'an tempere wyth
almaunde mylke; an make it hot, an caste þer-to Sugre an Salt, an serue
forth.

.xxvij. **Soupes dorye.**—Take gode almaunde mylke y-draw wyth wyn,
an let hem boyle to-gederys, an caste þer-to Safroun an Salt; an þan take
Paynemayn, an kytte it an toste it, an wete it in wyne, an ley it on a
dysshe, an caste þe syrip þer-on.   And þan make a dragge of powder
Gyngere, Sugre, canel, Clowes, Maces, an caste þer-on When it is y-dressid,
an serue þanne forth for a potage gode.

.xxviij. **Soupes Jamberlayne.**[2]—Take Wyne, Canel, an powder of
Gyngere, an Sugre, an of eche a porcyoun, þan take a straynoure & hange it
on a pynne, an caste ale þer-to, an let renne twyis or þryis throgh, tyl it
renne clere; an þen take Paynemaynne an kyt it in maner of brewes, an
toste it, an wete it in þe same lycowre, an ley it on a dysshe, an caste
blawnche powder y-now þer-on; an þan caste þe same lycour vp-on þe
same soppys, [an] serue hem forth in maner of a potage.

.xxix. **Lyode Soppes.**—Take Mylke an boyle it, an þanne take ȝolkys of
eyroun y-tryid fro þe whyte, an draw hem þorwe A straynoure, an caste hem
in-to þe mylke, an sette it on þe fyre an hete it, but let it nowt boyle; an
stere it wyl tyl it be somwhat þikke; þenne caste þer-to Salt & Sugre, an
kytte fayre paynemaynnys in round soppys, an caste þe soppys þer-on, an
serue it forth for a potage.

.xxx. **Soupes dorroy.**—Shere Oynonys, an frye hem in oyle; þanne take
Wyne, an boyle with Oynonys, toste whyte Brede an do on a dysshe, an
caste þer-on gode Almaunde Mylke, & temper it wyth wyne: þanne do þe
dorry a-bowte, an messe it forth.

[3].xxxj. **Brawn en Peuerade.**—Take Wyne an powder Canel, and draw it
þorw a straynour, an sette it on þe fyre, and lette it boyle, an caste þer-to
Clowes, Maces, an powder Pepyr; þan take smale Oynonys al hole, an

---

[1] leaf 10.   [2] Chamberlain.   [3] leaf 10 bk.

par-boyle hem in hot watere, an caste þer-to, and let hem boyle to-gederys; þan take Brawn, an lesshe it. but nowt to þinne. An ȝif it sowsyd be, lete it stepe a whyle in hot water tyl it be tendere, þan caste it to þe Sirip; þen take Sawnderys, an Vynegre, an caste þer-to, an lete it boyle alle to-gederys tyl it be y-now; þen take Gyngere, an caste þer-to, an so serue forth ; but late it be nowt to þikke ne to þinne, but as potage shulde be.

.**xxxij. Auter brawn en peuerade.**—Take myghty brothe of Beef or of Capoun, an þenne take clene Freysshe Brawn, an sethe it, but not y-now; An ȝif it be Freysshe Brawn, roste it, but not I-now, an þan leche it in peeys, an caste it to þe brothe. An þanne take hoole Oynonys, & pylle hem, an þanne take Vynegre þer-to, and Canelle, and sette it on þe fyre, an draw yt þorw a straynoure, and caste þer-to; þen take Clowys, Maces, an powder Pepyr, an caste þer-to, and a lytil Saunderys, an sette it on þe fyre, an let boyle tylle þe Oynonys an þe Brawn ben euyne sothyn, an nowt to moche; þan take lykoure y-mad of Bred an Vinegre an Wyne, an sesyn it vp, an caste þer-to Saffroun to make þe coloure bryth, an Salt, an serue it forth.

.**xxxiij. Oyle Soppys.**—Take a gode quantyte of Oynonys, an mynse hem not to smale, an sethe in fayre Water : þan take hem vp, an take a gode quantite of Stale Ale, as .iij. galouns, an þer-to take a pynte of Oyle fryid, an caste þe Oynonys þer-to, an let boyle alle to-gederys a gode whyle ; then caste þer-to Safroune, powder Pepyr, Sugre, an Salt, an serue forth alle hote as tost*es*, [1]as in þe same maner for a Mawlard & of a capou, & *hoc quære*.[2]

.**xxxiv. Chardewardon.**—Take Pere Wardonys, an sethe hem in Wyne or in fayre water; þan take an grynd in a morter, an drawe hem þorwe a straynoure wyth-owte ony lycoure, an put hem in a potte w*ith* Sugre and clarifyd hony, an Canel y-now, an lete hem boyle ; þan take it fro þe fyre, an let kele, an caste þer-to ȝolkys of Raw eyroun, tylle it be þikke; & caste þer-to pouder Gyngere y-now, an serue it in manere of Fysshe;[3] an ȝif if it be in lente, lef þe ȝolkys of Eyroun. & lat þe remenaunt boyle so longe tylle it be þikke, as þow it had be tempe*ry*d wyth þe ȝolkys, in þe maner of charde quynce ; an so serue hem in maner of Rys.

.**xxxv. Perys en Composte.**—Take Wyne an Canel, & a gret dele of Whyte Sugre, an set it on þe fyre & hete it hote, but let it nowt boyle, an draw it þorwe a straynoure ; þan take fayre Datys, an pyke owt þe stonys, an leche hem alle þinne, an caste þer-to ; þanne take Wardonys, an pare hem and sethe hem,

---

[1] lf. 11.   [2] 'look for this : see this,' generally *q.v.*
[3] For *Rys*; see Douce MS. No. 55, and the end of this recipe. A. also reads *fische.*

an leche hem alle þinne, & caste þer-to in-to þe Syryppe : þanne take a lytil
Sawnderys, and caste þer-to, an sette it on þe fyre ; an ȝif þow hast charde
quynce, caste þer-to in þe boyling, an loke þat it stonde wyl with Sugre, an
wyl lyid wyth Canel, an caste Salt þer-to, an let it boyle ; an þan caste yt
on a treen vessel, & lat it kele, & serue f[orth].

.xxxvj. Vele, kede, or henne in Bokenade.—Take Vele, Kyde, or Henne,
an boyle hem in fayre Water, or ellys in freysshe brothe, an smyte hem in
pecys, an pyke hem clene ; an þan draw þe same brothe þorwe a straynoure,
an caste þer-to Percely, Sawge, Ysope, Maces, Clowys, an let boyle tyl þe
flesshe be y-now ; þan sette it from þe fyre, & a-lye it vp with raw ȝolkys of
eyroun, & caste þer-to pouder Gyngere, Veriows, Safroun, & Salt, & þanne
serue it forth for a gode mete.

[1].xxxvij. Autre Vele en bokenade.—Take Vele, an Make it clene, and
hakke it to gobettys, an sethe it ; an take fat brothe, an temper vp þine
Almaundys þat þou hast y-grounde, an lye it with Flowre of Rys, and do
þer-to gode powder of Gyngere, & Galyngale, Canel, Maces, Quybybis, and
Oynonys y-mynsyd, & Roysonys of coraunce, & coloure yt wyth Safroun, and
put þer-to þin Vele, & serue f[orth].

.xxxviij. Storion in brothe.—Take fayre Freysshe Storgeoun, an choppe
it in fayre water ; þanne take it fro þe fyre, an strayne þe brothe þorw a
straynoure in-to a potte, an pyke clene þe Fysshe, an caste þer-to powder
Pepir, Clowes, Maces, Canel ; & þanne take fayre Brede, and stepe it in þe
same lycowre, & caste þer-to, an let boyle to-gederys, & caste þen Safroun
þer-to, Gyngere, an Salt, & Vynegre, & þanne serue it forth ynne.[2]

.ixl.[3] Oystres en grauey.—Take gode Mylke of Almaundys, an drawe it
wyth Wyne an gode Fysshe broþe, an sette it on þe fyre, & let boyle ; &
caste þer-to Clowes, Maces, Sugre an powder Gyngere, an a fewe parboylid
Oynonys y-mynsyd ; þan take fayre Oystrys, & parboyle hem in fayre Water,
& caste hem þer-to, an lete hem boyle to-gederys ; & þanne serue hem forth.

.xl. Oystrys in grauy bastard.—Take grete Oystrys, an schale hem ; an
take þe water of þe Oystrys, & ale, an brede y-straynid, an þe water also,
an put it on a potte, an Gyngere, Sugre, Saffron, powder pepir, and Salt,
an let it boyle wyl ; þen put yn þe Oystrys þer-to, and dresse it forth.

.xlj. Gelyne in dubbatte.—Take an Henne, and rost hure almoste y-now,
an choppe hyre in fayre pecys, an caste her on a potte ; an caste þer-to
Freysshe broþe, & half Wyne, Clowes, Maces, Pepir, Canelle, an stepe it with

---

[1] lf. 11 bk. [2] *i.e.* into the dining-room. [3] *i.e.* i from xl.

þe Same broþe, fayre brede & Vynegre : an whan it is y-now, serue it
forth.

[1].**xlij. Conyng, Mawlard, in gely or in cyuey.**—Take Conynge, Hen,
or Mawlard, and roste hem alle-most y-now, or ellys choppe hem, an frye
hem in fayre Freysshe grece ; an frye myncyd Oynenons, and caste alle in-to
þe potte, & caste þer-to fayre Freysshe brothe, an half Wyne, Maces, Clowes,
Powder pepir, Canelle ; þan take fayre Brede, an wyth þe same brothe stepe,
an draw it þorw a straynoure wyth vynegre ; an whan it is wyl y-boylid,
caste þo lycoure þer-to, & powder Gyngere, & Salt, & sesyn it vp an *serue*
f[orth].

.xliij. Mortrewes of Fysshe.—Take Gornard or Congere, a-fore þe navel
wyth þe grece (for be-hynde þe navel he is hery[2] of bonys), or Codlyng,
þe lyuer an þe Spaune, an sethe it y-now in fayre Water, and pyke owt þe
bonys, and grynde þe fysshe in a Morter, an temp*er* it vp wyth Almaunde
Mylke, an caste þer-to gratyd brede ; þan take yt vp, an put it on a fayre
potte, an let boyle ; þau caste þer-to Sugre and Salt, an serue it forth as
other Mortrewys.   And loke þat þow caste Gyngere y-now a-boue.

.xliiij. Mortrewys de Fleyssh.—Take Porke, an seþe it wyl ; þanne take
it vppe and pulle a-way þe Swerde,[3] an pyke owt þe bonys, an hakke it and
grynd it smal ; þenne take þe sylf brothe, & temp*er* it w*ith* ale ; þeu take
fayre gratyd brede, & do þer-to, an seþe it, an coloure it w*ith* Saffroun, & lye
it w*ith* ȝolkys of eyroun, & make it euen Salt, & caste pouder Gyngere,
a-bouyn on þe dysshe.

.xlv.—For to make Blawnche Perrye.—Take þe Whyte of the lekys, an
seþe hem in a potte, an presse hem vp, & hacke he*m* smal on a bord.   An
nym gode Almaunde Mylke, an a lytil of Rys, an do alle þes to-gederys, an
seþe an stere it wyl, an do þer-to Sugre or hony, an dresse it yn ; þanne
take powderd Elys, an seþe hem in fayre Water, and broyle hem, an kytte
hem in long pecys.   And ley .ij. or .iij. in a dysshe, and putte þin[4] perrey
in a-noþer dysshe, [5]an serue þe to dysshys to-gederys as Venysou*n* w*ith*
Furmenty.

.xlvj. Poumes.—Take fayre buttys of Vele & hewe hem, and grynd hem
in a morter, & wyth þe ȝolkys of eyroun, & w*ith* þe whyte of eyroun ;
an caste þer-to powder Pepyr, Canel, Gyngere, Clowys powþ*er*, & datys
y-mynced, Safroun, & raysonys of Coraunce, an sethe in a panne wyth fayre
water, an let it boyle ; þan wete þin handys in Raw eyroun, þan take it an

---

[1] leaf 12.   [2] Hairy.   [3] Rind, skin.   [4] Thine.   [5] lf. 12 bk.

rolle it in þin hondys, smaller or gretter, as þow wolt haue it, an caste it in-to boyling water, an let boyle y-now; þan putte it on a Spete round, an lete hem rosty; þen take flowre an ʒolkys of eyroun, an þe whyte, an draw hem þorwe a straynowre, an caste þer-to pouder Gyngere, an make þin[1] bature grene with þe Ius of Percely, or Malwys, in tyme of ʒere Whete, an caste on þe pommys as þey turne a-boute, & serue f[orth].

.**xlvij. Cawdelle Ferry.**—Take ʒolkys of eyroun Raw, y-tryid fro the whyte; þan take gode wyne, and warme it on þe potte on a fayre Fyre, an caste þer-on ʒolkys, and stere it wyl, but let it nowt boyle tylle it be þikke; and caste þer-to Sugre, Safroun, & Salt, Maces, Gelofres, an Galyngale y-grounde smal, & flowre of Canelle; & whan þow dressyst yn, caste blanke pouder þer-on.

.**xlviij. Tayloures.**—Take a gode mylke of Almaundys y-draw with Wyne an Water, an caste hym in-to a potte, and caste gret Roysouns of corauns, Also mencyd Datys, Clowes, Maces, Pouder Pepir, Canel, Safroun, & a gode dele Salt, & let boyle a whyle; þan take it and ly[2] it wyth Flowre of Rys, or ellys with Brede y-gratyd, & caste þer-to Sugre, & serue forth lyke Mortrewys, & caste pouder of Gyngere a-boue y-now.

.**xlix. Bryndons.**—Take Wyn, & putte in a potte, an clarifiyd hony, an Saunderys, pepir, Safroun, Clowes, Maces, & Quybibys, & mynced Datys, Pynys and Roysonys of Corauns, & a lytil Vynegre, [3]& sethe it on þe fyre; an sethe fygys in Wyne, & grynde hem, & draw hem þorw a straynoure, & caste þer-to, an lete hem boyle alle to-gederys; þan take fayre flowre, Safroun, Sugre, & Fayre Water, ande make þer-of cakys, and let hem be þinne Inow; þan kytte hem y lyke lechyngys,[4] an caste hem in fayre Oyle, and fry hem a lytil whyle; þanne take hem owt of þe panne, an caste in-to a vesselle with þe Syrippe, & so serue hem forth, þe bryndonys an þe Sirippe, in a dysshe; & let þe Sirippe be rennyng, & not to styf.

.**l. A potage on fysshday.**—Take an Make a styf Poshote of Milke an Ale; þan take & draw þe croddys þorw a straynoure wyth[5] whyte Swete Wyne, or ellys Rochelle Wyne, & make it sum-what rennyng an sum-what stondyng, & put Sugre a gode quantyte þer-to, or hony, but nowt to moche; þan hete it a lytil, & serue it forth al a-brode in þe dysshys; an straw on Canel, & Gyngere, and ʒif [þou] haue Blank powder, straw on and kepe it a[s] whyte as yt may be, & þan serue f[orth].

---

[1] Thine.   [2] Lye; allay.   [3] leaf 13.
[4] long thin strips.   [5] MS. with wyth.

.lj. Cawdelle de Almaunde.—Take Raw Almaundys, & grynde hem, an temper hem vp with gode ale, and a lytil Water, and draw it þorw a straynoure in-to a fayre potte, & late it boyle a whyle : & caste þer-to Safroun, Sugre, and Salt, & þan serue it forth al hotte in maner of potage.

.lij. Gyngaudre.—Take þe Lyuerys of Codlyngys, Haddok, Elys, or þe Hake hed, or Freysshe MylweH hedys, þe Pouches, & þe Lyuerys, an sethe hem in fayre Water ; þan take hem vp on a fayre bord, & mynce smal þe pouches ; þan take gode freysshe brothe of Samoun, or Turbut, or of Elys, & cast þe mynced pouches þer-to, & pouder Pepyr, & let boyle ; þan take þe brothe, þe pouches & þe lyuerys wer sodonn in, in a stipe [1] or on fayre brede, & draw þorw a straynoure, & þan mynce þe lyuer in fayre pecys ; & [2]whan þe pouches haue boylid, an þe licoure, caste þe leuer þer-to, an let boyle a whyle : þan caste þer-to þe lyuerys, Wyne, Venegre, Safroun, Salt, & late it boyle a whyle, and serue forth þat rennyng.

.Liij. Rapeye.—Take half Fygys & halfe Roysonys, and boyle hem in Wyne ; þan bray hem in a morter, an draw wyth the same lycoure þorw a straynoure so þikke þat it be stondynge ; þanne take Roysons of Corauns, Pynys, Clowys, Maces, Sugre of Siprys, an caste þer-to : þan putte it on a potte ; þan take Saunderys a fewe, Pepir, Canel, an a litel Safroun ; an ʒif it be noʒt stondyng, take [a] lytil flowre of Amidons, an draw it þorw a straynwoure, an caste þer-to Salt, & serue forth stondyng.

.Liiij. Rapeye.—Take almaundys, an draw a gode mylke þer-of, and take Datys an mynce hem smal, an put þer-on y-now ; take Raw Appelys, an pare hem and stampe hem, an drawe hem vppe with wyne, or with draf of Almaundys, or boþe ; þan caste pouder of Gyngere, Canel, Maces, Clowes, & caste þer-on Sugre y-now ; þan take a quantyte of flowre of Rys, an þrowe þer-on, & make it chargeaunt, an coloure it wyth Safroun, an with Saunderys, an serue forth ; an strawe Canel a-boue.

.lv. Iuschelle of Fysshe.—Take fayre Frye of Pyke, and caste it raw on a morter, an caste þer-to gratid brede, an bray hem as smale as þow mayste ; & ʒif it be to stondyng, caste þer-to Almaunde mylke, an bray hem to-gederys, an stere it to-gederys, & caste þer-to a littel Safroun & Salt, an whyte Sugre, an putte al in a fayre Treen bolle, & toyle[3] it to-gederys wyth þin hond, an loke þat it be noʒt to chargeaunt, but as a man may pore it out of þe bolle ; and þan take a Chafoure or a panne, an caste þer-in fayre grauey of pyke or of Freysshe Samoun, y-draw þorw a straynoure, & sette

---

[1] ? meaning.   [2] lf. 13 bk.   [3] *Twille* in Douce MS.

[1] it on þe fyre; þanne take fayre Percely an Sawge, an caste þer-to, an lat it
boyle, an caste þer-to a lytil Safroun an Salt; and whan it hath y-boylid
a whyle, stere it faste, an caste þe Stuffe þer-to, an stere it euermore; an
whan alle is oute of þe bolle, caste a litil an a litil in-to þe chafoure, or
þe panne; stere it soffter an sofftere, tylle it come to-gedere; þan gader it
to-gederys with a ladelle or a Skymoure, softe, tille it be round to-gedere;
þanne take it fro þe fyre, an sette þe vesselle on a fewe colys, an late it
wexe styf be hys owne acord; þan serue forth.

.lvj. **Charlette.**—Take Mylke, an caste on a potte, with Salt and Safroun
y-now; þan hewe fayre buttys of Calf or of Porke, noȝt to fatte, alle smal, an
kaste þer-to; þan take Eyroun, þe whyte an the ȝolke, & draw þorw a straynoure; an whan þe lycoure ys in boyling, caste þer-to þin Eyroun and Ale,
& styre it tylle it Crodde; þan presse it a lytil with a platere, an serue
forth; saue, caste þer-on broþe of Beeff or of Capoun.

.lvij. **Charlet a-forcyd ryally.**—Take gode Mylke of Almaunde; take
tender Porke, an hew it smal, an bray it on a morter; take eyroun, an draw
þorw a cloþe; temper vppe þin flesshe þer-with, an caste on þe potte; take
þe mylke, an sette it ouer þe fyre; sesyn it wyth Salt an Safroun caste þer-on;
boyle it, an when yt komyth on hy, a-lye it with wyne, an sette it a-doun;
take vppe an ley it on a cloþe, an presse it a lytil; ondo it a-ȝen, & caste
þer-on pouder Gyngere, Galyngale, Sugre y-now; menge it to-gederys, presse
it a-aȝen, seþe [2] þe broþe wyl; take styf Almaunde mylke y-temperyd with
Freysshe brothe, & caste þer-on Saffroun an Sugre y-now, an a lytil Salt,
& boyle it, þan take and set it owt; leche now þin mete, & ley þer-of in a
dysshe; take þe sewe, & ley a-boue; take Maces & Sugre, & caste þer-on, &
serue f[orth].

[3].lviij. **Let lory.**—Take Mylke, an sette it ouer þe fyre; take Salt &
Safroun, an caste þer-to; take Eyroun, þe ȝolke an þe Whyte y-strainyd a lyte,[4]
& caste it þer-to; whan þe Mylke his skaldyng hote, caste þe stuf þer-to,
an þenne stere yt tyll it crodde; and ȝif þou wolt haue it a-forsyd with
lyȝt coste, Take Mylke, & make it skaldyng hote, & caste þer-to Raw ȝolkes of
Eyroun, Sugre, pouder Gyngere, Clowes, Maces, an let not fully boyle; & so
hote, dresse it forth, an ley it on þe crodde; & ȝif þou wolt a-forse it in maner
of charlet, do it in fastyng dayis, & serue it forth.

.lix. **Furmenty** with **purpaysse.**—Make þin Furmenty in þe maner as I
sayd be-fore, saue temper it vp with Almaunden, Mylke, & Sugre, & Safroun,

---

[1] leaf 14.   [2] MS. seye.   [3] leaf 14 bk.   [4] lyte = little.

þan take þin Purpays as a Freysshe Samoun, & sethe it in fayre Water; & when he is I-sothe y-now, bawde it & leche it[1] in fayre peeys, & serue wyth Furmenty in hote Water.

.lx. **Trype of Turbut or of Codelynge.**—Take þe Mawes of Turbut, Haddok, or Codelyng, & pyke hem clene, & skrape hem, & Wasshem clene, and parboyle hem in gode Freysshe broþe of Turbut or Samoun, or Pyke; þan kytte Percely smalle, & caste þer-to, & kytte þe Mawys of a peny brede, & caste alle togederys in-to a potte, & let it boyle to-gederys; & whan þey bin soþin tendyr, caste þer-to Safroun, & Salt, & Veryous, & pouder Gyngere, & serue f[orth].

.lxj. **A goos in hogepotte.**—Take a Goos, & make hure clene, & hacke hyre to gobettys, & put yn a potte, & Water to, & sethe to-gederys; þan take Pepir & Brennyd brede, or Blode y-boylyd, & grynd y-fere Gyngere & Galyngale & Comyn, & temper vppe with Ale, & putte it þer-to; & mynce Oynonys, & frye hem [2]in freysshe grece, & do þer-to a porcyon of Wyne.

.lxij. **Conyngys in graueye.**—Take Conyngys, & make hem clene, & hakke hem in gobettys, & sethe hem, oþer larde hem & Rost hem; & þanne hakke hem, & take Almaundys, & grynde hem, & temper hem vppe with gode Freysshe brothe of Flesshe, & coloure it wyth Safroun, & do þer-to a porcyon of flowre of Rys, & do þer-to þen pouder Gyngere, Galyngale, Canel, Sugre, Clowys, Maces, & boyle it onys & seþe it; þen take þe Conyngys, & putte þer-on, & dresse it & serue it forth.

.lxiij. **Harys in Cyueye.**—Take Harys, & Fle hem, & make hem clene, an hacke hem in gobettys, & sethe hem in Water & Salt a lytylle; þan take Pepyr, an Safroun, an Brede, y-grounde y-fere, & temper it wyth Ale; þan take Oynonys & Percely, y-mynced smal to-gederys, & sethe hem be hem self, & afterward take & do þer-to a porcyon of Vynegre, & dresse in.

.lxiiij. **Capoun in consewe.**—Take a Capoun, & make hem[3] clene, & sethe hym in Water, percely, Saucreye & Salt; & whan he his y-now, quarter hym; þan grynde Almaundys, & temper vppe wyth þat brothe of þe Capoun; or ellys take þe ʒolkys of Eyroun, & make it chargeaunt, & strayne þe Almaundys & boyle it; take Sugre a goode porcyoun, & do þer-yn; & when it ys y-boylid, ley þe Capoun in þe dysshe, & put þat Sew a-boue, & strawe þer-vppe-on Sugre, & send it yn with almaȝ.

.lxv. **Hennys in bruette.**—Take þe hennys, & skalde hem, & ope hem, & wasshe hem clene, & smyte hem to gobettys, & sethe hem wyth fayre porke;

---

[1] *leche it*, repeated in MS.   [2] leaf 15.   [3] ? for *hym*; but see p. 19, No. lxxij.

þan take Pepyr, Gyngere, & Brede, y-grounde y-fere, and temper it vppe with þe same brothe, or ale draft, & coloure it with Safroun, & seþe it to-goderys, & serue forth.

.lxvj. **Bruette Sareson.**—Take Almaundys & draw a gode mylke [1] & flowre of Rys, & Porke & Brawen of Capoun y-sode, or Hennys smale y-grounde, & boyle it y-fere, & do in-to þe mylke; & þan take pouder Gyngere, Sugre, & caste a-boue, an serue forth.

.lxvij. **Bruet of Almaynne.**—Take Almaundys, & draw a gode mylke þer-of with Water; take Capoun, Conyngys or Pertriches; smyte þe Capoun, or kede, or Chykonys, Conyngys: þe Pertriche shal ben hol: þan blaunche þe Fleyssh, an caste on þe mylke; take larde & [mynce] it, & caste þer-to; take an mynce Oynonys & caste þer-to y-nowe, do Clowes & smal Roysonys þer-to; caste hol Safroun þer-to, þan do it to þe fyre, & stere it wyl; whan þe fleysshe ys y-now, sette it on þe fyre, an do þer-to Sugre y-now; take pouder Gyngere, Galyngale, Canel, & temper þe pouder wyth Vynegre, & caste þer-to; sesyn it with salt, & serue forth.

.lxviij. **Bruet of Almaynne in leute.**—Take fyne þikke Mylke of Almaundys; take **datys**, an mynce hem smal þer-on; take Sugre y-nowe, & straw þer-on, & a lytil flowre of Rys; sylt, [2] & serue forth whyte, & loke þat it be rennyng.

.lxix. **Whyte Mortrewes.**—Take Almaunde Mylke & Floure of Rys, & boyle it y-fere; þenne take Capoun & Hennys, & sethe hem and bray hem as smal as þou may, & ly [3] it with an Ey [4] or to, & also a-lye it vppe with þe mylke of Almaundys, & make hem chargeaunt as Mortrewes schuld be, & dresse hem forth, & caste Canel a-boue, or Gyngere. Blanke pouder is best.

.lxx. **Fauntempere.**—Take Almaunde Mylke, & Floure of Rys, Sugre, an gode pouþer Gyngere, Galyngale, Canel, & gode Erbys, and stampe hem [&] grynd hem þorw a cloþe, & caste þer-to, & boyle yt, an a-lye it wyth ȝolkys of Eyroun, & make it more boyle; þan take Maces, Quybibes, & Geloferys, & caste þer-to whan that þou schalt dresse it yn.

[5] .lxxj. **Murrey.**—Take Porke an Vele, & sethe it, & grynd it, & draw it with þe self brothe; þen take bred y-gratyd, & pouder of Gyngere & of Galyngale, & Houy, an caste þer-to, & boyle it y-fere; & make it chargeaunt, & coloure it with Saunderys & serue f[orth].

.lxxij. **Talbottys.**—Take an Hare, an fle hem clene; þen take þe blode, & Brede, an Spycery, an grynde y-fere, & draw it vppe with þe brothe;

---

[1] lf. 15 bk.   [2] ?sprinkle.   [3] Allay; mix.   [4] Egg.   [5] leaf 16.

þan take Wyne or Ale, an cast þer-to, & make gobettys, & þanne serue it forth.

.lxxiij. **Conyngys in cyveye.**—Take Conyngys, an fle hem, & seþe hem, & make lyke þou woldyst make a sewe, saue alle-to-choppe hem, & caste Safroun & lyer þer-to, & Wyne.

.lxxiiij. **Arbolettys.**—Take Milke, Boter an Chese, & boyle in fere; þen take eyroun, & cast þer-to; þan take Percely & Sawge & hacke it smal, & take pouder Gyngere & Galyngale, and caste it þer-to, and þan serue it forth.

.lxxv. **Spyneye.**—Take þe Flowþerys of Hawthorun; boyle hem & presse hem, bray hem smal, temper hem vppe wyth Almaunde Milke, & lye it with Abyndoun [1] & Gratyd brede & flowre of Rys; take Sugre y-now & put þer-to, or Hony in defawte, & colowre it wyth þe same þat þe flowrys ben, & serue f[orth].

.lxxvj. **Brasele.**—Take Dace, Troutys, & Roche, an roste hem on a gredelle; þan seþe in Wyne, & caste Veryous þer-to, powder of Gyngere, & Galyngale, & dresse it yn.

.lxxvij. **Crem de Coloure.**—Take an make þicke Milke of Almaundys, & do it in a potte, & sethe it ouer þe fyre; þan take a fayre Canvas, an put it þer-on, & late renne out þe Water; þen take þe halfyndele, & put it in a pot of erþe; þen take the oþer halfyndele, & parte it [in] to,[2] & make þe half ȝelow, & do þer-yn Wyn, Sugre, Clowes, Maces, powder of Canelle; take [blank in MS.] & grynd a lytel in a morter; [3] þan temper it vppe wyth almaunde mylke, & do euery of hem in a potte, an loke þat it be y-like chargeauut, & sette it ouer þe fyre, an boyle it a lytyl, an serue forth.

.lxxviij. **Colouryd Sew with-owt fyre.**—Take fowre pounde of Almaundys, & ley in Water ouer eue, an blanche hem, and on þe morwe grynde hem ryth wyl, an draw þer-of a þicke mylke; þan take Rys, and wasshem clene, an gryud hem wyl, & draw hem vppe wyth þe Mylke þorw a straynoure, an do it on a bolle, & parte it in þe vesselle, an do in al whyte Sugre, an euery vesselle Clowes, Maces, Quybibes, & pouder Canelle; An lete þat on party ben whyte, þat oþer ȝelow, & þat oþer grene with Percely; And ley of euery a leche [4] in a dysshe, an loke þat Mylke be temperyd wyth wyne, an þat [5] oþer with Rede wyn.

.lxxix. **Apple Muse.**—Take Appelys an sethe hem, an Serge [6] hem þorwe a Sefe in-to a potte; þanne take Almaunde Mylke & Hony, an caste þer-to, an

---

[1] Amydon.   [2] Two.   [3] lf. 16 bk.   [4] a strip.   [5] MS. þan.   [6] Sift.

gratid Brede, Safroun, Saunderys, & Salt a lytil, & caste all in þe potte & lete hem sethe; & loke þat þou store it wyl, & serue it forth.

.lxxx. **Salomene.**—Take gode Wyne, an gode pouder, & Brede y-ground, an sugre, an boyle it y-fere; þan take Trowtys, Rochys, Perchys, oþer Carpys, oþer alle þese y-fere, an make hem clene, & aftere roste hem on a Grydelle; þan hewe hem in gobettys: whan þey ben y-sothe, fry hem in oyle a lytil, þen caste in þe brwet; aud whan þou dressist it, take Maces, Clowes, Quybibes, Gelofrys, an cast a-boue, & serue forth.

.lxxxj. **Blaundysorye.**—Take Almaunde Mylke, an flowre of Rys, and brawn of Capounys or of hennys, & pouder Gyngere, & boyle it y-fere, & make it chargeaunt; an whan þou dressest yn, nym Maces, Quybibes, & caste a-boue, & serue f[orth].

[1].lxxxij. **Blamang.**—Take Rys, an lese [2] hem clene, & wasshe hem clene in flake Water, & þan sethe hem in Watere, & aftyrward in Almaunde Mylke, & do þer-to Brawn of þe Capoun aftyrward in-to a-noþer almaunde Mylke, an tese it smal sumdele with a pyn, an euer as it wolt caste [3] þer-to, stere it wel; nym Sugre and caste þer-to, þen make it chargeaunt; þen take blawn-chyd Almaundys, an frye hem, an sette hem a-boue, whan þou scruyst ynne; & ȝif þou wolt, þou myȝte departe hem with a Cawdelle Ferry y-wreten [4] before [No. xlvij. p. 15, and cxxxix. p 31], an þan serue forth.

.lxxxiij. **Vyaund de cyprys bastarde.**—Take gode wyne, & Sugre next Aftyrward, & caste to-gedere; þenne take whyte Gyngere, and Galyngale, & Canel fayre y-mynced; þen take Iuse of Pereile & Flowre of Rys, & Brawn of Capoun & of Chykonnys I-grounde, & caste þer-to; An coloure it wyth Safroun & Saunderys, an a-ly it with ȝolkys of Eyroun, & make it chargeaunt; an whan þou dressest it yn, take Maces, Clowes, Quybibes, and straw a-boue, & serue forth.

.lxxxiiij. **Vyaund de ciprys Ryalle.**—Take þe to del [5] ȝolkys of eyron, þe þridde dele Hony; take Clowes & kutte hem; take Roysonys, tak brawn of Capoun, & hewe it smal; caste al in a potte, & lat boyle & store it wyl; take wyne an boyle hem, & make a Syryppe; take of [6] þe potte al a-bowte, þer as it hangyth, & late it boyle wyl tille it be as chargeaunt as it may; take þin þombe [7] & pylt [8] þer-on, & ȝif it cleuey, let it boyle, & ȝif it nowt, sette it owt a-non in a clen bolle, an wete þin bolle in þe Syrippe, and caste þin mete þer-on; & whan þow dressist þi mete, leche it & caste þin [9] Syryppe a-bouyn vppe-on, & serue forth.

---

[1] lf. 17 (? *Blamanger*).   [2] pick.   [3] stick.   [4] Written.
[5] Two parts.   [6] off.   [7] Thumb.   [8] Put.   [9] Thy.

.lxxxv. **Gaylede.**—Take Almaunde Mylke & Flowre of Rys, & do þer-to Sugre or Hony, & Powder Gyngere & Galyngale; þen take figys, [1]an kerue hem a-to, or Roysonys y-hole,[2] or hard Wastel y-dicyd[3] and coloure it with Sauuderys, & sethe it & dresse hem yn.

.lxxxvj. **Rys.**—Take a porcyoun of Rys, & pyke hem clene, & sethe hem welle, & late hem kele; þen take gode Mylke of Almanndys & do þer-to, & seþe & stere hem wyl; & do þer-to Sugre an hony, & serue f[orth].

.lxxxvij. **Maumenye ryalle.**—Take Vernage, oþer strong Wyne of þe beste þat a man may fynde, an putte it on a potte, & caste þer-to a gode quantyte of pouder Canelle, & sette it on þe fyre, an ȝif it an hete; & þanne wrynge it soft þorw a straynoure, þat þe draf go nowt owte, & put on a fayre potte, & pyke fayre newe pynys, & wasshe hem clene in Wyn, & caste a gode quantyte þer-to, & take whyte Sugre þer-to, as moche as þe lycoure is, & caste þer-to; & draw a few Sawnderys wyth strong wyne þorwe a stray-noure, an caste þer-to, & put alle ou on[4] potte, & caste þer-to Clowys, a gode quantyte, & sette it on þe fyre, & ȝif it a boyle; þen take Almaundys, & draw hem with mythty Wyne; & at þe firste boyle ly it vppe with Ale, & ȝif it a boyle, & sette it on þe fyre, and caste þer-to tesyd brawn, (of[5] defaute of Pertriche or Capoun,) a gode quantyte of tryid Gyngere perase,[6] & sesyn it vppe with pouder Gyngere, & Salt & Safroun; & ȝif it is to stondyng, a-ly it with Vernage or swete Wyne, & dresse it Flat with þe backe of a Sawcere in þe Vernage or myȝthty Wyne, & loke þat þou haue Sugre y-nowe, & serue forth hote.

.lxxxviij. **Mammenye bastarde.**—Take a potelle of Clarifiyd Hony, & a pounde of Pynys, & a pounde of Roysouns Coraunce, & [a] pound of Saunderys, & pouder canelle, & .ij. galouns of Wyne or Ale, & a pound of Pepir, & caste alle on a potte, & skym yt; þan take .iij. pounde of Amyndons, & a galon of Wyne, & a gode galon of Venegre, & let stepe vp to-gederys, & draw þorw a straynoure; [7]an whan þe potte boylith, caste þe lycoure þer-to, an lat it be alle stondyng; þan take pouder Gyngere, Salt & Safron, an sesyn it vppe, an serue alle flat on a dysshe, aH hote, an caste pouder Gyngere þer-on, an serue f[orth].

.lxxxix. **Elys in Gauncelye.**—Take Elys, an fle hem, & sethe hem in Water, an caste a lytil Salt þer-to; þan take Brede y-Skaldyd, an grynd it, an temper it with þe brothe an with Ale · þan take Pepir, Gyngere, an Safroune, an grynd alle y-fere; þan neme Oynonys, an Percely, an boyle

---

[1] lf. 17 bk.   [2] ? unstoned.   [3] diced, cut into small squares.
[4] In one.   [5] In.   [6] ? meaning.   [7] lf. 18.

it in a possenet wel, þen caste alle to-gederys, an sethe y-fere & serue f[orth].

.lxxxx. **Hennys in Gauncelye.**—Take Hennys, an roste hem; take Mylke an Garleke, an grynd it, an do it in a panne, an hewe þin hennys þer-on with ȝolkys of eyron, an coloure it with Safroun an Mylke, an serue forth.

.lxxxxj. **Vyolette.**—Nym Almaunde Mylke, an flowre of Rys, and pouder Gyngere, Galyngale, Pepir, Datis, Fygys, & Rasouys y-corven, an coloure it with Safroun, an boyle it & make it chargeaunt; an whan þou dressyste, take þe flowres, an hew hem, an styre it þer-with; nyme þe braunchys with þe flowres, an sette a-boue and serue it Forth.

.lxxxxij. **Oystrys in bruette.**—Take an schene[1] Oystrys, an kepe þe water þat cometh of hem, an strayne it, an put it in a potte, & Ale þer-to, an a lytil brede þer-to; put Gyngere, Canel, Pouder of Pepir þer-to, Safroun an Salt; an whan it is y-now al-moste, putte on þin Oystrys: loke þat þey ben wyl y-wasshe for[2] þe schullys: & þan serue forth.

.lxxxxiij. **Walkys[3] in bruette.**—Take [Walkys] an sethe in Ale, þen pyke hem clene; þan wasshem in Water an Salt be hem-self, & fyrst wyth Ale & Salt, an do so whele þey ben slepyr[4]; þen putte hem in [5]Vynegre, an ley Perceli a-boue, an serue ynne.

.lxxxxiiij. **Tenche in bruette.**—Take þe Tenche, an sethe hem & roste hem, an grynde Pepir an Safroun, Bred and Ale, & tempere wyth þe brothe, an boyle it; þen take þe Tenche y-rostyd, an ley hym on a chargeoure; þan ley on þe sewe a-boue.

.lxxxxv. **Tenche in cyueye.**—Take a tenche, an skalde hym, roste hym, grynde Pepir an Safroun, Brede an Ale, & melle it to-gederys; take Oynonys, hakke hem, an frye hem in Oyle, & do hem þer-to, and messe hem forth.

.lxxxxvj. **Tenche in Sawce.** —Take a tenche whan he is y-sothe, and ley him on a dysshe; take Percely & Oynonys, & mynce hem to-gederys; take pouder Pepir, & Canelle, & straw þer-on; take Vynegre, an caste Safroun þer-on, an coloure it, an serue it forth þanne alle colde.

.lxxxxvij. **Chykonys in bruette.**—Take [an] Sethe Chykonys, & smyte hem to gobettys; þan take Pepir, Gyngere, an Brede y-grounde, & temper it vppe wyth þe self brothe, an with Ale; an coloure it with Safroun, an sethe an serue forth.

.lxxxxviij. **Blamanger of Fyshe.**—Take Rys, an sethe hem tylle they brekyn, & late hem kele; þan caste þer-to mylke of Almaundys; nym

---

[1] for schele.   [2] on account of.   [3] Whelks.   [4] Slippery; slimy.   [5] lf. 18 bk.

Perche or Lopstere, & do þer-to, & melle it; þan nym Sugre with pouder Gyngere, & caste þer-to, & make it chargeaunt, and þan serue it forth.

.**xxxxix. Sardeyne**ȝ.—Take Almaundys, & make a gode Mylke of Flowre of Rys, Safroun, Gyngere, Canelle, Maces, Quybibeȝ; grynd hem smal on a morter, & temper hem vppe with þe Mylke; þan take a fayre vesselle, & a fayre parte of Sugre, & boyle hem wyl, & rynsche þin dysshe alle a-bowte with-ynne with Sugre or oyle, an þan serue forth.

¹.**C. Roseye.**—Take Almaunde Mylke an flowre of Rys, & Sugre, an Safroun, an boyle hem y-fere; þan take Red Rosys, an grynd fayre in a morter with Almaunde mylke; þan take Loches, an toyle² hem [with] Flowre, an frye hem, & ley hem in dysshys; þan take gode pouder, and do in þe Sewe, & caste þe Sewe a-bouyn þe lochys, & serue forth.

.**Cj. Eyron en poche.**—Take Eyroun, broke hem, an sethe hem in hot Water; þan take hem Vppe as hole as þou may; þan take flowre, an melle with Mylke, & caste þer-to Sugre or Hony, & a lytel pouder Gyngere, an boyle alle ȝ-fere, & coloure with Safroun; an ley þin Eyroun in dysshys, & caste þe Sewe a-boue, & caste on pouder y-now. Blawnche pouder ys best.

.**Cij. Muskelys in bruette.**—Take þe Muskelys whan þey ben y-sothe, & pyke owt þe Muskele of þe schulle, & pyke a-way ye here: þau take brede, an pepir & Safroun y-grounde, & temper it vp with þe brothe; & ȝif þou wolt, a-lye it with Wyne or with Ale, & serue f[orth].

.**Ciij. Fygeye.**—Take Fygys, an sethe hem tylle þey ben neysshe, þan bray hem tylle þey ben smal; þenne take hem vppe an putte hem in a potte, & Ale þer-to; þan take Bred y-gratyd, an Pyneȝ hole, & caste þer-to, & let boyle wyl; & atte þe dressoure, caste on pouder Canel y-now, & serue forth: & ȝif þow wolt colour yt in .iij. maners, þou myȝt, with Saunderys, Safroun, & of hym-self, and ley on pouder y-now, & serue f[orth].

.**Ciiij. Bolas.**—Take fayre Bolasse, wasshe hem clene, & in Wyne boyle hem þat þey be but skaldyd bywese, & boyle hem alle to pomppe,³ & draw hem þorw a straynoure, & a-lye hem with flowre of Rys, & make it chargeaunt, & do it to þe fyre, & boyl it; take it of, & do þer-to whyte Sugre, gyngere, Clowys, Maces, Canelle, & store it wyl to-gederys: þanne take gode perys, ⁴& sethe hem wel with þe Stalke, & sette hem to kele, & pare hem clene, and pyke owt þe corys; þan take datis, & wasshe hem clene, & pyke owt þe Stonys, & fylle hem fulle of blaunche poudere: þan take þe

¹ leaf 19.   ² Rub, cover.   ³ Pulp.   ⁴ lf. 19 bk.

Stalke of þe Perys, take þe Bolas, & ley .iij. lechys in a dysshe, & sette þin perys þer-yn.

.Cv. **Lorey de Boolas.**—Take Bolas, & seþe hem a lytil, & draw hem þorw a straynoure, & caste hem in a broþe ; & do þer-to Brede y-gratyd, & boyle y-fere, & ʒolkys of eyroun y-swengyd, & a-lyid ; take Canel, and Galyngale, Skemyd hony, & do þer-to, & sethe wyl, & serue forth.

.Cvj. **Rapeye of Fleysshe.**—Take lene Porke y-sode & y-grounde smalle, & tempere it vppe with þe self broþe, & do it in a potte, an caste þer-to a lytil honye, & boyle it tyl it be chargeaunt ; & a-lye it wyth ʒolkys of Eyroun, & coloure it with Saunderys, & dresse forth, and pouder Marchaunt.

.Cvij. **Sore Sengle.**—Take Elys or Gurnard, & parte hem half in Wyne, & half in watere, in-to a potte ; take Percely and Oynonys & hewe hem smalle ; take Clowes or Maces & caste þer-on ; take Safroun, & caste þer-to, & sette on þe fyre, & let boyle tylle it be y-now ; þen sette it a-doun ; take poudere Gyngere, Canelle, Galyngale, & temper it vppe with Wyne, & cast on þo potte & serue forth.

.Cviij. **Prymerose.**—Take oþer half-pound of Flowre of Rys, .iij. pound of Almaundys, half an vnce of hony & Safroune, & take þe flowre of þe Pryme-rose, & grynd hem, and temper hem vppe with Mylke of þe Almaundys, & do pouder Gyngere þer-on : boyle it, & plante þin skluce[1] with Rosys, & serue f[orth].

.Cix. **Gelye de chare.**—Take caluys fete, & skalde hem in fayre water, an make hem alle þe whyte. Also take howbys of [2]Vele, & ley hem on water to soke out þe blode ; þen take hem vppe, an lay hem on a fayre lynen cloþe, & lat þe water rennyn out of [hem] ; þan Skore[3] a potte, & putte þe Fete & þe Howhys þer-on ; þan take Whyte Wyne þat wolle hold coloure, & cast þer-to a porcyon, an non oþer lycoure, þat þe Fleysshe be ouer-wewyd[4] with-alle, & sette it on þe fyre, & boyle it, & Skeme it clene ; an whan it is tendyr & boylid y-now, take vppe þe Fleyshe in-to a fayre bolle, & saue þe lycoure wyl ; & loke þat þow haue fayre sydys of Pyggys, & fayre smal Chykenys wyl & clene skladdyd & drawe, & lat þe leggys an þe fete on, an waysshe hem in fayre water, & caste hem in þe fyrste brothe, an sethe it a-ʒen ouer þe fyre, & skeme it clene ; lat a man euermore kepe it, an blow of þe grauy. An in cas þe lycoure wast[5] a-way, caste more of þe same wyne þer-to, & put þin honde þer-on ; & ʒif þin hond waxe clammy, it is a syne of godenesse,

---

[1] viscous compound?   [2] leaf 20.   [3] Scour.
[4] See other *Cookery*, No. 174, *wese.*   [5] Waste.

an let not þe Fleyshe be moche sothe,[1] þat it may bere kyttyng; þan take it
vppe, & ley it on a fayre cloþe, & sette owt þe lycoure fro þe fyre, & put a
few colys vnder-nethe þe vesselle þat þe lycoure is yn; þan take pouder of
Pepir, a gode quantyte, & Safron, þat it haue a fayre Laumbere coloure, & a
gode quantyte of Vynegre, & loke þat it be sauery [of] Salt & of Vynegre,
fayre of coloure of Safroun, & putte it on fayre lynen cloþe, & sette it vnder-
nethe a fayre pewter dysshe, & lat it renne þorw þe cloþe so ofte tylle it
renne clere : kytte fayre Rybbys of þe syde of þe Pygge, & lay ham on a
dysshe, an pulle of þe lemys of þe Chykenys, eche fro oþer, & do a-way þe
Skynne, & ley sum in a dysshe fayre y-chowchyd,[2] & pore þin [3] gelye þer-on,
& lay Almaundys þer-on, an Clowys, & paryd Gyngere, & serue forth.

[4].Cx. **Gelye de Fysshe.**—Take newe Pykys, an draw hem, and smyte hem
to pecys, & sethe in þe same lycoure þat þou doste Gelye of Fleysshe ; an whan
þey ben y-now, take Perchys and Tenchys, & seþe ; & Elys, an kutte hem in
fayre pecys, and waysshe hem, & putte hem in þe same lycoure, & loke þine
lycoure be styf y-now ; & ʒif it wolle notte cacche,[5] take Soundys of watteryd
Stokkefysshe, or ellys Skynnys, or Plays, an caste þer-to, & sethe ouer þe
fyre, & skeme it wyl ; & when it ys y-now, let nowt þe Fysshe breke ; þenne
take þe lycoure fro þe fyre, & do as þou dedyst be [6] þat oþer Gelye, saue,
pylle þe Fysshe, & ley þer-off in dysshis, þat is, perche & suche ; and Flowre
hem, & serue forthe.

.Cxj. **Tannye.**— Take almaunde Mylke, & Sugre, an powdere Gyngere, & of
Galyngale, & of Canelle, and Rede Wyne, & boyle y-fere : & þat is gode tannye.

.Cxij. **Sturmye.**—Take gode mylke of Almaundys y-drawe with wyne ;
take porke an hew it Smalle ; do it on a Morter, and grynde it ryth smalle ;
þen caste it in þe same Mylke, & caste it on a potte ; take Sawnderys & flowre
of Rys ; melle hem with þe Mylke, draw hem þorw a straynoure, & caste it
[in] a clene pot, loke þat it be chargeaunt y-now ; take Sugre, an putte þer-on,
& Hony ; do it ouer þe fyre, & let it sethe a gret whyle ; sture yt wyl ; take
Eyroun hard y-soþe, take þe whyte, & hew hem as smalle as þow myʒth, caste
hem on þe potte ; take Safroune & caste þer-to, with powder Gyngere,
Canelle, Galyngale, Clowys, & loke þat þou haue powder y-now ; caste it in
þe potte, temper it with Vynegre ; take Salt & do þer-to, menge hem wylle
to-gederys, Make a Siryppe ; þe .ij. dele schalle ben wyne, & þe .ij. dele
Sugre or hony ; boyle it & stere it, & Skeme it clene ; þer-on wete [7]þin
dysshes, & serue forth.

---

[1] boiled.   [2] Y-couched ; laid.   [3] Thine.   [4] 3 lf. 20 bk.
[5] stick ; see other *Cookery*, No. 174.   [6] By, with.   [7] leaf 21.

.Cxiij. **Bruette saake.**—Take Capoun, skalde hem, draw hem, smyte hem to gobettys, Waysshe hem, do hem in a potte; þenne caste owt þo potte, waysshe hem a-ȝeu on þe potte, & caste þer-to half wyne half Broþe ; take Percely, Isope, Waysshe hem, & hew hem smal, & putte on þe potte þer þe Fleysshe is ; caste þer-to Clowys, quybibes, Maces, Datys y-tallyd, hol Safroune ; do it ouer þe fyre ; take Canelle, Gyngere, tempere þiu powajes with wyne ; caste in-to þe potte Salt þer-to, hele [1] it, & whan it is y-now, serue it forth.

.Cxiiij. **Tayleȝ.**—Take a chargeaunt Mylke of Almaundys, an draw with wyne [2]; take Fygys & Roysonys a gode porcyon, to make it chargeaunt, waysshe hem clene, & caste hem on a morter, grynd hem as small as þou myȝt, temper hem vppe with þin [3] Mylke, draw hem þorw a straynoure, also chargeauntly as þou myȝth ; caste it iu a clene potte, do it to þe fyre ; take Datys y-taylid a-long, & do þer-to; take Flowre of Rys, & draw it þorw a straynoure, and caste þer-to, & lat it boyle tylle it be chargeaunt; sette it on þe fyre ; take pouder Gyngere & Canelle, Galyngale; temper with Vynegre, & caste þer-to Sugre, or hony; caste þer-to, sesyn it vppe with Salt, & serue forth.

.Cxv. **Quynade.**—Take Quynces, & pare hem clene, caste hem on a potte, & caste þer-to water of Rosys ; do it ouer þe fyre, & hele [4] it faste, & let it boyle a gode whyle tyl þey ben neysshe ; & ȝif þey wol not ben neysshe, bray hem in a Morter smal, draw hem þorw a straynoure ; take gode Mylke of Almandys, & caste in a potte & boyle it ; take whyte Wyne & Vynegre, an caste þer-to þe Mylke, & let it stonde a whyle ; take þan a clene canvas, & caste þe mylke vppe-on, & with a platere [5]stryke it of þe cloþe, & caste it on þe potte ; gedyr vppe þe quynces, & caste to þe creme, & do it ouer þe fyre, & lat boyle ; take a porcyon of pouder of Clowys, of Gyngere, of Graynys of Perys, of Euery a porcyon ; take Sugre y-now, with Salt, & a party of Safroun, & alle menge to-gederys ; & when þou dressyst forth, plante it with foyle of Syluer.

.Cxvj. **Blaunche de ferry.**—Take Almaundys, an draw þer-of an Chargeaunt Mylke; take Caponys & sethe hem ; & whan þey ben y-now, take hem vppe, & ley hem on a fayre bord, & strype of þe Skyn, & draw out þe Brawn & hew hem smal ; do hem on a Morter, & grynd hem smal ; caste on a potte, & fayre whyte Salt, & boyle hem ; & whan þey bey boylid, sette it out, & caste on whyte Wyne or Venegre, & make it quaylo [6]; take a clene cloþe and lete it be tryid a-brode, & stryke it wyl vnder-nethe alle þe whyle þat þer wol auȝt out þer-of; þan caste Blaunche powder þer-on, or pouder Gyngere

---

[1] Cover.   [2] MS. *caste in to þe potte*, struck through after *wyne*.
[3] Thine.   [4] Cover.   [5] lf. 21 bk.   [6] Curdle.

y-mellyd w*ith* Sugre; stryke it clene, take a newe Erþen potte, oþer a clene bolle, & caste þin mete þer-on, þer plantyng Anys in comfyte.

.**Cxvij. Sauge.**—Take Gyngere, Galyngale, Clowys, & grynde i*n* a morter; þan take an handfulle of Sawge, & do þer-to, grynd wyl to-gederys; take Eyroun, & sethe hem harde, nym þe ȝolkys, grynde hem w*ith* þe Sawge & w*ith* þe spycis, & temp*er* it vppe w*ith* Venegre or eysel, or w*ith* Alegere; take þe whyte of þe Eyro*un*, & sethe hem, & mynce hem smal, & caste þer-to; when it is y-temperyd, take Brawn of hennys or Fyssches, & ley on dysschys, & caste þin mete a-boue.

.**Cxviij. Murreye.**—Take Molberys, & wryng hem þorwe a cloþe; nym Vele, hew it, sethe it, grynd it smal, & caste þer-to; nym gode Spycery, Sugre, & caste þer-to; take Wastylbrede y-gratyd, [1]and ȝolkys of Eyroun, & lye it vppe þer-w*ith*, & caste gode pouder a-boue y-now, & þan serue forth.

.**Cxix. Vyaunde de cyprys** i*n* **lente.**—Take gode þikke mylke of Almaundys, & do it on a potte; & nyme þe F[le]ysshe[2] of gode Crabbys, & gode Samou*n*, & bray it smal, & tempere yt vppe w*ith* þe forsayd mylke; boyle it, an lye it w*ith* floure of Rys or Amyndou*n*, an make it chargeaunt; when it ys y-boylid, do þer-to whyte Sugre, a gode quantyte of whyte V*er*nage Pime; [3] w*ith* þe wyne, Pome-garnade. Whan it is y-dressyd, straw a-boue þe grayne of Pome-garnade.

.**Cxx. Whyte Mortrewys of Porke.**—Take lene Porke, & boyle it; blaunche Almandys, & grynd hem, & temp*er* vppe w*ith* þe brothe of þe porke, & lye hem vppe w*ith* þe Flowre of Rys, an lete boyle to-gederys, but loke þat þe porke be smal grounde y-now; caste þer-to Myncyd Almaundys y-fryid in freyssche grece; þen sesyn hem vppe alle flatte in a dysshe; þrow þer-to Sugre y-now & Salt; & atte þe dressoure, strawe þer-on pouder Gyngere y-mellyd w*ith* Almaundys.

.**Cxxj. Rapeye.**—Take Fygys & Roysonys, & grynd hem in a Mortere, & tempere hem vppe w*ith* Almaunde Mylke, & draw hem þorw a cloþe; þen take gode Spycys, & caste þer-to; take Perys, seþe hem & pare hem, & do a-way þe core, & bray hem in a mortere, & caste to þe oþ*er*; take gode Wyne, & Blake Sugre or Hony, & caste þer-to a lytil, & let it boyle in fere; & whan þow dressyst yn, take Maces & Clowes, Quybibys & Graynys, & caste a-boue.

.**Cxxij. A rede Morreye.**—Take Molberys, and wrynge a gode hepe of hem þorw a cloþe; nym Vele, hew it & grynd it smal, & caste þer-to; nym gode Spycery [an] Sugre, & caste þer-[4]to; take Wastilbrede & grate it, & ȝolkys

---

[1] leaf 22.   [2] MS. *Fysshe* (? intentionally).   [3] ? meaning.   [4] lf. 22 bk.

of Eyronn, & lye it vppe þer-with, & caste gode pouder of Spycery þer-an a-bouen; & þan serue it forth.

.Cxxiij. Strawberye.—Take Strawberys, & waysshe hem in tyme of ȝere in gode red wyne; þan strayne þorwe a cloþe, & do hem in a potte with gode Almaunde mylke, a-lay it with Amyndoun oþer with þe flowre of Rys, & make it chargeaunt and lat it boyle, and do þer-in Roysonys of coraunce, Safroun, Pepir, Sugre grete plente, pouder Gyngere, Canel, Galyngale; poynte it with Vynegre, & a lytil whyte grece put þer-to; coloure it with Alkenade, & droppe it a-bowte, plante it with þe graynys of Pome-garnad, & þan serue it forth.

.Cxxiiij. Chyryoun.—Take Chyryis,[1] & pike out þe stonys, waysshe hem clene in wyne, þan wryng hem þorw a cloþe, & do it on a potte, & do þer-to whyte grece a quantyte, & a partye of Floure of Rys, & make it chargeaunt; do þer-to hwyte Hony or Sugre, poynte it with Venegre; A-force it with stronge pouder of Canelle & of Galyngale, & a-lye it with a grete porcyoun of ȝolkys of Eyroun; coloure it with Safroun or Saunderys; & whan þou seruyste in, plante it with Chyrioun, & serue f[orth].

.Cxxv. Vyolette.—Take Flourys of Vyolet, boyle hem, presse hem, bray hem smal, temper hem vppe with Almaunde mylke, or gode Cowe Mylke, a-lye it with Amyndoun or Flowre of Rys; take Sugre y-now, an putte þer-to, or hony in defaute; coloure it with þe same þat þe flowrys be on y-peyntid a-boue.

.Cxxvj. Rede Rose.—Take þe same, saue a-lye it with þe ȝolkys of eyroun, & forþer-more as vyolet.

.Cxxvij. Prymerose.—Ryȝth as vyolette.

.Cxxviij. Flowrys of hawþorn.[2]—In þe same maner as vyolet.

[3].**Cxxix. A potage on a Fysdaye.**—Take an sethe an .ij. or .iij. Applys y-p[ar]ede,[4] & strayne hem þorw a straynoure, & Flowre of Rys þer-with; þan take þat whyte Wyne, & strayne it with-alle; þan loke þat it be nowt y-bounde to moche with þe Floure of Rys, þan ȝif it a-boyle; þen caste þer-to Saunderys & Safroun, & loke it be marbylle;[5] þan take Roysonys of corauns, & caste þer-on, & Almaundys y-schredyd þer-on y-nowe; & mynce Datys Smale, & caste þer-on, & a lytil Hony to make it doweet, or ellys Sugre; þenne caste þer-to Maces & Clowys, Pepir, Canelle, Gyngere, & oþer spycery y-now; þen take Perys, & sethe hem a lytil; þen reke hem on þe colys tyl þey ben tendyr; þan smale schrede hem rounde; & a lytil or þou serue it in, þrow hem on þe potage, & so serue hem in almost flatte, noȝt Fullyche.

.Cxxx. Brewes in Lentyn.—Take a fewe Fygys, & seþe hem & draw hem

<hr>

[1] MS. Chyrþis. [2] MS. Hawiorn. [3] leaf 23. [4] MS. y-pede. [5] i.e. variegated.

þorw a straynoure with Wyne; þen putte þer-to a lytil Hony; þen toste
Brede, & Salte it; & so broune & rennyng as Brwes, serue hem in, & straw
pouder Canelle y-now þer-on atte þe dressoure, & serue it forth.

.Cxxxj. **A potage colde.**—Take Wyne, & drawe a gode þikke Milke of
Almaundys with Wyne, ȝif þou mayste; þen putte yt on a potte, caste þer-to
Pouder Canelle & Gyngere & Saffroun; þen lat it boyle, & do it on a cloþe; &
ȝif þou wolt, late hym ben in dyuers colourys, þat on whyte with-owte
Spyces, & þat oþer ȝelow with Spicerye.

.Cxxxij. **Sauke[1] Sarsoun.**—Take Almaundys, & blaunche hem, & frye
hem in oyle oþer in grece, þan bray hem in a Mortere, & tempere hem with
gode Almaunde mylke, & gode Wyne, & þen þe þrydde perty schal ben
Sugre; & ȝif it be noȝt þikke y-nowe, a-lye it with Alkenade, & Florche[2] it
a-bouyn with Pome-garned, [3]& messe it; serue it forth.

.Cxxxiij. **Rapeye.**—Take Pykys or Tenchys, oþer freysshe Fysshe, & frye
it in Oyle; þen nyme crustys of whyte brede, & Raysonys & Canelle, an bray
it wyl in a mortere, & temper it vppe wyth gode wyne; þen coloure it with
Canelle, or a litil Safroun: þan boyle it, & caste in hol Clowys & Quybibes,
& do þe Fysshe in a dysshe, & þan serue forth.

.Cxxxiiij. **Apple Moyle.**—Nym Rys, an bray hem wyl, & temper hem with
Almaunde mylke, & boyle it; & take Applys, & pare hem, an smal screde
hem in mossellys; þrow on sugre y-now, & coloure it with Safroun, & caste
þer-to gode pouder, & serue f[orth].

.Cxxxv. **Applade Ryalle.**—Take Applys, & seþe hem tylle þey ben tendyr,
& þau lat hem kele; þen draw hem þorw a straynour; & on flesshe day caste
þer-to gode fatte broþe of freysshe beef, an whyte grece, & Sugre, &
Safroun, & gode pouder; & in a Fysshe day, take Almaunde mylke, & oyle
of Olyff, & draw þer-vppe with-al a gode pouder, & serue forth. An for
nede, draw it vppe with Wyne, & a lytil hony put þer-to for to make it þan
dowcet; & serue it forth.

.Cxxxvj. **A potage of Roysons.**—Take Raysonys, & do a-way þe kyrnellys;
& take a part of Applys, & do a-way þe corys, & þe pare,[4] & bray hem in a
mortere, & temper hem with Almande Mylke, & melle hem with flowre of
Rys, þat it be clene chargeaunt, & straw vppe-on pouder of Galyngale & of
Gyngere, & serue it forth.

.Cxxxvij. **Chykons in dropeye.**—They schul ben fayre y-boylid in fayre
watere tyl þey ben y-now, þen take hem fyrst, & choppe hem smal: & whan

þey ben y-now, tempere vppe a gode Almaunde mylke of þe same, & with
Wyne: a-lye it with Amyndon, oþer with ¹floure of Rys: þen take fayre
freysshe grece, & putte Alkenade þer-to, & gader his coloure þer-of, & ley þe
quarterys .v. or .vj. in a dysshe, as it wole come a-bowte, & Salt it atte þe
dressoure, sprynge with a feþer or .ij. here & þere a-bowte þe dysshe; & ȝif
þou lyst, put þer-on pouder of Gyngere, but noȝt a-boue, but in þe potage,
& þan serue forth.

.**Cxxxviij. Pumpes.**—Take an sethe a gode gobet of Porke, & noȝt to lene,
as tendyr as þou may; þan take hem vppe & choppe hem as smal as þou
may; þan take clowes & Maces, & choppe forth with-alle, & Also choppe forth
with Roysonys of coraunce; þan take hem & rolle hem as round as þou may,
lyke to smale pelettys, a .ij. inches a-bowte, þan ley hem on a dysshe be hem
selue; þan make a gode Almaunde mylke, & a lye it with floure of Rys, & lat
it boyle wyl, but loke þat it be clene rennyng; & at þe dressoure, ley
.v. pompys in a dysshe, & pore þin potage þer-on. An ȝif þou wolt, sette on
euery pompe a flos campy ² flour, & a-boue straw on Sugre y-now, & Maces:
& serue hem forth.   And sum men make þe pellettys of vele or Beeff, but
porke ys beste & fayrest.

.**Cxxxix. Caudel Ferry departyd with a blamanger.**—Take Fleysshe of
Capoun, or of Porke, & hakke hem smal, & do it in a mortere an bray it wyl,
& temper it vppe with capoun broþe þat it be wyl chargeaunt; þan nym
mylke of Almaundys, take ȝolkys of eyrown, & Safroun, & melle hem
to-gederys þat it be ȝelow, & do þer-to pouder Canelle, & styke þer-on Clowis,
Maces, & Quybibis, & serue f[orth].

.**Cxl. Egredouncye.**—Take Porke or Beef, wheþer þe lykey, & leche it
þinne þwerte³; þen broyle it brown a litel, & þen mynce it lyke Venyson;
choppe it in sewe, þen caste it in ⁴a potte & do þer-to Freyssh brothe; take
Erbis, Oynonys, Percely & Sawge, & oþer gode erbis, þen lye it vppe with
Brede; take Pepir & Safroun, pouder Canel, Vynegre, or Eysel Wyne, Broþe
an Salt, & let ȝet⁵ boyle to-gederys, tylle þey ben y-now, & þan serue it
forth renny[n]g.

.**Cxlj. Noteye.**—Take a gret porcyoun of Haselle leuys, & grynd in a morter
as smal as þou may, whyl þat þey ben ȝonge; take þan, & draw vppe a þriʄt
Mylke of Almaundys y-blaunchyd, & temper it with Freysshe broþe; wryng
out clene þe Ius of þe leuys; take Fleysshe of Porke or of Capoun, & grynd it
smal, & temper it vppe with þe mylke, & caste it in a potte, & þe Ius þer-to,

¹ leaf 24.   ² ? field-flower.   ³ MS. ywerte.   ⁴ lf. 24 bk.   ⁵ It.

do it ouer þe fyre & late it boyle; take flour of Rys, & a-lye it; take & caste Sugre y-now þer-to, & Vynegre a quantyte, & pouder Gyngere, & Safrou̅n it wel, & Salt; take smal notys, & broke hem; take þe kyrnellys, & make hem whyte, & frye hem vppe in grece; plante þer-with þin mete & serue forth.

.Cxlij. **Vyande Ryalle**.—Nyme gode Mylke of Almaundys, & do it in a potte, & sette it ouer þe fyre, & styre it tyl it boyle almost; þen take flour of Rys & of þe selue Mylke, au draw it þorwe a straynoure, & so þer-with a-lye it tylle it be Chargeaunte, & store it faste þat it crouste noȝt; þen take [*gap in MS.*] owte of grece, & caste it þorw a Skymoure, & colour þat Sewe þer-with; þan take Sugre in confyte, & caste in y-now; sesyn it with Salt & ley þre lechys iu a dysshe, & caste Aneys in comfyte þer-on, & þanne serue forth.

.Cxliij. **Lampreys** iu **galentyn**.—Take Brede, & stepe it with Wyne & Vynegre, & caste þer-to Canelle, & draw it þorw a straynoure, and do it in a potte, & caste pepir þer-to; þan take Smale Oynonys, mynce hem, frye hem in Oyle, & caste þer-to a fewe Saunderys, 'an let hem boyle a lytil; þen take þe lampronys & skalde hem with [*gap in MS.*] & hot watere, & sethe & boyle hem in a dysshe, & cast þe Sewe vppe-on, & serue forth for a potage.

.Cxliiij. **Schyconys** with **þe bruesse**.—Take halfe a dosyn Chykonys, & putte hem in-to a potte; þen putte þer-to a gode gobet of freysshe Beef, & lat hem boyle wyl; putte þer-to Percely, Sawge leuys, Saucrey, noȝt to smal hakkyd; putte þer-to Safrou̅n y-now; þen kytte þin Brewes, & skalde hem with þe same broþe; Salt it wyl; & but þou haue Beef, take Motou̅n, but fyrste Stuffe þin chekons iu þis wyse: take & seþe hard Eyrou̅n, & take þe ȝolkys & choppe hem smal, & choppe þer-to Clowys, Maces, Hole Pepir, & Stuffe þin chekonys with-al; Also put hole gobettys & marye with yune; Also þen dresse hem as a pertryche, & fayre coloure hem, & ley vppe-on þis browes, & serue in with Bakoun.

.Cxlv. **Blaunche Perreye.**—Take Pesyn, & waysshe hem clene, & þen take a gode quantyte of fyne leye, & putte it on a potte, & a lytil water þer-to; & whan þe ley is seþin hot, caste þe Pesyn þer-to, & þer late hem soke a gode whyle; þen take a quantyte of wollen cloþe, & rubbe hem, & þe holys[2] wyl a-way; þenne take a seve or a wheterydoun, & ley þin pesyn þer-on, & go to þe water, & waysshe hem clene a-way þe holys, þen putte hem in a potte, & þey wyl alle to-falle with a lytil boylynge, to pereye, sauc þe whyte Pepyn is þer-in, & þat is a gode syȝth; þen Salt hem, & serue hem forth.

[1] leaf 25.   [2] Hulls, shucks.

.Cxlvj. **Ry꜀th so Caboges**[1] Ben scruyd, sauc men sayn it is gode Also to ley hem in a bagge ouerny꜀th in renuyug streme of watere, & a-morwe sette vppe watere, & when þe water is skaldyng hot, þrow hem þer on, & hoole hem in þere wyse be-forsayd, & serue forth.

[2].**Cxlvij. Brwes in lentyn.**—Take Water & let boyle, and draw a lyer þer-to of Brede, of þe cromys, with wyne ꜀-now; lete alle ben wyne almost; þen put þer-to hony a gode quantyte, þat it may ben dowcet, þan putte pouder Pepir þer-to, Clowys, Maces, and Saunderys, & Salt, & skalde þin[3] brewes tender, & serue f[orth].

.**Cxlviij. Whyte Pesyn in grauey.**—Take Whyte Pesyn, & hoole hem in þe maner as men don Caboges, or blaunche perry; þan sethe hem with Almaunde mylke vppe, putte þer-to Sugre ꜀-now, & fryid Oynonys & Oyle, & serue f[orth].

.**Cxlix. A Potage.**—Take an sethe a fewe eyron) iu red Wyne; þan take & draw hem þorw a straynoure with a gode mylke of Almaundys; þen caste þer-to Roysonys of Coraunce, Dates y-taylid, grete Roysonys, Pynes, pouder Pepir, Sawndrys, Clouys, Maces, Hony ꜀-now, a lytil doucete, & Salt; þau bynde hym vppe flat with a lytyl flowre of Rys, & let hem ben Red with Saunderys, & serue hym in flatte; & ꜀if þou wolt, in fleyssh tyme caste vele y-choppid þer-on, not to smale.

.**Cl. Cawdel out of lente.**—Take & make a gode mylke of Almaundys y-draw vppe with wyne of Red, whyte is beterre; ꜀if it schal be whyte, þan strayne ꜀olkys of Eyroun þer-to a fewe. Put[4] þer-to Sugre & Salt, but Sugre ꜀-now; þen when it begynnyth to boyle, sette it out, & almost flatte; serue it then forth, & euer kepe it as whyte as þou may, & at þe dressoure droppe Alkenade þer-on, & serue forth; & ꜀if þou wylt haue hym chargeaunt, bynd hym vppe with fflour [of] Rys, oþer with whetyn floure, it is no fors. And ꜀if þou wolt, coloure hym with Safroun, & straw on pouder y-now, & Sugre y-now, & serue f[orth].

.**Clj. Creme Bastarde.**—Take þe whyte of Eyroun a grete hepe, & putte it on a panne ful of Mylke, & let yt boyle; [5]þen sesyn it so with Salt an hony a lytel, þen lat hit kele, & draw it þorw a straynoure, an take fayre Cowe mylke an draw yt with-all, & seson it with Sugre, & loke þat it be poynant & doucet: & serue it forth for a potage, or for a gode Bakyn mete, wheder þat þou wolt.

.**Clij. Capoun in Salome.**—Take a Capoun & skalde hym, Roste hym, þen

[1] i.e. Cabbages in just the same way.   [2] lf. 25 bk.   [3] Thiue.   [4] MS. but.   [5] lf. 26.

take þikke Almaunde mylke, temper it wyth wyne Whyte oþer Red, take a
lytyl Saunderys & a lytyl Safroun, & make it a marbyl coloure, & so atte þe
dressoure þrow on hym in ye kychoun, & þrow þe Mylke a-boue, & þat is
most commelyche, & serue forth.

.Cliij. **Pompys.**—Take Beef, Porke, or Vele, on of hem, & raw, alle to-
choppe it atte þe dressoure, þan grynd hem in a morter as smal as þou may,
þan caste þer-to Raw ȝolkys of Eyroun, wyn, an a lytil whyte [sugre]: caste
also þer-to pouder Pepyr, & Macys, Clowes, Quybibys, pouder Canelle,
Synamoun, & Salt, & a lytil Safroun; þen take & make smale Pelettys
round y-now, & loke þat þou haue a fayre potte of Freysshe broþe of bef or
of Capoun, & euer þrow hem þer-on & lete hem sethe tyl þat þey ben y-now;
þen take & draw vppe a þryfty mylke of Almaundys, with cold freysshe
broþe of Bef, Vele, Moton, oþer Capoun, & a-lye it with floure of Rys & with
Spycerye; & atte þe dressoure ley þes pelettys .v. or .vj. in a dysshe, & þen
pore þin sewe aneward,[1] & serue in, or ellys make a gode þryfty Syryppe &
ley þin[2] pelettys atte þe dressoure þer-on, & þat is gode seruyse.[3]

'LECHE VYAUNDEZ.

.I. **Brawn in comfyte.**—Take Freysseh Brawn & sethe yt y-now, & pare
it & grynde it in a mortere, & temper it with Almand mylke, & draw[5] it
þorw a straynoure in-to a potte, & caste þer-to Sugre y-now, & powder of
Clowys, & let boyle; þen take floure of Canelle, & pouder of Gyngere; &
þen take it out of þe potte, an putte it in a lynen cloþe & presse it, but lat it
boyle so longe in þe potte tylle it be alle þikke; þan take it vppe & presse it
on a cloþe, & þen leche it fayre with a knyff, but not to þinne; & þan ȝif þou
wolt, þou myȝht take þe Rybbys of þe bore al bare, & clete[6] hem enlongys
þorw þe lechys, an so serue forth a leche or to in euery dysshe.

.ij. **Blaunche Brawen.**—Take Freysshe Braun, & mynce hem smal, & take
gode þikke mylke of Almaundys y-blaunchyde, & putte alle in-to a potte, &
Sugre, & lat boyle alle to-gederys tyl it be ryȝt styffe; þen caste it vppe, &
caste it in a fayre cold basyn, & lette it stonde þer-in tyl it be cold; & þen
leche .ij. or .iij. in a dysshe, & serue forth.

.iij. **Pynade.**—Take Hony & gode pouder Gyngere, & Galyngale, & Canelle,
Pouder pepir, & graynys of parys, & boyle y-fere; þan take kyrnelys of
Pynotys & caste þer-to; & take chyconys y-soþe, & hew hem in grece, &

---

[1] on it.   [2] Thine.   [3] four blank pages follow.
[4] lf. 27 bk.   [5] MS. *dray*.   [6] Set, see Douce MS. No. 48.

caste þer-to, & lat seþe y-fere; & þen lat droppe þer-of on a knyf; & ȝif it cleuyth & wexyth hard, it ys y-now; & þen putte it on a chargere tyl it be cold, & mace[1] lechys, & serue wi*th* oþer metys; & ȝif þou wolt make it in spycery, þen putte non chykonys þer-to.

.iiij. **Gyngerbrede.**—Take a quart of hony, & sethe it, & skeme it clene; take Safroun, pouder Pepir, & þrow þer-on; take gratyd Brede, & make it so chargeaunt[2] þat it wol be y-lechyd; þen take pouder Canelle, & straw þer-on y-now; þen make yt[3] square, lyke as þou wolt leche yt; take when þou lechyst hyt, an caste Box leves a-bouyn, y-stykyd þer-on, on clowys. And ȝif þou wolt haue it Red, coloure it wi*th* Saunderys y-now.

.v. **Leche lumbarde.**—Take Datys, an do a-way þe stonys, & sethe in swete Wyne; take hem vppe, an grynd hem in a mortere; draw vppe þorw a straynoure wi*th* a lytyl whyte Wyne & Sugre, And caste hem on a potte, & lete boyle tylle it be styff; þen take yt vppe, & ley it on a borde; þan take pouder of Gyngere & Canelle, & wryng it, & molde it to-gederys in þin hondys, & make it so styf þat it wolle be lechyd; & ȝif it be noȝt styf y-nowe, take hard ȝolkys of Eyron & kreme[4] þer-on, or ellys grated brede, & make it þicke y-now; þen take clareye, & caste þer-on in maner of a Syryppe, when þou shalt *s*erue it forth.

.vj. **Auter maner leche lumbarde.**—Take fayre Hony, and clarifi yt on þe fyre tylle it wexe hard; þen take hard ȝolkys of Eyroun, & kryme[4] a gode quantyte þer-to, tyl it be styf y-now; an þenne take it vppe, & ley it on a borde; þen take fayre gratyd Brede, & pouder pepir, & molde it to-gederys wi*th* þine hondys, tylle it be so styf þat it wole ben lechyd; þan leche it; þen take wyne & pouder Gyngere, Canelle, & a lytil claryfyid hony, & late renne þorw a straynour, & caste þis Syryp þer-on, when þou shalt *s*erue it out, instede of Clereye.

.vij. **Soupes of Salomere.**—Take boylid Porke, & hew yt an grynd it; þen take cowe Mylke, & Eyroun y-swonge, & Safrou*n*, & mynce Percely bladys, & caste þer-to, & let boyle alle y-fere; & dresse vppe-on a cloþe, & keruc þer-of smal lechys, & do hem in a dysshe; þen take almaunde mylke & flowre of Rys, and Sugre an Safroun, & boyle it alle y-fere; þen caste þin[5] sewe on þin[5] lechys, & serue forth alle hote.

[6] .viij. **Lette lardes.**—Take kowe mylke, & do þer-to Eyroun y-swonge; þan take ryȝt fatte Porke y-sothe, & hew it smalle, & sethe it; take pouder Gyngere, Galyngale, or Pepir; caste þer-to, colour it wyth Safroun, & caste

---

[1] A. *make.*   [2] stiff.   [3] lf. 28.   [4] Crimme; crumble.   [5] Thine.   [6] lf. 28 bk.

all þese to-gederys, & boyle it, & gadre þe croddes to hepe with-al; þen take
vppe þe croddys to hepe with Ale, & presse hem on a cloþe; þan kerue þer-of
lechys, & Roste it on a gredyre, & strawe Sugre y-now alle a-bowte; & ȝif
þou wolt make þat on syde Rede, an þat oþer ȝelow, Take Pannes, & make as
I haue sayd, & coloure þat on panne with Saunderys, an þat other with
Saffroune, an ley on a cloþe to-gederys, þe Rede fyrste on þe cloþe, an [lat]
þe ȝelow be abouyn þe Rede, & presse hem to-gederys, & that on syde wol
ben rede, & þat oþer ȝelow.   An ȝif þow wolt haue it Motley, take þre pottys,
& make letlardys in eche, & coloure þat on with Saunderys, & þat oþer wyth
Safroune, & þe þrydde on a-nother degre, so þat þey ben dyuerse; an when
þey boyle, caste al to-gederys in-to on, an stere hem a-bowte with þin hond,
& þan presse hem, and he wol be Motley whan he ys lechyd.

.ix. **Mange Moleynne.**—Take Almaundys, an blaunche hem, an draw þorw
a straynoure a þicke mylke in-to an potte; þan take brawn of a Capoun, an
hew it smalle, an do it in a potte, an lye it with Floure of Rys; an do þer-to
whyte grece, & sethe alle to-gederys; an when it is y-sothe, take vppe of þe
fyre, & do þer-in Sugre y-now; þen take blaunchyd Almaundys, & frye hem,
& ley .iij. lechys on a dysshe, & on euery leche prycke .iij. Almaundys; an
þan serue it forth.

.x. **Vyaund de leche.**—Take whyte Wyne a god quantite, [1]an putte it on
a potte; þen putte þer-to raw ȝolkys of eyroun y-tryid, & pouder of clowys,
& pouder canel y-now, an Safroun y-now; þan lat it boyle tyl it be ryȝth
chargeaunte, an þen sette it doun; & take an sette ouer a panne of cowe milke,
& þrow Saunderys y-nowe þer-on; þen make a styf poshotte[2] of Ale; þen take
þe croddys, an lat it honge on a pyn in a cloþe, an lat it cleue euer þerue-
owt;[3] þen take þe cawdel forsayd, & melle hem to-gederys in a cloþe, with
þe poshotte;[2] þen put þer-on Sugre, Canel, pouder Gyngere y-now; presse
hem vp sware,[4] an leche it, & serue it forth.

.xj. **Vyaund leche.**—Take cowe Mylke, & set it ouer þe fyre, & þrow
þer-on Saunderys, & make a styf poshotte of Ale; þan hang þe croddys þer-of
in a pynne, in a fayre cloþe, and lat it ouer-renne; þan take it & put hony
þer-to, & melle it y-fere; þen feche þe croddys of þe deye,[5] & melle hem to-
gederys, & lay it on a chesefatte or it be torne, .iij. fold or iiij. fold, in lynen
cloþe, & salt it, & leche it; & þanne serue it forth.

.xij. **Vyaund leche.**—Take Eyroun, þe whyte & þe ȝolke, and caste hem
in a morter, an broke hem wyl; þan take cowe mylke & caste þer-to, & menge

---

[1] lf. 29.   [2] Posset.   [3] Throughout?   [4] Square.   [5] Dairymaid.

hem wyl to-gederys; þan put al in a panne, & lat boyle; & with ale make it to a poshotte; þen hange þe croddys in a pynne, & let it ouer-renne; melle þe croddys with hony; þen take þe bladys of Barlyche, or of Percely, & stampe hem, & wrynge þorw a cloþe; & so alle þe grene, melle it a-mong þe croddys; þenne take þe cruddys þat comon fro þe deye, melle hem to-gederys, presse hem, & serue hem forth; an þe coloure wyl ben þan Motley.

.xiij. **Vyaund leche.**—Take a gode quantyte of Brawn, an Hony, & a lytil brede, & let sethe to-gederys pouder Pepir, Clowys, ¹Maces, an Safroun, & draw it þorwe a straynoure, & chafe it a litel, & caste it in fayre dysshis, an let it kele, & þan serue f[orth].

.xiiij. **Vyaunde leche.**—Take Hony a gode quantite; þen take pouder Pepir, & Safroun, & Canel, & caste þer-to; & þen caste it on a dysshe, & let it kele, & serue forth.

.xv. **Storioun² leche.**—Take an howe³ of vele, & let boyle, butte fyrst late hym ben stepid .ij. or .iij. owrys in clene Water to soke out þe blode, & whan it is tender y-sothe, take hym vppe as fast as þou may; þan take harde ȝolkys of Eyroun redy sothe, & caste also þer-to, & pouder Pepir y-now, & also choppe a-mong þe ȝynes⁴ of þe fete clene y-pikyd, & a lytil Salt, nowt to moche, & presse hem on a clowte tyl a-morwe⁵; þan leche it, & lay hem in dysshis, an pore þer-[on] a quantyte of Venegre, & Pepir, & Percely, & Oynonys smal mencyd, & serue forth.

.xvj. **Chare de wardoun leche.**—Take Perys, & soþe ham, & Pike ham & stampe ham, & draw hem þorw a straynoure, & lye it with Bastard; þen caste hem in-to a potte, & Safroun with-al, and boyle with Maces, Clowes, pouder Canel, Quibibes, &⁶ a litel pouder Pepir, & Rolle hem vppe with Brede, þe cromes with-in þin hondys, & serue forth.

.xvij. [**Vyaund leche**].—Take calfes fete an hepe, & lat stepe in cold watere; þen boyle hem smal; þan take þe broþe & gode Milke of Almaundys, & choppe þe Syneys⁷ in-to þe same milk rythte smal; þan boyle it ouer þe fyre, & coloure it with Saunderys, & put Sugre y-now in-to þe potte; & ȝif þou wolt haue hym of .ij. colour, þan take an coloure but half with Saunderys, & caste þat oþere half in a dysshe, & lat it kele; & whan it is cold, þen þat is y-colouryd with Saunderys, het it, & cuene⁸ melle it hote; caste hem a-bouyn þe oþer, & lat kele, an þan serue forth. Than take Sugre, a quantyte ⁹of swete Wyne, & Blaunche pouder þer-on, & make Sawce þer-of; And so colde, ley it in þe dysshis, be-helyd,¹⁰ & serue f[orth].

---

¹ lf. 29 bk.   ² Sturgeon.   ³ Hock.   ⁴ Sinews.   ⁵ To-morrow.
⁶ MS. & an.   ⁷ Sinews.   ⁸ Euenly.   ⁹ lf. 30.   ¹⁰ Covered.

.xviij. Vyaund leche.—Take a Tenche, au steue hym in a potte with Wyne; when he is y-now, pyke owt þe bonys, take an stampe hem in a morter; þen take a lytil of þicke Almaunde mylke, & putte þer-to; þen take hem vppe, & putte hem in þe broþe forsayde, þat it was y-soþe in, & þat y-straynid; caste þer-to Maces, Clowes, pouder Pepir, & Pouder Cauelle; þan caste Safron þer-to; þen caste him in a dysshe, & lat hem kele; þen put Vynegre, pouder Gyngere, Cauel y-now in þe botmond[1] þer-of, vnneþe y-helyd.[2]

.xix. Pome dorres.—Take Fylettys of Raw porke, & grynd hem wyl; do Salt [and] pouder Pepir þer-to; þan take þe Whyte of the Eyroun [and] þrow þer-to, & make hem so hard þat þey mow ben Rosted on a Spete; make hem round as an Appil: make fyre with-owte smoke; þen take Almaunde mylke, & y-boutyd[3] flour, do hem to-gederys; take Sugre, & putte in þin[4] bature; þen dore hem with sum grene þing, percely or ȝolkys of Eyroun, to-geder, þat þey ben grene; & be wyl war þat þey ben nowt Browne; & sum men boyle hem in freysshe broþ or þey ben spetid; & whan þey ben so boylid, þen þey must ben sette an kelid, & þan Spete hem, & dore hem with ȝolkys of Eyroun y-mengyd with þe Ius of haselle leuys.

.xx. Yrchouns.—Take Piggis mawys, & skalde hem wel; take groundyn Porke, & knede it with Spicerye, with pouder Gyngere, & Salt & Sugre; do it on þe mawe, but fille it nowt to fulle; þen sewe hem with a fayre þrede, & putte hem in a Spete as men don piggys; take blaunchid Almaundys, & kerf hem long, smal, & scharpe, & frye hem in grece & sugre; take a litel prycke, & prykke þe yrchons, An putte in þe holes þe Almaundys, every hole half, & eche fro oþer; ley hem þen to þe fyre; when þey ben rostid, dore hem sum wyth [5]Whete Flowre, & mylke of Almaundys, sum grene, sum blake with Blode, & lat hem nowt browne to moche, & s[erue] f[orth].

.xxj. An Entrayle.—Take a chepis wombe; take Polettys y-rostyd, & hew hem; þen take Porke, chese, & Spicery, & do it on a morter, & grynd alle y-fere; þen take it vppe with Eyroun y-swonge, & do in þe wombe, & Salt, & soþe hem tyl he be y-nowe, & serue forth.

.xxij. For to make floure Rys.—Take Rys, an lese hem clene; þen drow hem wyl in þe Sonne, þat þey ben drye; þan bray hem smal y-now; & þerow a crees bunte syfte hem, & for defaute of a bonte, take a Renge.[6]

.xxiij. Pome-Garnez.—Take lene Raw Porke, & lene raw Flesshe of hennys, & raw eyroun, & rent þe flesshe fro þe bonys, & hew it smal; take

---

[1] Bottom.   [2] Scarcely covered.   [3] Bolted, sifted.   [4] Thine.   [5] lf. 30 bk.   [6] Ring strainer.

þanne Salt, Gyngere, & Safroun, Salt, Galyngale, þer-of y-now, & caste it in
a morter, & bray it smal; take þan þin fleysshe, & caste it in-to þat morter to
þe Spycery, & þat it be wyl y-grounde; þanne make þer-of pelettys, as it were
Applys, be-twene þin hondys; loke þou haue a fayre panne sething ouere þe
fyre, & do þer-on þin pelettys, & late hem nowt sethe to swythe, & þan lat
hem kele; & whan þey ben cold, ȝif hem a fayre spete of haselle, & be-twyn
euery, loke þer be an ynche, & lay hem to þe fyre: & þan make þin baturys,
þe on grene, & þat oþer ȝelow; þe grene of Percely.

.**xxiiij. Waffres.**—Take þe Wombe of A luce, & seþe here wyl, & do it on
a morter, & tender chese þer-to, grynde hem y-fere; þan take flowre an
whyte of Eyroun & bete to-gedere, þen take Sugre an pouder of Gyngere, &
do al to-gederys, & loke þat þin Eyroun ben hote, & ley þer-on of þin
paste, & þan make þin waffrys, & serue yn.

[1].**xxv. Hagws of a schepe.**—Take þe Roppis[2] with þe talour,[3] & parboyle
hem; þan hakke hem smal; grynd pepir, & Safroun, & brede, & ȝolkys of
Eyroun, & Raw kreme or swete Mylke: do al to-gederys, & do in þe grete
wombe of þe Schepe, þat is, the mawe; & þan seþe hym an serue forth ynne.

xxvj. Frawnchemyle.—Nym Eyroun with þe whyte, & gratid Brede, &
chepis talow, Also grete as dyse; nym Pepir, Safroun, & grynd alle to-
gederys, & do in þe wombe of þe chepe, þat is, þe mawe; & seþe hem wyl,
& serue forth.

xxvij. Appraylere.—Take þe fleysshe of þe lene Porke, & seþe it wel: &
whan it is soþe, hew it smal; nym þan Safroun, Gyngere, Canel, Salt,
Galyngale, old chese, myid[4] Brede, & bray it smal on a morter; caste þin[5]
fleysshe in to þe spicery, & loke þat it be wil y-ground, & temper it vppe
with raw Eyroun; þan take a longe Pecher, al a-bowte ouer alle þat it be
ransched;[6] þan held[7] out þin grece, & fulle þi Pechir of þin farsure, & take
a pese of fayre Canneuas, & doble it as moche as þou may ceuyr þe mouþe
with-al, & bynd it fast a-bowte þe berde,[8] & caste hym to seþe with þin
grete Fleysshe, in lede oþer in Cauderoun, for it be wyl soþin; take þen
vppe þin Pecher, & breke it, an saf þin farsure; & haue a fayre broche,
& broche it þorw, & lay it to þe fyre; & þan haue a gode Bature of
Spiceryc, Safroun, Galyngale, Canel, & þer-of y-now, & flowre, & grynd
smal in a morter, & temper it vp with raw Eyroun, & do þer-to Sugre of
Alisaunder[9] y-now; & euer as it dryit, baste it with bature, & sette forth
in seruyce.

---

[1] If. 31.　　　[2] Guts.　　　[3] Tallow; fat.　　　[4] Crumbed.　　　[5] Thine.
[6] Rinsed.　　　[7] Cast.　　　[*] Rim.　　　[9] Alexandria.

.xxviij. Cokyntryce.—Take a Capoun, & skald hym, & draw hem clene, & smyte hem a-to in þe waste ouerþwart; take a Pigge, & skald hym, & draw hym in þe same maner, & smyte hem also in þe waste; take a nedyl & a þrede, & sewe þe fore partye of the [1]Capoun to þe After parti of þe Pygge; & þe fore partye of þe Pigge, to þe hynder party of þe Capoun, & þan stuffe hem as þou stuffyst a Pigge; putte hem on a spete, & Roste hym: & whan he is y-now, dore hem with ȝolkys of Eyroun, & pouder Gyngere & Safroun, þenne wyth þe Ius of Percely with-owte; & þan serue it forth for a ryal mete.

.xxix. Milke Rostys.—Take swete Mylke, an do it in a panne; take Eyroun with alle þe whyte, & swenge hem, & caste þer-to; colour it with Safroun, & boyle it so þat it wexe þikke; þan draw it þorw a straynoure, & uym that leuyth,[2] & presse it: & whan it is cold, larde it, & schere on schevres,[3] & roste it on [4] a Gredelle, & serue f[orth].

.xxx. Alows de Beef or de Motoun.—Take fayre Bef of þe quyschons,[5] & motoun of þe bottes, & kytte in þe maner of Stekys; þan take raw Percely, & Oynonys smal y-scredde, & ȝolkys of Eyroun soþe hard, & Marow or swette, & hew alle þes to-geder smal: þan caste þer-on poudere of Gyngere & Saffroun, & tolle hem to-gederys with þin hond, & lay hem on þe Stekys al a-brode, & caste Salt þer-to; þen rolle to-gederys, & putte hem on a round spete, & roste hem til þey ben y-now; þan lay hem in a dysshe, & pore þer-on Vynegre & a lityl verious, & pouder Pepir þer-on y-now, & Gyngere, & Canelle, & a fewe ȝolkys of hard Eyroun y-kremyd þer-on; & serue forth.

.xxxj. To make Stekys of venson or bef.—Take Venyson or Bef, & leche & gredyl it vp broun; þen take Vynegre & a litel verious, & a lytil Wyne, & putte pouder perpir þer-on y-now, and pouder Gyngere; & atte þe dressoure straw on pouder Canelle y-now, þat þe stekys be al y-helid þer-wyth, & but a litel Sawce; & þan serue it forth.

.xxxij. A Siryppe pur vn pestelle.—Take gode Wyne, & a-lye yt [6]with raw ȝolkys of Eyroun; þan late hem boyle to-gederys a whyle; þen put pouder Pepir, & þrow it þer-on; loke þat it be bytyng of Pepir. Take Clowys, macys, Safroun, & caste þer-to; & atte þe dressoure þorw on þin Sirip on þi pestelle, & kreme hard ȝolkys of Eyroun þer-to, & serue forht.

.xxxiij. Pygge y-farsyd.—Take raw Eyroun, & draw hem þorw a straynoure; þan grate fayre brede; take Safroun & Salt, & pouder of Pepir, & Swet of a schepe, & melle alle to-gederys in a fayre bolle; þen broche þin

---

[1] lf. 31 bk.   [2] Take what remains.   [3] Shivers; thin strips.
[4] MS. & on.   [5] Cushions.   [6] lf. 32.

Pygge; þen farce hym, & sewe þe hole, & lat hym roste; & þan serue forth.

.xxxiiij. **Poddyng of Capoun necke.**—Take Percely, gysour, & þe leuer of þe herte, & perboyle in fayre water; þan choppe hem smal, & put raw ȝolkys of Eyroun .ij. or .iiij. þer-to, & choppe for-*with*. Take Maces & Clowes, & put þer-to, & Safroun, & a lytil pouder Pepir, & Salt; & fille hym vppe & sew hym, & lay him a-long on þe capon Bakke, & prycke hym þer on, and roste hym, & serue f[orth].

.xxxv. **Capoun or gos farced.**—Take Percely, & Swynys grece, or Sewet of a schepe, & parboyle hem to-gederys til þey ben tendyr; þan take harde ȝolkys of Eyroun, & choppe for-*with*; caste þer-to Pouder Pepir, Gyngere, Canel, Safroun, & Salt, & grapis in tyme of ȝere, & clowys y-nowe; & for defawte of grapis, Oynons, fyrst wil y-boylid, & afterward alle to-choppyd, & so stuffe hym & roste hym, & serue hym forth. And ȝif þe lust, take a litil Porke y-sode, & al to-choppe hit smal a-mong þat oþer; for it wol be þe better, & namely [1] for þe Capoun.

.xxxvj. **Pokerounce.**—Take Hony, & caste it in a potte tyl it wexe chargeaunt y-now; take & skeme it clene. Take Gyngere, Canel, & Galyngale, & caste þer-to; take whyte Brede, & kytte to trenchours,[2] & toste ham; take þin paste whyle it is hot, & sprede it vppe-[3]on þin trenchourys *with* a spone, & plante it *with* Pynes, & serue f[orth].

.xxxvij. **Sauoge.**—Take Pigis fete clene y-pekyd; þan tak Freysshe broþe of Beff, & draw mylke of Almaundys, & þe Piggys þer-in; þen mence Sawge; þan grynd hym smal, & draw owt þe Ius þorw a straynoure; þan take clowys y-now, & do þer-in pouder Gyngere, & Canelle, Galyngale, Vynegre, & Sugre y-now; Salt it þan, & þanne serue forth.

.xxxviij. **A Kyde a-Forsyde.**—Take a pigge, & make hym clene, and Skynne hym, & Fylle it ful of suche mete as þou dost a capoun; þan take þe fleysshe, & vntrusse hym on a spete, in þe maner of a kede, & roste hym; & endore hym *with* ȝolkys of Eyroun as an kede, & þan serue forth.

.xxxix. **Eyroun in lentyn.**—Take Eyroun, & blow owt þat ys *with*-ynne atte oþer ende; þan waysshe þe schulle clene in warme Water; þan take gode mylke of Almaundys, & sette it on þe fyre; þan take a fayre canvas, & pore þe mylke þer-on, & lat renne owt þe water; þen take it owt on þe cloþe, & gader it to-gedere *with* a platere; þen putte sugre y-now þer-to; þan take þe halvyndele, & colour it *with* Safroun, a lytil, & do þer-to pouder Canelle;

---

[1] MS. *a namely.*   [2] two trenchers, big slices.   [3] lf. 32 bk.

þan take & do of þe whyte in the neþ*er* ende of þe schulle, & in þe myddel þe ȝolk, & fylle it vppe w*ith* þe whyte; but noȝt to fulle, for goyng ouer; þan sette it in þe fyre & roste it, & *serue* f[orth].

.xl. Puddyng of p*ur*paysse.—Take þe Blode of hym, & þe grece of hym self, & Ote-mele, & Salt, & Pepir, & Gyngere, & melle þese to-goderys wel, & þan putte þis in þe Gutte of þe purpays, & þan lat it seþe esyli, & not hard, a good whylys; & þan take hym vppe, & broyle hym a lytil, & þan *serue* f[orth].

.xli. Raynolleȝ.—Nym sode Porke & chese, & seþe y-fere, & caste þer-to gode pouder Pepir, Canelle, Gyngere, Clowes, Mac[e]ȝ, [1]an close þin comade in dow, & frye it in freysshe grece ryȝt wel; an þanne serue it forth.

.xlij. Froyse in lentynne.—Take Fygis & Roysonys, & grynde hem in a mortere, & draw vppe w*ith* kreme of Almaundys; þan take Rys þorw a cloþe; þan take þe Luce, an þe Perche, & þe Schrympe, & seþe hem, & do a-way þe bonys, & þe hedys, & grynde hem in an Mortere, & draw hym vppe w*ith* þe creme of þe Almaundys; þen take Rys, & do hem on a potte ouer þe fyre, Whan þey ben clene, w*ith* a lytil Watere, late hem seþe til þey ben dryȝe, & þat þey schorge; þan take & hew on a borde, & do þer-to; þen take Sugre, & Safroun a goode quantyte, & gode pouder, & caste þer-to, & boyle it y-fere, & frye it in oyle, & make þer-of a Froyse, & *serue* f[orth].

.xliij. Payn pur-dew.—Take fayre ȝolkys of Eyrou*n*, & trye hem fro þe whyte, & draw hem þorw a straynoure, & take Salt and caste þer-to; þan take fayre brede, & kytte it as troundeȝ rounde; þan take fayre Boter þat is claryfiyd, or ellys fayre Freysshe grece, & putte it on a potte, & make it hote; þan take & wete wyl þin troundeȝ in þe ȝolkys, & putte hem in þe panne, an so frye hem vppe; but ware of cleuyng to the panne; & whan it is fryid, ley hem on a dysshe, & ley Sugre y-nowe þer-on, & þanne serue it forht.

.xliiij. Meselade.[2]—Take Eyroun, þe ȝolkys an þe whyte to-gedere, & draw hem þorw a straynoure; & þan take a litil Botere, & caste in a fayre frying panne; & whan þe boter is hot, take þe drawyn Eyroun, & caste þer-to; þan take a Sawcere, an gadre þe Eyroun to-gedere in þe panne, as it were þe brede of a pewter dysshe; & þan take fayre peceȝ of Brede, þe mountance of a mosselle of Brede, vppe-on þe Eyroun, & turne þan [thy][3] brede downward in þe panne; þanne [4]take it of þe panne, & caste fayre whyte

Sugre þer-to, & serue forth; an to euery good meslade take a þowsand Eyroun or mo.

.**xlv. Brawune fryeȝ.**—Take Brawune, & kytte it þinne; þan take þe ȝolkys of Eyroun, & sum of þe whyte þer-with; þan take mengyd Flowre, an draw þe Eyroun þorw a straynoure; þen take a gode quantyte of Sugre, Saferoun, & Salt, & caste þer-to, & take a fayre panne with Freyssche gres, & set ouer þe fyre; & whan þe grece is hote, take þe Brawn, an putte in bature, & turne it wyl þer-yn, an þan putte it on þe panne with þe grece, & late frye to-gederys a lytil whyle; þan take it vppe in-to a fayre dyssche, & caste Sugre þer-on, & þan serue forth.

.**xlvj. Longe Fretoure.**—Take Milke, an make fayre croddes þer-of, in þe maner of a chese al tendyr; þan take owt þe whey as clene as þou may, & putte it on a bolle; þan take ȝolkys of Eyroun & Ale, & menge floure, & cast þer-to, a gode quantyte, & draw it þorw a straynoure in-to a fayre vesselle; þan take a panne with fayre grece, & hete it on þe fyre, but lat it nowt boyle, & þan ley þin creme a brode; þan take a knyff, & kytte a quantyte þer-of fro þe borde in-to þe panne, & efte a-noþer, & let it frye; & whan it is brownne, take it vppe in-to a fayre dyssche, and caste Sugre y-now þer-on, & serue forth.

.**xlvij. Rapeye.**—Take dow, & make þer-of a þinne kake; þanne take Fygys & raysonys smal y-grounde, & temper hem with Almaunde Milke; take pouder of Pepir, & of Galyngale, Clowes, & menge to-gederys, & ley on þin kake a-long as bene koddys, & ouer-caste þin kake to-gederys, & dewte on þe eggys, an frye in Oyle, & serue forth.

.**xlviij. Ryschewys in lente.**—Take Fygys & sethe hem uppe in Ale; þan take whan þey ben tendyr, & bray hem smal on a Mortere; [1]þan take Almaundys, & schrede hem þer-to smal; take Perys, & schrede hem þer-to; take datys, & schrede hem þer-to; & nym Milwel or lenge, þat is wel y-wateryd, & tese þer-to; þan make þin farsure, & rolle a-long in þin hond, & ley hem in flowre; þan make þin bature with ale & Floure, & frye hem vppe brown in Oyle; ryȝt so, make round-lyke Fretourys in þe maner be-for-sayd, & frye hem vppe, & þat ben y-clepid Ragons, & þanne serue hem forth.

.**xlix. Hanoney.**—Take an draw þe Whyte & þe ȝolkys of þe Eyroun þorw a straynoure; þan take Oynonys, & schrede hem smal; þan take fayre Boter or grece, & vnneþe kyuer þe panne þer-with, an frye þe Oynonys, & þan caste þe Eyroun in þe panne, & broke þe Eyrouns & þe Oynonys to-gederys;

[1] leaf 34

an þan lat hem frye to-gederys a litel whyle; þan take hem vp, an serue
forth alle to-broke to-gederys on a fayre dyssche.

.l. Hagas de Almaynne.—Take Fayre Eyroun, þe ȝolke & þe Whyte, &
draw hem þorw a straynour; þan take Fayre Percely, & parboyle it in a
potte with boyling broþe; þan take þe ȝolkys of Eyroun hard y-sothe, &
hew þe ȝolkys & þe Percely smal to-gederys; þan take Sugre, pouder
Gyngere, Salt, & caste þer-to; þen take merow, & putte it on a straynourys
ende, & lat hange in-to a boyling potte; & parboyle it, & take it vppe, &
let it kele, & þan kytte it in smal pecys; þan take þe drawyn Eyroun,
& put hem in a panne al a-brode, & vnneþe ony grece in þe panne, & cowche
ye ȝolkys & þe Percely þer-on in þe panne, & þan cowche of þe Marow pecys
þer-on, & þan fold vppe eche kake by-neþe eche corner in .iiij. square, as
platte, and turne it on þe panne oneȝ; let lye a litel whyle; þan take it vp
& serue f[orth].

¹.lj. Cryspeȝ.—Take Whyte of Eyroun, Mylke, & Floure, & a lytel Berme,
& bete it to-gederys, & draw it þorw a straynoure, so þat it be renneng, &
not to styf, & caste Sugre þer-to, & Salt; þanne take a chafer ful of freysshe
grece boyling, & put þin hond in þe Bature, & lat þin bature renne down
by þin fyngerys in-to þe chafere; & whan it is ronne to-gedere on þe chafere,
& is y-now, take & nym a skymer, & take it vp, & lat al þe grece renne
owt, & put it on a fayre dyssche, & cast þer-on Sugre y-now, & serue forth.

.lij. Ryschewys of Marow.—Take fayre Flowre & raw ȝolkys of Eyroun,
& Sugre, & Salt, & pouder of Gyngere, & Safroun, & make fayre cakes; &
þan take marow, Sugre, & pouder of Gyngere, & ley it on þin cake, & fold
hem to-gederys, & kytte hem in þe maner of Rysschewes, & frye hem in
freyssche grece, & þanne serue forth.

.liij. Lesynges de chare.—Take fayre Buttys of Porke; hewe hem, &
grynd hem, & caste þer-to Raw ȝolkys of Eyroun, & þen putte it in-to a
fayre Vesselle; & take Roysonys of corauns, & dates myncyd, & pouder
of Gyngere, Pepir, & Safroun, & Sugre, an melle all þes to-gederys; &
make fayre past of Sugre & Safroun, & Salt; temper þer-in, & make
.ij. fayre flat cakys þer-of, & lay þe stuf þer-on al a-brode on þe cake al
flat; & þan take þat oþer cake, & lay hym al a-brode þer-on; & þan kytte
[the] cakys þorw with an knyf in maner of lesyngys; & þan make fayre
bature of Raw ȝolkys of Eyroun, Sugre, & Salt, & close þe sydys of þe
lesyngȝ þer-with, & þan frye hem in fayre grece, & serue forth.

.liiij. Fretoure.—Take whete floure, Ale ȝest, Safroun, & Salt, & bete

¹ leaf 34 bk.

alle to-goderys as þikke as þou schuldyst make oþer bature in fleyssche tyme; & þan take fayre Applys, & kut hem in ma¹ner of Fretourys, & wete hem in þe bature vp on downne, & frye hem in fayre Oyle, & caste hem in a dyssche; & caste Sugre þer-on, & serue forth.

.lv. **Chawettys Fryidde.**—Take & make fayre past of flowre & water, Sugre, & Safroun, & Salt; & þan make fayre round cofyns þer-of; & þen fylle þin cofyns with þin stuf, & keuere þin cofyns with þe same past, & frye hem in gode Oyle, & serue f[orth].

.lvj. **Tansye.**— Take fayre Tansye, & grynd in a morter; þanne take Eyroun, þe ȝolkys & þe whyte, & stray[ne] hem þorw a straynoure; & strayne also þe Ius of þe Tansye, & melle to-goderes; & take fayre Freysche grece, & put þer-on ouer þe fyre, tylle it melte; þan caste þe stuf þer-on, & gadere to-gedere with a Sawcer or a dysshe, as þou wolt it, lasse oþer more, & turne it in þe panne; & þan serue it forth.

.lvij. **Froyse out of Lentyn.**—Take Eyroun & draw þe ȝolkes & þe whyte þorw a straynoure; þan take fayre Bef or vele, & sethe it tyl it be y-now; þan hew cold oþer hote, & melle to-goderys þe eggys, þe Bef, or vele, & caste þer-to Safroun, & Salt, & pouder of Pepir, & melle it to-goderys; þan take a fayre Frying-panne, & sette it ouer þe fyre, & caste þer-on fayre freysshe grece, & make it hot, & caste þe stuf þer-on, & stere it wel in þe panne tyl it come to-goderys wel; cast on þe panne a dysshe & presse it to-goderys, & turne it onys, & þanne serue it forth.

.lviij. **Ryschewys close & Fryez.**—Take Fygys, & grynd hem smal in a mortere with a lytil Oyle, & grynd with hym clowys & Maces; & þan take it vppe in-to a vesselle, & cast þer-to Pynez, Saundrys, & Roysonys of Coraunce, & meneyd Datys, Pouder Pepir, Canel, Salt, Safroun; ²þan take fyne past of flowre an water, Sugre, Safroun, & Salt, & make fayre cakys þer-of; þan rolle þin stuf in þin hond, & couche it in þe cakys, & kyt it, & folde hym as Ruschewys, & frye hem vppe in Oyle; and serue forth hote.

.lix. ³**Nese Bekys.**—Take Fygys & grynd hem wel; þan take F[re]ysshe ⁴ Samoun & goode Freysshe Elys wyl y-sothe, & pyke owt þe bonys, & grynd þe Fyssche with þe Fygis, & do þer-to powder Gyngere, Canelle; & take fayre past [of]⁵ Flowre, & make fayre cakys ryth þinne, & take of þe fars, & lay on þe cake, & close with a-noþer; þen take a Sawcere, & skoure þe sydis, & close þe cake, & Frye hem wyl in Oyle; & ȝif þou wolt haue hym

¹ leaf 35. ² leaf 35 bk. ³ ? MS. N or M. ⁴ MS. *Fyssche* ; A. *fresshe.* ⁵ *of* added from A.

partye, coloure hym w*ith* Safroun, Percely, & Sawnderys ; & serue forth for a gode fryid mete.

.lx. Myleȝ in Rapeye.—Take Fygys & wasche hem clene, and boyle hem in wyne, & grynd hem smal, & draw hem vppe w*ith* þe Wyne þat þey were sothyn in ; þan take flowre of Rys, & Wyne, & draw þorw a straynoure, & do þer-to pouder Gyng*er*, Canelle, Maceȝ, Quybibeȝ, & þen take Freyssche Samoun, oþe[r] Pike or gode Freysssche Codlyng ; seþe it wyl, & pike owt þe bonys ; þan take perys y-coryd, & grynde hem ryȝth smal & wyl w*ith* þe Fyssche ; þan take hard ȝolkys of Eyroun soþin, & grynd it wyth-al, & do it in-to þin veselle, & take w*ith* Sugre & pouder Gynger, & meng it w*ith* þe farcere [1] wyl, & presse hem to-gederys ; þan make a gode bature [2] of Almaunde mylke & Floure, & do þer-in, & frye hem wyl in Oyle, & ley hem yn a dyssche, & pore on þe Sew, & serue forth.

.lxj. Cruste Rolle.—Take fayre smal Flowre of whete ; nym Eyroun & broke þer-to, & coloure þe past w*ith* Safroun ; rolle it on a borde also þinne as p*ar*chement, rounde a-bowte as [3] an oblye ; [4] frye hem, & serue forth ; and þus may do in lente, but do away þe Eyroun, & nym mylke of Almaundys, & frye hem in Oyle, & þen serue forth.

.lxij. Chawettys a-forsed.—Take Merybonys & Porke ; hew it an Raw ȝolkys of Eyroun, & melle to-gederys w*ith* pouder Canelle, Pepir, Gyngere, & Safroun, & Sugre y-now ; kyuere hem, frye hem vp in Grece, & s*er*ue forth.

.lxiij. Fretoure owt of lente.—Take Flowre, Milke, & Eyroun, & grynd Pepir & Safroun, & make þer-of a bature ; pare Applys, & ster hem, & frye hem vppe.

.lxiiij. Towres.—Take & make a gode þikke bature of ȝolkys of Eyroun, & marow y-now þer-on, pouder pepir, Maceȝ, clowes, Safroun, Sugre, & Salt ; & ȝif þou wolt, a litel soþe Porke or vele y-choppid ; þer-to take þen þe whyte of Eyroun, & strayne hem in-to a bolle ; þan putte a lytil Saffroun & Salt to þe whyte, & sette a panne w*ith* grece ouer þe fyre, & be-war þat þin grece be nowt to hote ; þan putte a litel of þe Whyte comade in þe panne, & late flete al a-brode as þou makyst a pancake ; þen, whan it is sumwhat styf, ley þin comade of þin Eyroun, þat is to saying, of þe ȝolkys, in þe myddel, & caste by þe cake round a-bowte, & close hym foure-square, & fry hem vp, & serue hem forth for Soperys in Somere. [5]

---

[1] Farcure ; stuffing.   [2] MS. *a gode a bature gode.*   [3] leaf 36.
[4] *Oble,* sacramental wafer.   [5] four pages and a quarter blank here in the MS.

¹HERE BEGYNNYTH DYUERSE BAKE METIS.

.I. **Tartes de chare.**—Take Freyssche Porke, & hew it, & grynd it on a mortere ; & take it vppe in-to a fayre vesselle ; & take þe whyte an þe ȝolkys of Eyroun, & strayne into a Vesselle þorw a straynoure, & tempere þin Porke þer-with ; þan take Pynez, Roysonys of Coraunce, & frye hem in freysshe grece, & caste þer-to pouder Pepir, & Gyngere, Canelle, Sugre, Safroun, & Salt, & caste þer-to, & do it on a cofynne, & plante þin cofynne a-boue with Pyneȝ, & kyt Datys, & gret Roysonys, & smal byrdys, or ellys hard ȝolkys of Eyroun ; & ȝif þou take byrdys, frye hem on a lytel grece or þow putte hem on þin cofynne, & endore with ȝolkys of Eyroun, & Safroun, & lat bake til it be y-now, & serue forth.

.ij. **A-noþer manere.**—Take Fygys, Roysonys, & Porke, & a lytel brede y-ground y-fere ; take hym vppe, & put Pepir y-now þer-to, & Maceȝ, Clowys, & make þin cofyn, & putte þin comade þer-on.

.iij. **A-noþer manere.**—Tak fayre porke y-broylid, & grynd it smal with ȝolkys of Eyroun ; þan take Pepir, Gyngere, & grynd it smal, & melle it with-al, & a lytel hony, & floryssche þin cofyns with-ynne & with-owte, & hele hem with þin ledys,² & late hem bake, & serue forth.

.iiij. **Daryoles.**—Take wyne & Fr[e]ssche broþe, Clowes, Maces, & Marow, & pouder of Gyngere, & Safroun, & let al boyle to-gederys, & put þer-to creme, (& ȝif it be clowtys, draw it þorwe a straynoure,) & ȝolkys of Eyroun, & melle hem to-gederys, & pore þe licoure þat þe Marow was soþyn yn þer-to ; þan make fayre cofyns of fayre past, & put þe Marow þer-yn, & mynce datys, & strawberys in tyme of ȝere, & put þe cofyns ³in þe ovyn, & late hem harde a lytel ; þan take hem owt, & put þe licoure þer-to, & late hem bake, & serue f[orth].

.v. **A-nother manere.**—Take Pike, Almaunde Milke, & boyle yt þikke, & let it kele ; þan take Eyroun & chese, & grynd y-fere, & do þer-to ; take pouder Sugre & caste þer-to, & put in þin cofyns, & noȝt y-helyd, & bake, & serue f[orth].

.vj. **Tartes of Fyssche.**—Take Fygys, & Roysoynys, & pike an sethe in Wyne ; þan take Costardys, Perys, & pare hem clene, & pike out þe core, & putte hem in a morter with þe frute ; þen tak Codlyng or haddok, oþer Elys, & seþe hem & pike owt þe bonys, & grynd alle y-fere, & do þer-to a lytel wyne, & melle to-gederys : an do þer-to Canelle, Clowys, Maceȝ, Quybibeȝ,

---

¹ lf. 37 bk.   ² Lids.   ³ leaf 38.

pouder Gyngere, & of Galyngale, & pepir, & Roysonys of coraunce, and coloure it with Safroun. When þou makyst þin cofyns, þan take gode fat Ele, & culpe hym, & take owt þe stonys of Datys, & farce hem; & blaunche Almaundys, & caste þer-to; but fyrste frye hem in Oylo, & couche al þis a-mong, & bete þin cofyns with þe ledys, & bake, & serue forth.

.vij. **Chawettys.**—Take buttys of Vele, & mynce hem smal, or Porke, & put on a potte; take Wyne, & caste þer-to pouder of Gyngere, Pepir, & Safroun, & Salt, & a lytel verþous,[1] & do hem in a cofyn with ȝolkys of Eyroun, & kutte Datys & Roysonys of Coraunce, Clowys, Maceȝ, & þen couere þin cofyn, & lat it bake tyl it be y-now.

.viij. **Chawettys.**—Take Porke y-sode, & mencyd Datys, and grynd hem smal to-gederys; take ȝolkys of Eyroun, & putte þer-to a gode hepe, & grene chese putte þer-to; & whan it ys smal y-now, take Gyngere, Canelle, & melle wyl þi commade þer-with, & put in þiu cofyns; þan take ȝolkys of Eyroun [2]hard y-sothe, an kerue hem in two, & ley a-boue, & bake hem; & so noȝt y-closyd, serue forth.

.ix. **Malmenye Furneȝ.**—Take gode Milke of Almaundys, & flowre of Rys, & gode Wyne crete, or þe brawn of a Capoune, oþer of Fesaunte, & Sugre, & pouder Gyngere, & Galyngale, & of Canelle, & boyle y-fere; & make it chargeaunt, & coloure it with Alkenade, oþer with Saunderys; & ȝif it be Red, a-lye it with ȝolkys of Eyroun; & make smal cofyns of dow, & coloure hem with-owte, & bake on an ovyn, & coloure with-ynne & wyth-oute; þen haue Hony y-boylid hote, & take a dyssche, & wete þin dyssche in þe hony, & with þe wete dyssche ley þe malmenye & þe cofyns; & whan þey ben bake, & þou dressest yn, caste a-boue blaunche pouder, Quybibeȝ, maceȝ, Gelofreȝ; & þanne serue it forth.

.x. **Rapeye.**—Take Dow, & make þer-of a brode þin cake; þen take Fygys & Roysonys smal y-grounde, & fyrst y-sode, An a pece of Milwelle or lenge y-braid with-al; & take pouder of Pepir, Galyngale, Cloweȝ, & mence to-gedere, & ley þin comede on þe cake in þe maner of a benecodde, y-rollyd with þin hond; þan ouer-caste thy cake ouer þi comade, as it wol by-clippe hit; & with a saweere brerde go round as þe comade lyith, & kutte hem, & so he is kut & close with-al, & bake or frye it, & þanne serue it forth.

.xj. **Tartes of Frute in lente.**—Take Fygys & sethe hem wyl tyl þey ben neyssche; þan bray hem in a morter, & a pece of Milwél þer-with; take ham vppe & caste roysonys of coraunce þer-to; þan take Almaundys & Dates[3]

---

[1] verjuice.   [2] lf. 38 bk.   [3] '& Dates' interlined by a later hand.

y-schrod þer-to; þan take pouder of Pepir & mong with-al; þen putte it on
þin cofynne, & Safroun þin cofynn a-bouc, & opyn hem a-bowte þe
myddel; & ouer-cast þe openyng vppon þe lede,[1] & bake hym a lytel, &
serue f[orth].

[2]**.xij. Vn Vyaunde Furne; san; noum de chare.**—Take stronge Dow, &
make a cake sumdele þicke, & make it tow; þan take larde; of Venysoun, or
a bere, or of a Berc, & kerue hem þinne as Fylettes of Porke, & lay þin
lardys square as a chekyr, & ley þer-vppe a tyne y-makyd of Eyroun vppe-
on þe tyne; ley þin farsure, y-makyd of Hennys, & of Porke, of Eyroun, &
myid brede, & Salt, & chese, yf þou it hast; & þat it bo makkyd at .iiij.
tymes. Fyrst make þus þin whyte farsure: grynd in a mortere, Gyngere,
Canelle, Galyngale; take then almaundys & flonre of Rys, and a party of
Fleysshe, & caste ther-to in a mortere, & grynd ry;th smal, & temper it
with Eyroun. þus make þin ;elow Farsure: nym Safroun, Gyngere, Canel,
Galyngale, Brede, & a partye of þin Fleyssche, & grynd it smal in þe
mortere, & temper it vppe with Eyroun. The þryd maner schal ben blake:
nym Gyngere, Canelle, Galyngale, Brede, Eyroun, & Old chese; nym þan
Percely, & grynd it smal in a mortere, & wryng it & do it vppe; & do it
to þin Fleyssche, & þer-with coloure þin fayre partye of Fleyssche, & ley a
party of þin Fleyssche on .iiij. quarterys, but þat þe brede be as þin cake;
take þen & ley þer-vppe-on þin Fleyssche, & lay þer-vppe-on a grece; a-bouc
þin grece ley þi cyrey; nym þin þridde cours of þin Flessche, & lay as
brode as þin cake, & þan grece, & þer a-bouyn, a cyrey. ¶ ley þe iiij. course
of þin Fleyssche on .iiij. quarterys as brode as þin cake, & þan grece, &
þan a-boue, a cyuey. The .v. cours of þin Fleyssche, ley as brode as þine
cake, & þen grece, & þan aboue, a cyuey. Nym þe .vj. cours, & lay as brode
as þin cake, & þan grece, & þan a cyuey. Nym þo .viij. cours of þe
Fleysshe, & lay as brode as þin cake on .iiij. quarterys, & grece, & þan a
cyrey; & a lytel bake hem, & serue forth.

[3]**.xiij. Vn Vyaunde furnez san; nom de chare**.—Take flowre, Almaunde
milke, & Safroune, & make þer-of .iiij. tynez, & frye þi tynez in Oyle; nym
þen Almaundys, & draw þer-of mylke ry;t þikke; nym mace;, Quybibe;, &
floure of Rys, Canelle, Galyngale; take þenne haddok, Creue;, Perchys,
Tenche;, & seþe; whan þey ben sothyn, take þin fyssche from þe bonys,
& bray it ry;t smal with þin Spicerye to-goderys, & make þer-of þin
farsure. Whan it is y-makyd, departe it in .iiij. partyis, þat o partye

---

[1] lid.   [2] leaf 39.   [3] leaf 39 back.

4

whyte, þat oþer ȝelow, þe þrydde grene, þe ferþe blak coloure with Fygys,
Roysonys, an Datys; take þe firste cours of þe Fyssche, of al þe .iiij.
cours, & ley on þin cyvey a-bouyn þin Fyssche, in .iiij. quarterys, as a
chekyr, as brode as þin cake, & caste a-bouyn Sugre of Alysaundre, &
þer-vppe-on þine tyne. Nym an-oþer cours, & ley on þi .iiij. quarterys
as brode as þin tyne, & þer-vppe-[on] þin Sugre. Nym þe þrydde cours
of þin Fyssche, & ley on .iiij. quarterys, & caste a-boue Sugre, & a tyne.
Nym [þe] .iiij. cours a-cordant to þin oþer, a-þenched[1] to-geder, an a-boue
a hole as a rose, & cetera.

.xiiij. **Pety Pernollys.**—Take fayre Floure, Safroun, Sugre, & Salt, &
make þer-of past; þan make smal cofyns; þen take ȝolkys of Eyroun, & trye
hem fro þe whyte; & lat þe ȝolkys be al hole, & noȝt to-broke, & ley .iij.
or .iiij. zolkys in a cofyn; and þan take marow of bonys, to or .iij.
gobettys, & cowche in þe cofynn; þan take pouder Gyngere, Sugre,
Roysonys of coraunce, & caste a-boue; & þan kyuere þin cofyn with þe
same past, & bake hem, & frye hem in fayre grece, & serue f[orth].

.xv. **Douceteȝ.**—Take Creme a gode cupfulle, & put it on a straynoure;
þanne take ȝolkys of Eyroun & put þer-to, & a lytel mylke; þen strayne it
þorw a straynoure in-to a bolle; þen take Sugre y-now, & put þer-to, or
ellys hony forde faute[2] of Sugre, þan coloure it with Safroun; þan take þin
cofyns, & put in þe ovynne lere, & lat hem ben hardyd; þan take a dysshe
y-fastenyd on þe pelys ende; & pore þin comade in-to þe dysshe, & fro þe
dysshe in-to þe cofyns; & when þey don a-ryse wel, take hem out, & serue
hem forth.

.xvj. **Crustade.**—Take vele, an smyte in lytel pecys in-to a potte, an
wayssche yt fayre; þan take fayre water, & lat yt boyle to-gedere with
Percely, Sawge, Saueray, & Ysope smal y-now an hew; & whan it is on
boylyng, take pouder Peper, CaneH, Clowys, Maces, Safroun, & lat hem
boyle to-gederys, & a gode dele of wyne þer-with. Whan þe fleyssche is
y-boylid, take it fro þe broþe al clene, & lat þe broþe kele; & whan it is
cold, take Eyroun, þe whyte & þe ȝolkys, & cast þorw a straynoure, & put
hem in-to the broþe, so many þat þe broþe be styf y-now; þen make fayre
cofyns, & cowche .iij. pecys or .iiij. of þe fleyssche in a cofyn; þan take
Datys, & kytte hem, & cast þer-to; þan take pouder Gyngere, & a lytel
verious, & putte in-to þe broþe & Salt; & þan putte þe broþe on þe cofyns,
bake a lytel with þe fleyssche or þou putte þin lycoure þer-on, & lat al

[1] ? pinched, A. reads, "a-þenched to-gedre aboue a hole, as a rose."   [2] leaf 40.

bake to-gederys tyl it be y-now; þanne [take] yt owt, and serue
hem forth.

.xvij. Crustade lumbard.—Take gode Creme, & leuys of Percely, &
Eyroun, þe ȝolkys & þe whyte, & breke hem þer-to, & strayne þorwe a
straynoure, tyl it be so styf þat it wol bere hym-self; þan take fayre
Marwe, & Datys y-cutte in .ij. or .iij. & Pruneȝ; & putte þe Datys an[1] þe
Pruneȝ & Marwe on a fayre cofynne, y-mad of fayre past, & put þe cofyn
on þe ovyn tyl it be a lytel hard; þanne draw hem out of þe ouyn; take þe
lycour & putte þer-on, & fylle it vppe, & caste Sugre y-now on, & Salt;
þan lat bake to-gederys tyl it be y-now; & ȝif it be in lente, lef þe Eyroun
& þe Marwe out, [2] & þanne serue it forth.

.xviij. Flathons.—Take Milke an ȝolkys of Eyroun, & draw it þorw a
straynoure with whyte Sugre, oþer blake Sugre, & mylt fayre botter, & putte
þer-to, & Salt; & make fayre cofyns, & sette hem on þe ouen tyl þey ben
hard; þan take a pele with a dyssche on þe ende, & fylle þe dyssche with
þin comade, & pore in-to þe cofyns, & lat bake a lytel whyle; þan take hem
out in-to a fayre dysscħ, & cast whyte sugre þer-on, & serue forth.

.xix. Venyson y-bake.—Take hoghes of Venysoŵ, & parboyle hem in
fayre Water an Salt; & whan þe Fleyssche is fayre y-boylid, make fayre
past, & cast þin Venyson þer-on; & caste a-boue an be-neþe, pouder Pepir,
Gyngere, & Salt, & þan sette it oŵ þe ouyn, & lat bake, & serue forth.

.xx. Pety Pernauntes.—Take fayre Flowre, Sugre, Safroun, an Salt, &
make þer-offe fayre past & fayre cofyng*es*; þan take fayre y-tryid ȝolkys
Raw, & Sugre, an pouder Gyngere, & Raysounys of Coraunce, & myncyd
Datys, but not to smal; þan caste al þis on a fayre bolle, & melle al to-
gederys, & put in þin cofyn, & lat bake oþer Frye in Freyssche grece.

.xxj. Quyncis or Wardoʊns i*n* past.—Take & make fayre Rounde cofyns
of fayre past; þan take fayre Raw Quynces, & pare hem with a knyf, & take
fayre out þe core þer-of; þan take Sugre y-now, & a lytel pouder Gyngere,
& stoppe þe hole fulle; & cowche .ij. or .iij. wardonys or quynceȝ in a
cofyn, & keuere hem, & lat hem bake; & for defaut of Sugre, take hony; but
þen putte pouder Pepir þer-on, & Gyngere, in þe maner be-for sayd.

.xxij. Lamproʊns y-bake.—Take lamprounys & skald hem with [*blank in
MS.*], & make fayre paste, & couche .ij. or iij lamprounys with pouder of
Gyngere, Salt, Pepir, & lat hem bake; & leche [3] Samoun in fayre brode
pecys, & bake hem in þe maner be-forsayd, & þanne serue forth.

---

[1] MS. in.   [2] leaf 40, back.   [3] leaf 41.

.**xxiij. Lamprays bake.**—Take & make fayre round cofyns of fyne past, & take Freyssche lampreys, & late hem blode .iij. fyngerys with-in þe tayle, & lat hem blede in a vesselle, & late hym deye in þe same vesselle in þe same blode; þan take broun Brede, & kyt it, & stepe it in þe Venegre, & draw þorw a straynoure; þan take þe same blode, & ponder of Canel, & cast þer-to tyl it be broun; þan caste þer-to pouder Pepir, Salt, & Wyne a lytelle, þat it be noȝt to strong of venegre. An skald þe Lampray, & pare hem clene, & couche hym round on þe cofyn, tyl he be helyd;[1] þan kyuere hym fayre with a lede, saue a lytel hole in þe myddelle, & at[2] þat hool, blow in þe cofynne with þin mowþe a gode blast of Wynde. And sodenly stoppe þe hole, þat þe wynd a-byde with-ynne, to reyse vppe þe cofynne, þat he falle nowt a-downe; & whan he is a lytel y-hardid in þe ouen, pryke þe cofyn with a pynne y-stekyd on a roddys ende, for brekyng of þe cofynne, & þan lat bake, & serue forth colde.   And when þe lamprey is take owt of þe cofynne & etyn, take þe Syrippe in þe cofynne, & put on a chargere, & caste Wyne þer-to, an pouder Gyngere, & lat boyle in þe fyre.   Than take fayre Paynemayn y-wette in Wyne, & ley þe soppis in þe cofynne of þe lamprey, & ley þe Syrippe a-boue, & ete it so hot; for it is gode lordys mete.

.**xxiiij. Tartes de chare.**—Take Freyssche Porke, & hew it; & grynd it in a mortere, & take it vppe in-to a fayre vesselle; & take þe whyte of Eyroun & þe ȝolke, y-tryid þorw a straynoure; & temper þin porke þer-with; & þan take Pyneȝ, & Raysonys of Coraunce, & frye hem in Freyssche grece, & caste þer-to [3]pouder Pepir & Gyngere, Canel, Sugre, Safroun, Salt, & caste þer-to; & do it on a cofynne, & plante þe cofynne a-boue with Pruneȝ, & with Datys, & gret Roysonys of Coraunce, & smal Byrdys, or ellys harde ȝolkys of Eyroun; & yf þow tage[4] Byrdys, frye hem in grece or þou putte hem in þe cofyn; & þan keuere þin cofynne; & þan endore it with ȝolkys of Eyroun, & with Safroune, & late yt bake tyll it be y-now; & þan serue forth.

.**xxv. Rastons.**—Take fayre Flowre, & þe whyte of Eyroun, & þe ȝolke, a lytel; þan take Warme Berme, & putte al þes to-gederys, & bete hem to-gederys with þin hond tyl it be schort & þikke y-now, & caste Sugre y-now þer-to, & þenne lat reste a whyle; þan kaste in a fayre place in þe oven, & late bake y-now; & þen with a knyf cutte yt round a-boue in maner of a crowne, & kepe þe cruste þat þou kyttyst; & þan pyke al þe cromys with-ynne to-gederys, an pike hem smal with þin knyf, & saue þe sydys & al þe

---

[1] covered.   [2] Harl. ellys. A. eH, altered to *at.*   [3] lf. 41, bk.   [4] take.

cruste hole w*ith*-owte; & þan caste þer-in clarifiyd Boter, & Mille [1] þe crome;
& þe [2] botere to-goderez, & keuere it a-ȝen w*ith* þe cruste, þat þou kyttest
a-way; þan putte it in þe ovyn aȝen a lytil tyme; & þan take it out, & serue
it forth.

.**xxvj. Darioles.**—Take Wyne, an Freyssche broþe, & Clowes, & Maces, &
Marwe, pouder Gyngere, Safroun, & lat al boyle to-goderys, & Creme, (ȝif it
be clowty, draw it þorw a straynoure,) & ȝolkys of Eyroun, & melle hem
to-goderys, & pore þe lycoure þat þe marwe was sothe in, þer-to; þen
make fayre cofyns, & put þe Marwe þer-in, & mence Datis, & Strawberys
in tyme of ȝere, & sette þe cofyns [3] in þe ovenne, & lat hem hard a lytelle,
& take hem out, & put þe lycoure þer-to, & lat bake; & serue forth.

.**xxvij. Pyeȝ de pareȝ.**—Take & smyte fayre buttys of Porke, & buttys
of Vele, to-goderys, & put it on a fayre potte, & do þer-to Freyssche [4] broþe,
& a quantyte of wyne, & lat boyle alle to-goderys tyl yt be y-now; þan take
it fro þe fyre, & lat kele a lytelle; þan caste þer-to ȝolkys of Eyroun, &
pouder of. Gyngere, Sugre, & Salt, & mynced Datys, & Roysonys of
Coraunce; þen make fayre past, and cofyunys, & do þer-on; kyuer it, &
let bake, & *serue* f[orth].

.**xxviij. Potrous.**—Take a schouyl of yrowȝ, & hete it brennyng hote; &
þan take it owt of þe fyre, & fille it fulle of Salt; þan make a pitte in þe
Salt al holow, þe schap of a treen dyssche; & sette þe panne & þe Salt
ouer þe fyre a-ȝen, tyl þe Salt be brennyng hote; & þan caste þin whyte
& þe ȝolkys of Eyroun in-to þe hole of þe Salte, & lat seþe ouer þe fyre tyl
it be half harde; & þan put a dyssche half fulle of Salt; & þan take a
dressoure knyf, & put vnderneþe þe Salt in þe panne, & hef [5] it vppe so fayre,
þat þe cofyn w*ith* þe Eyroun broke noȝt; þan sette it on þe dyssche wyth
þe Salt, & þan serue it forth.

.**xxix. Flampoyntes bake.**—Take fayre Buttes of Porke, & seþe hem in
fayre Watere, & clene pyke a-way þe bouys & þe Synewes, & hew hem &
grynd hem in a mortere, & *temper* w*ith* þe Whyte of Eyroun, & Sugre, &
pouder of Pepir, & Gyngere, & Salt; þan take neyssche Cruddis, grynd hem,
& draw þorw a straynoure; & caste þer-to Aneys, Salt, pouder Gyngere,
Sugre; & þan take þe Stuffe of þe Porke, & putte it on euelong cofyn of
fayre past; & take a feþer, & endore þe Stuffe in þe cofyn w*ith* þe cruddys;
& whan it is bake, take Pyneȝ, & clowys, & plante þe cofyn a-boue, a rew
of on, & rew of a-noþer; & þan serue f[orth].

---

[1] melle A. (mix).   [2] MS. þe þe.   [3] Cofyns A., fyre Harl.   [4] leaf 42.   [5] Heave; lift.

.xxx. Sew trappe.—Take .ij. lytel erþen pannys, & sette on þe colys[1] tyl
þey ben hote; make a dyssche-fulle of þikke bature of Floure & Watere; take
& grece a lytel þat oþer panne, & do þe bater þer-on; & lat renne al a-bowte
þe panne, so þat þe pan be al [2]y-helyd; take & sette þe panne a-ȝen ouer þe
fyre of colys; do þat oþer panne a-boue þat oþer panne, tyl it be y-baken
y-now; whan it is y-bake, þat it wol a-ryse fro þe eggys of þe panne, take
kydes Fleyssche & ȝong porke, & hew it; take Percely, ysope, & Sauerey
[and hew hit][3] smal y-now; & þrow a-mong þe Fleyssche;[4] & do it in a panne,
& þe cofynne, do it to þe colys; hele it with þat oþer panne, & do colys
a-bouyn, & lat baken wyl; whan it is y-now, take Eyroun, & breke hem;
take þe ȝolkes, & draw þorw a straynoure: caste to þe ȝolkys Hwyte Sugre,
Gyngere, Canelle, Galyngale; sture it wyl to-gederys; take al þis, & sette
a-down þe panne, & cast in a-bouyn þe cofynne in þe panne: sture it
to-gederys; hele it aȝenward with þat oþer panne, & lay colys a-boue, & lat
bake wyl tyl it be y-now; take yt owt of þe panne, & do it out y-hole, or
as moche as þow wolt, & þanne serue it forth.

.xxxj. Herbelade.—Take Buttes of Porke, & smyte hem in pecys, & sette
it ouer þe fyre; & seþe hem in fayre Watere; & whan it is y-soþe y-now, ley
it on a fayre bord, & pyke owt alle þe bonys, & hew it smal, & put it in a
fayre bolle; þan take ysope, Sawge, Percely a gode quantite, & hew it smal,
& putte it on a fayre vesselle; þan take a lytel of þe broþe, þat þe porke was
soþin in, & draw þorw a straynoure, & caste to þe Erbys, & ȝif it a boyle; þenne
take owt þe Erbys with a Skymoure fro þe broþe, & caste hem to þe Porke in
þe bolle; þan mynce Datys smal, & caste hem þer-to, & Roysonys of Coraunce,
& Pyneȝ, & drawe þorw a straynoure ȝolkys of Eyroun þer-to, & Sugre, &
pouder Gyngere, & Salt, & coloure it a lytel with Safroune; & toyle yt with
þin hond al þes to-gederys; þan make fayre round cofyns, & harde hem
a lytel in þe ovyn; þan take hem owt, & wyth a [5]dyssche in þin hond, fylle
hem fulle of þe Stuffe; þan sette hem þer-in a-ȝen; & lat hem bake y-now,
& serue forth.

.xxxij. A bake Mete.—Take an make fayre lytel cofyns; þan take Perys,
& ȝif þey ben lytelle, put .iij. in a cofynne, & pare clene, & be-twyn euery
pere, ley a gobet of Marow; & yf þou haue no lytel Perys, take grete, & gobet
ham, & so put hem in þe ovyn a whyle; þan take þin commade lyke as þou

---

[1] A. *on þe colys*, Harl. vp colde.   [2] leaf 42 back.   [3] Added from A.
[4] A. adds "[take salt and do þer-to, take the fleysshe] and do hit on þe panne."
[5] leaf 43.

takyst to Dowcetys, & pore þer-on; but lat þe Marow & þe Pecyȝ[1] ben sene;
& whan it is y-now, serue f[orth].

.xxxiij. A bake Mete Ryalle.—Take & make litel cofyns, & take
Chykonys y-soþe; oþer Porke y-soþe, & smale y-hackyd; oþer of hem boþe:
take Clowys, Maces, Quybibes, & hakke with-alle, & melle yt with cromyd
Marow, & lay on Sugre y-now; þan ley it on þe cofynne, & in þe myddel
lay a gobet of marow, & Sugre round a-bowte y-now, & lat bake; & þis
is for soperys.

.xxxiiij. Crustade Ryal.—Take & pyke owt þe marow of bonys as hool
as þou may; þen take þe bonys, an soþe hem in Watere, or[2] that þe broþe be
fat y-now; þen take Almaundys, & wayssche hem clene, & bray hem, &
temper hem vppe with þe fat broþe; þan wyl þe mylke be broun; þen take
pouder Canelle, Gyngere, & Sugre, & caste þer-on; þan take & make fayre
cofyns, & lat hem hard in þe ovyn; þan take Roysonys of coraunce, & ley in
þe cofynne, & taylid Datys y-kyt a-long; þen take Eyroun a fewe, y-straynid,
& swenge a-mong þo Milke þe ȝolke; þen take the botmon of þe cofynne þer
þe Marow schal stonde, & steke þer gret an long gobettys þer-on vppe-
ryȝt, & lat bake a whyle; þen pore þin comade þer-on halful, & lat bake;
& whan yt A-rysith, it is y-now; þen serue forth.

.xxxv. Crustade.—Take a cofyn, & bake hym drye; þen take Marw-
[3]bonys & do þer-in; þenne nym hard ȝolkys of Eyroun, & grynde hem smal,
& lye hem vppe with Milke; þan nym raw ȝolkys of Eyroun, & melle hem
a-mong chikonys y-smete, & do þer-inne; & yf þou luste, Smal birdys; &
a-force wyl þin comade with Sugre or hony; þan take clowys, Maceȝ, Pepir,
& Safron, & put þer-to, & salt yt; & þan bake, & serue forth.

.xxxvj. Crustade gentyle.—Take a Cofyn y-bake; þan grynd Porke or
Vele smal with harde ȝolkys[4] of Eyroun; þan lye it with Almaunde Milke,
& make hem stondyng; take Marow of bonys, & ley on þe cofynne, & fylle
hem fulle with þin comade, & serue f[orth].

.xxxvij. Doucettes.—Take Porke, & hakke it smal, & Eyroun y-mellyd
to-gederys, & a lytel Milke, & melle hem to-gederys with Hony & Pepir, &
bake hem in a cofyn, & serue forth.

.xxxviij. Doucettes a-forcyd.—Take Almaunde Milke, & ȝolkys of Eyroun
y-melled to-gederys, Safroun, Salt, & hony; dry þin cofyn, & ley þin Maribonys þer-on, & caste þin comade þer-on, & serue f[orth].

.xxxix. Daryoles.—Take Milke an Eyroun, & þe fatte of þe Freyssche

---

[1] A. perys.   [2] A. til that.   [3] leaf 43 back.   [4] A. adds *and rawe ȝolkes.*

broþe, Pepir, & Safroun, & Hony; dry þin cofyn, & caste þin comade þer-on, & serue forth.

.xl. **Daryoles.**—Take croddys of þe deye, & wryng owt þe whey; & take ȝolkys of Eyroun nowt to fewe, ne noȝt to many, and strayne hem boþe togederys þorw a straynour, & þan hard þin cofynne, & ley þin marew þer-in; & pore þin comade þer-on, an bake hem, & serue hem forth.

.xlj. **Flathouns** in **lente.**—Take & draw a þrifty Milke of Almaundes; temper with Sugre Water; þan take hardid cofyns, & pore þin comad þer-on; blaunche Almaundis hol, & caste ther-on Pouder Gyngere, Canelle, Sugre, Salt, & Safroun; bake hem, & serue f[orth].

Amen.

[¹ CONUIUIA

Quædam Antiqua, viz.

Conuiuium

1. Regis H. 4. in coronatione suâ A° Dⁿⁱ· 1399. apud Westmonaster*ium*.
2. Conuiuium Regis supradicti in nuptiis A° Dⁿⁱ· apud Wynton*iam*.
3. Conuiuium Domini de La Grey, incerti temporis.
4. Conuiuium Ricardi Flemming Episcopi Lincolniensis, incerti temporis : ille tamen ibidem Episcopus institutus a Papa A° D° 1420, circa annum nonu*m* Regis H. 5.
5. Conuiuium ad funeralia Nicholai Bubbewith, Episcopi Bathonen*sis* et Wellen*sis*, die 4° Dec. A° D° 1424, a° 3° H. 6.
6. Conuiuium Johannis Stafford, qui successit Nicholao Bubbewith præfato, in inductu suo ad Episcopatum Bathonen*sis* et Wellensis, die 16 Sept. A° D° 1425.
7. Conuiuium in nuptijs Comitis Devoniæ, incerti tempor*is*.]

[*Harl.* 279, *leaf* 45.]

Conuiuium do*mi*ni Henr*ici* Regis quarti, In coronacione sua apud Westmon*asterium*. ²

Le pr*i*mer cours.

Braun en peu*er*arde.
Viaund Ryal.
Teste de senglere enarme}.
Graund chare.
Syngnettys.
Capoun de haut grece.
Fesaunte.

Heroun.
Crustade Lumbarde.
Storicoun, graunt luc*es*.
A Sotelte.

Le .ij. cours.

Venyson en furmenty.³
Gely.

---

¹ Leaf 57. This *Contents* (between square brackets) is in a much later hand, probably 18th century.

² Did Chaucer get any of it, in return for his humorous *Purse* appeal?

³ A. *en formede*.

Porcelle farce enforce.
Pokokkys.
Cranys.
Venyson Roste.
Conyng.
Byttore.
Pulle endore.
Graunt tartez.
Braun fryez.
Leche lumbarde.
A Sotelte.

Le .iij. cours.
Blaundesorye.
Quyneys in comfyte.
Egretez.
Curlewys.

Pertryche.
Pyionys.
Quaylys.
Snytys.
Smal byrdys.
Rabettys.
Pome dorreng.
Braun blanke leche.
Eyroun engele.[1]
Frytourys.
Doucettys.
Pety perneux.
Egle.
Pottys of lylye.
A Sotelte.

Conuiuium Regis supradicti in nupcijs apud Wyntoniam.

Le .j. cours.
Fylettys in galentyne.
Vyaund Ryalle.
Grosse chare.
Signettys.
Capoun of haut grece.
Fesauntys. [leaf 45, back.]
Chewetys.
A Sotelte.

Le .ij. cours.
Venyson with furmente. Potage.
Gelye.
Porcellys.
Conynge.
Bittore.
Pulcynges farce₃.
Pertryche.
Leche fryez.
Braun bruse.
A Sotelte.

Le .iij. cours
Creme de Almaundys.
Perys in Syryppe.
Venyson Rostyd.
Kyde.
Wodecokke.
Plouere.
Rabettys.
Quaylys.
Snytys.
Feldefare.
Smale byrdys.
Crustade.
Sturgeoun.
Fretoure.
A Sotelte.

Ibidem conuiuium de pissibus.

Le .j. cours.
Vyaund Ryal.
Sew lumbarde.

---

[1] *i.e.* iced eggs.

Salt Fysshe.
Laumpreys pouderyd.
Pyke.
Breme.
Samoun Rostyd.
Crustade Lumbarde.
A sotelte.

Le .ij. cours.

Purpayis en furmente.
Gely.
Breme.
Samoun.
Congre.
Gurnarde.
Plays.
Lampreys in past.
Leche fryez.
Panteryse.
Coronys for a sotelte.

Le .iij. cours.

Creme of Almaunde.
Perys in syrippe.
Tenche enbrace.
Troutez.
Floundrys fryid.   [leaf 46.]
Perchys.
Lamprey Rostyd.
Elys Rostyd.
Lochys & colys.

Sturioun.
Crabbe au Creuoys.
Graspeys.
Egle coronys in sotelte.

In Festo Sancte Trinitatis in cena.

Le .j. cours.

Brewys.
Chykonys y-boylid.
Pygge en Sage.
Spaulde de Motoun.
Capoun Rostyd.
Pastelade.

Le .ij. cours.

Venysoun en broþe.
Kyde Rostyd.
Heronsewys.
Peioun.
Venysoun Rostyd.
Rabettys.
Pety perneux.

Le iij. cours.

Gely.
Quaylys.
Samaca.
Pescodde.
Blaunderellys.
Strawberys.

Conuiuium domini de la Grey.

Le .j. cours.

Rys Moleynȝ.
Vyaunde bruyse.
Bakunde Heryng.
Gros Salt fysshe.
Salt Samoun.
Salt Elys.

Fryid Marlyng.
Grete Pyke.
Bakyn Elys.

Le .ij. cours.

Compost   }
Brode canelle. } Potage.
Codlyng.

Ruchet.
Rochys.
Cheucyne.
Flampoyne.
Halybutte.
Plays fryid.
Trayne Roste.
Vn Lechemete.

Le .iij. cours.

Gelye.   [leaf 46, back.]
Creme of Almaundys.

Trowtys.
Storione.
Purpays.
Wylkys.
Elys & Lamprouns Rostyd.
Tenche.
Perche.
Breme de Mere.
Pyuenade in paste.
Leche lumbarde.
Chesmeyne.

Conuiuium Flemmynge, Lincolniensis Episcopi.

Le .j. cours.

Perrey fyn. ⎫
Rapeye.   ⎬ potage.
Grete taylys of Milwelle,
An lenge.[1]
Samoun pollys.
Salt Elys with galentyne.
Gode Pyke an fat.
Grosse tarteȝ.

Le .ij. cours.

Lampreys in galentyne.
Vyand Ryal.
Haddok.
Gurnard.
Plays.
Halybutte.

Elys an Lampronys Rostyd.
Flampayn.

Le .iij. cours.

Mammenye.
Creme de .ij. colourys.
Troutys.
Storioun.
Samon freysshe.
Perche.
Walkys.
Breme de Mere.
Crabbe.
Purpeys Rostyd.
Goions fryid.
Doucetys.

Conuiuium Johannis Chaundelere, Episcopi Sarum, in introitu episcopatus sui : in carnibus.

Le .j. cours.

Furmenty en Venyson.
Vyaund cyprys.
Capoun boilys.
Swan.
Fesaunt.
Pecokke.

Pomys en gele.   [leaf 47.]
Vn lechemete.
Tart Ryal.
Vn sotelte.   Agnus dei.

Le .ij. cours.

Vyaund Ryal.   ⎫
Blandyssorye. ⎬ Potage.

[1] i.e. "Great tails of Milwell and Ling : " see next page, col. 2, near foot.

Porcellys
Kyde.
Crane.
Venysoun Rostyd.
Heronsewes.
Pulsous farce.
Pertryge.
Vn leche.
Crustade Ryal.
Vn sotelte : a Lebarde.

Le .iij. cours.

Mammenye Ryal.
Vyand.

Bittore.
Curlewe.
Pyioun.
Rabettys.
Doderellys.
Quaylys.
Larkys.
Vyaunt Ardant.
Vu lechemete.
Frytourys Lumbard.
Payn Puffe.
Gele.
Vu Sotelte : Aquila.

Conuiuium domini Nicholai Bubbewyth, nuper episcopi Bathonensis & Wellensis ad funeralia; videlicet, quarto die decembris, anno domiui Millesimo. CCCC^{mo} vecessimo quarto : in carnibus :—

Le .j. cours.

Nomblys de Roo.
Blamangere.
Braun, cum Mustard.
Chynes de porke.
Capoun Roste de haut grece.
Swan Roste.
Heroun Rostyd.
Aloes de Roo.
Puddyng de Swan necke.
Vn Lechemete.
Vn bake, videlicet Crustade.

Le .ij. cours.

Ro Styuyd.
Mammenye.
Connyng Rostyd.
Curlew.
Fesaunt Rostyd.
Wodecokke Roste.   [leaf 47, back.]
Pertryche Roste.
Plouer Roste.

Snytys Roste.
Grete byrdes Rosted.
Larkys Rostyd
Vennysoun de Ro Rostyd.
Yrchouns.
Vn leche.
Payn puffe.
Colde bakemete.

Conuiuium de piscibus pro viris Religiosis ad funeralia predicta.

Le .j. cours.

Elys in sorry.
Blamanger.
Bakoun heryng.
Mulwyl taylys.
Lenge taylys.
Jollys of Samoun.
Merlyng soþe.
Pyke.
Grete Plays.

Leche barry.
Crustade Ryal.

Le .ij. cours.

Mammenye.
Crem of Almaundys.
Codelyng.
Haddok.
Freysse hake.
Solys y-soþe.

Gurnyd broylid with a syryppe.
Brem de Mere.
Roche.
Perche.
Menus fryid.
Yrehouns.
Elys y-rostyd.
Leche lumbard.
Grete Crabbys.
A cold bakemete.

Conuiuium Johannis Stafforde, Episcopi Wellensis in inductu Episcopatus sui, videlicet .xvj.º die Septembris, Anno domini millessimo CCCCᵐᵒ vicessimo quinto [1425].

Le .j. cours.

Furmenty with venysoun.
Mammenye.
Brawnne.
Kede Roste.
Capoun de haut Grece.
Swan.
Heyroun.
Crane.
A leche.   [leaf 48.]
Crustade Ryal.
Frutoure Samata.
A soltelte, a docter of lawe.

Le .ij. cours.

Blaunche Mortrewys.
Vyand Ryal.
Pecoke.
Conyng.
Fesaunte.
Tele.
Chykonys doryd.
Pyions.
Veysoun Rostyd.
Gullys.
Curlew.

Cokyntryche.
A leche.
Pystelade chaud.
Pystelade fryid.
Frytoure damaske.
A sotelte, Egle.

Le .iij. cours.

Gely.
Creme Moundy.
Pety Curlewe.
Egret.
Pertryche.
Venysoun Roste.
Plovere.
Oxyn kyū.
Quaylys.
Snytys.
Herte de Alouse.
Smale byrdys.
Doweet Ryal.
Petelade Fryid.
Hyrchouns.
Eggys Ryal.
Pomys.
Brawn fryid.

A sotelto, Sent Andrewe.
Frute.
Waffrys.
Vyn dowce.

Pro inferiori parte Aule, & in alijs locis.

Le .j. cours.

Furmenty with venysoun.
Mammenye.
Brawn.
Kede Roste.
Capoun.

Leche.
A bakemete.

Le .ij. cours.

Mortrewys.
Pygge.
[1] Conynge.
Peionys.
Ckykons.
Venysoun Rosted.
Leche.
Frutoure.
Bakemete chaud.
Bakemete fryid.

A Ryal Fest in þe Feste at þe weddyng of þe Erle of Deuynchire.

Le .j. cours.

Furmenty with Venysoun.
Vyand Goderygge.
Vele Roste.
Swan with chawderoun.[2]
Pecokke.
Crane.
Vn leche.
Vn Fryid mete.
Vn pasty, cooperta.
A sotelte: Ceruus.

Le .ij. cours.

Mammenye.
Vyand Motlegh.
Kede.
Conyng.
Herons.
Chykonys endoryd.
Venyson Rosted.
I. leche.
Vn Fryid mete.
I. paste Crustade.

A colde Bakemete.
A sotelte: Homo.

Le .iij. cours.

Gely.
Datys in comfyte.
Fesaunt.
Gullys.
Poper.
Mawlard de la Ryuer.
Peionys
Pertryche.
Curlew.
Pomez endoryd.
I. Leche.
Payn Puffe.
A sotelte : Arbor.

Pro inferiori parte Auli.

Le .j. cours.

Venyson en Broþe.
Spawdys[3] de Motoun.
Kyde.

[1] leaf 48 back.   [2] A. chaudewyne.   [3] *Spaut* or *Spaud*, Shoulder.

Doke.

Chykonys Roste.

Pygge in Sawge.

Venysoun bake.[1]

Le. ij. cours.

Caudel Ferry.

Pyionys.

Gullys.

Rabettys.

Venysoun Roste.[2]

Doucetys.

Vn Leche.[3]

[1] A. *venysoune rostid.*

[2] A. adds *in syrup.*

[3] A. adds ' mete,' and also adds *Vn fryide mete* after.

[End of Harl. MS. 279.]

COOKERY BOOK II.

HARLEIAN MS. 4016, ab. 1450 A.D.

[*This Contents is not in the MS., but is made up from the titles therein.*]

COOKERY BOOK II.

HARLEIAN MS. 4016, ab. 1450 A.D.

[1][T]his is the purviaunce made for Kinge Richard, beinge with þe Duc of lancastre at the Bisshoppes place of Durham at Londone, the xxiii day of September, the yere of the kinge forsaid .xij./ [A.D. 1387.]

First begynnyng for a-chatry.

Xiiij. oxeñ lying in salte.
IJ. oxeñ ffreyssh.
Vi[xx.][2] hedes of shepe fressh.
Vi[xx.] carcas of shepe fressh.
Xij. Bores.
Xiiij. Calvys.
Cxl. pigges.
CCC. maribones.
Of larde and grece, ynogh.
IIJ. toñ of salt veneson.
IIJ. docs of ffressh veneson.

The pultry.

L. Swannes.
CCx. Gees.
L. capons of hie grece.
Viii. dusseñ oþer capons.
Lx. dd[3] Hennes.
CC. copuH Conyngges.
IIIJ. Fesauntes.
V. Herons and Bitores.
Vi. kiddes.

V. dissoñ pullayñ for Gely.
Xij. dd.[3] to roste.
C. dd. peions.
Xij. dd. partrych.
Viij. dd. Rabettes.
X. doseñ Curlewes.
Xij. doseñ Brewes.
Xij. Cranes.
Wilde fowle ynogh.
VJ[xx.] galons melke.
Xij. galons Creme.
Xl. galons of Cruddes.
IIj. bushelȝ of Appelles.
Xj. thousand egges.

¶ The first course.

Veneson with Furmenty.
A potage called viaundbruse.
Hedes of Bores.
Grete Flessh.
Swannes rosted.
Pigges rosted.
Crustade lumbard in paste.
And a Sotelte.

[1] fol. 1. [2] six score. [3] dozens.

¶ The seconde course.

A potage called Gele.
A potage de Blandesore.
Pigges' rosted.
Cranes' rosted.
Fesauntes rosted.
Herons rosted.
Chekens endored.
Breme.
[1] Tartes.
Broke braune.
Conyngges rosted.
And a sotellte.

¶ The thirde course.

Potage. bruete of Almondes.
Stwde lumbarde.
Venyson rosted.
Chekenes rosted.
Rabettes rosted.
Partrich rosted.
Peions rosted.
Quailes rosted.
Larkes rosted.
Payne puff/.
A Dissh of Gely.
Longe Frutours.
And a Sotelte.

¶ Atte the stalling of John Stafford, Archibisshoppe of Caunterbury, the xxj yere of king Harry the vj. [A.D. 1443.]

Brawne with Mustard.
Furmenty with Veneson.
Mawmeny.
Fesaunte.
Swan.
Capon.
Carpeis of Veneson.
Heron sewe.
Grete breme.
Leche cremy ryaH.
Custard ryoH.
A sotelte. Seint Andrew, sitting on
   an hie Auter of a-state, with bemes
   of golde; afore him knelyng, þe
   Bisshoppe in pontificalibus; his
   Croser kneling behinde him, coped.

¶ The second course.

Bruet Mon amy.
Viaund cypre.

Crane rosted.
Veneson rosted.
Conyng.
Betore.
Partrich.
Curlewe.
Graunte carpe.
Leche Frutour.
Tard riaH.

A sotelte: þe Trinite sitting in a son
   of gold, with a crucyfix in his
   honde. Seint Thomas in þat one
   side, Seint Austin in that oþer,
   my lorde kneling in pontificalibus
   afor him. behinde him, his croser
   coped with the armes of Rouches-
   tre. behinde him, in þat o side, a
   blak Monke, prior[2] of Cristes chirch;
   in þat other side, the Abbot of
   Seint Austyus.

[1] fol. 1b.

[2] fol. 2.

¶ **The thirde course.**

Creme Vine.
Gely departed.
Browes.
Chekenos boiled.
Melons p̄puH.
Plouer rosted.
Rabettes.
Votrelleꝛ.
Rales.
Quayles.
Dew doues.

Blanke singuler leche.
Frutoure Rasyñ.
Qnynes bakyñ.
A sotelte. A godhede in a soñ of
gold glorified aboue; in the soñ
the holy giste voluptable. Seint
Thomas kneling a-for him, with þe
poynt of a swerd in his hede,[1] & a
Mitre there-vppoñ, crownyng S. T.
in dextera parte, maria tenens
mitram; in sinistra parte, Johannes
Baptista; et in iiij. partibus, iiij.
Angeli incensantes.

Here Beginnethe A Boke of Kokery.

Hare in Wortes.—Take Colys, and stripe hem faire fro the stalkes. Take
Betus and Borage, auens,[2] Violette, Malvis, parsle,
betayñ, pacience, þe white of the lekes, and þe croppe of þe netle; parboile,
presse out the water, hew hem smaH, And do there-to mele. Take goode
broth of ffressh beef, or other goode flessh and mary bones; do it in a potte,
set on þe fire; choppe the hare in peces, And, if þou wil, wassh hir in þe same
broth, and theñ drawe it thorgh A streynour with the blode, And þeñ put
aH oñ the fire. And if she be añ olde hare, lete hire boile weH, or þou cast
in thi wortes; if she be yonge, cast in aH togidre at ones; And lete hem
boyle til þei be ynogh, and cesoñ hem with salt. And serue hem forth. The
same wise thou may make wortes of A Gose of a niȝt,[3] powdryng of beef,
or eny other fressh flessh.

[4] **Buttered Wortes.** ¶ Take al maner of good herbes that thou may gete,
and do bi ham as is forsaid; putte hem oñ þe fire with faire water; put
þere-to clarefied buttur a grete quantite. Whañ thei ben boyled ynogh,
salt hem; late none otemele come there-in. Dise brede smaH in disshes, and
powre oñ þe wortes, and serue hem forth.

Cabochis. ¶ Take faire Cabochis, pike hem and wassh hem, and parboyle

---

[1] 'honde' crost through, and 'hede' written after.   [2] MS. aneus.   [3] night.   [4] fol. 2b.

hem; theñ presse oute the water oñ a faire borde, choppe hem, and cast hem in a faire potte with goode fressh broth and with Mary-bones, And lette hem boyle; theñ take faire grate brede, and cast there-to, safcroñ,[1] salt, and lete boyle ynogh, And theñ serue hit forth.

Growelle fforce. ¶ Take Groweñ y-made of ffressh beef; And whañ it is y-soddeñ ynogh, drawe it thorgh a Streynour into a fair potte; theñ take lene porke, and setñ it; grynde it smañ in a morter, and temper it with the seid broth, and cast togidre, And lete it boyle til hit be ynogh, And cast thereto Sapheroñ and salt, and serue it forth.

Nombles of Veneson. ¶ Take Nombles and kut hem smañ, whañ they beñ rawe; þeñ take fressh broth, water, and wyne, of eche of hem y-lyche moche, pouder of peper, Caneñ, and boyle hem till it be almost ynogh, And theñ cast powder ginger there-to, And a lituñ vynegre; salt and cesoñ it vppe, and serue it forth for a gode potage.

Venysoñ in broth. ¶ Take rybbes of venysoñ, and wassh hem faire in Water, And streyñ the Water thorgh a Streynour into a faire potte, and cast þe Venysoñ thereto, parcely, Sauge, powder of peper, cloueȝ, Maces, Vinegre, salt, And late hem boile til þei be ynow, & serue it forth.

[2]**Furmenty with venysoñ.** ¶ Take faire whete, and kerve it in a morter, And vanne a-wey clene the duste, and wassh it in faire watere and lete it boile tiñ hit broke; theñ do awey the water clene, and caste there-to swete mylke, and sette it ouer the fire, And lete boile til it be thik ynogh, And caste there-to a goode quantite of tryed rawe yolkes of egges, and caste thereto Sapheroñ, sugur, and salt; but late it boile no more theñ, but sette it oñ fewe coles, lest the licoure wax colde.   And þeñ take fressh venysoñ, and water hit; seth hit and bawde hit; And if hit be salt, water hit, sethe hit, and leche hit as hit shañ be serued forth, and put hit [in a vesseñ with feyre water, and buille it][3] ayeñ; and as hit boyleth, blowe a-wey the grece, and serue it forth with ffurmenty, And a litul of þe broth in the Dissh añ hote with the flessh.

Bourreys. ¶ Take pipes, hertes, neres, myltes, and of the rybbes of þe Swyne, or elles take (if thou wilt) Mallard or Goos, and choppe hem smañ, And theñ parboile it in faire water, And take it vp, and pike it clene, And putte into a potte, And cast there-to Ale ynogh, Sauge, Salt, And lete boile right ynowe, &þeñ serue it forth.

Mortreus de Chare. ¶ Take porke, and seth it ynow; and take it vppe, and bawde hit, and hewe it and grinde it, and in a morter; And cast thereto

grated brede, and then drawe the same broth thorgh a streynour, And temper
hit with ale, and do al into a potte, and lete boile, and aley hit with yolkes
of egges, And then lete it boile no more, And caste thereto powder of ginger,
Salt, And put hit in disshes in maner of Mortrewes, And cast thereto powder
of ginger, & serue it forth.

Brawne in confite. ¶ Take fressh brawne, and myce [1] it smaH, and take
Almondes, and blanche hem, and grinde hem, and drawe hem thorgh a
straynour.

[2] **Brawne in confite.** ¶ Take fressh brawne, and seth it ynowe; pare hit,
and grinde hit in a morter, and temper it with almond mylke, and draw it
thorgh a Streynour into a potte, and cast thereto Sugour ynowe, and pouder
of Clowes, and lete boyle ; and take floure of CaneH, or powder, a goode
quantite, and caste there-to. And lete boyle, and caste there-to powder of
ginger ; And then take it vp oute of the potte, And put in a lynnen clothe
and presse it ; lete hem boile so long in þe potte that it be thik, And then take
hit vppe, and presse it in the clothe ; And then leche hit faire, but not to
thyn ; And then take the ribbes of þe boor, and al bare, and set hem enlonge
the leches, And serue it forthe .ij. or iij. leches in a dissh.

Blaunche brawne. ¶ Take fressh Brawne, and myce it smaH ; And take
Almondes, and blaunche hem, and gryude hem thorgh a Streynour into stuffe
mylke, And put al into a potte, and sugur, And boyle al togidre til hit be
right stuff ; And then take it vp, And cast hit in-to a faire basyn, And lete
it stonde there til hit be aH colde ; And þen take a knyfe And leche it faire,
but not to thyn, And þen serue hit forthe, a leche. or ij. in a dissh.

Browne in egurdouce.[3] ¶ Take mighti broth of beef or of Capon, or take
faire fressh brawne, and seth hit, but not ynow, And then leche hit, And
cast hit into the broth ; then take hole oynones, pike hem,[4] And cast hem al
hole there-to ; then take Vynegre and CaneH, and sette on þe fire, and hete
hem, and drawe hem þorgh a Streynoure, and cast hit there-to. Then take
clowes, Maces, powder of peper, and cast thereto, and a lituH Sawndres,
And sette hit ouer þe fyre and lete boyle til þe oynones and the brawne
ben even sodde, and not to moche ; then take licour made of brede, vynegre,
[5]and wyn, and seson it vppe, and caste thereto a litul saferon to coloure hit,
and salt, And serve it forth.

Brawne in peuard.[6] ¶ Take wyn, pouder of CaneH, drawe hit thorgh a

---

[1] micer, michier, dépecer, mettre en pièces.—Hippeau. Gloss.   [2] fol. 3b.
[3] D. calls this " Braune en peneruade," it is recipe 55 there.   [4] D. pile, i.e. peel.
[5] fol. 4.   [6] Braune en peueruade, D.

Streynour, set hit ouer the fire, lete hit boile, caste there-to Maces, cloues, powder of Peper ; take smale onyons hole, parboyle hem, caste there to ; lete hem boile togider ; then take Brawne, leche hit, but not to thin ; And if hit be saused, let stepe hit in Hote water til hit be tender, then cast hit into þe siripe ; take Saundres, Vynegre, and caste there-to, And lete boile al togidre til hit be ynowe ; then take powder of ginger, caste thereto ; lete hit not be thik ne to thyn, butte as potage shulde be ; And serve hit forthe.

Garbage. ¶ Take faire Garbage, chikenes hedes, ffete, lyvers, And gysers, and wassh hem clene ; caste hem into a faire potte, And caste fressh broth of Beef, powder of Peper, Caneh, Clowes, Maces, Parcely and Sauge myced smaH ; then take brede, stepe hit in þe same brothe, Drawe hit thorgh a streynour, cast thereto, And lete boyle ynowe ; caste there-to pouder ginger, vergeous, salt, And a lituH Safferon, And serve hit forthe.

Pigge or chiken in Sauge. ¶ Take a pigge, Draw him, smyte of his hede, kutte him in .iiij. quarters, boyle him til he be ynow, take him vppe, and lete cole, smyte him in peces ; take an hondefuH. or .ij. of Sauge, wassh hit, grynde it in a morter with hard yolkes of egges ; then drawe hit vppe with goode vinegre, but make hit not to thyn ; then seson hit with powder of Peper, ginger, and salt ; then cowche thi pigge in disshes, and caste þe sirippe þer-vppon, and serue it forthe.

Stwed Beeff. ¶ Take faire Ribbes of ffresh beef, And (if thou wilt) roste hit [1]til hit be nygh ynowe ; then put hit in a faire possenet ; caste þer-to parcely and oynons mynced, reysons of corauns, powder peper, canel, clowes, saundres, safferon, and salt ; then caste there-to wyn and a lituH vynegre ; sette a lyd on þe potte, and lete hit boile sokingly on a faire charcole til hit be ynogh ; þon lay the fllessh, in disshes, and the sirippe there-vppon, And serve it forth.

Stwed Mutton. ¶ Take faire Mutton that hath ben roste, or elles Capons, or suche oþer flessh, and mynce it faire ; put hit into a possenet, or elles bitwen ij. siluer disshes ; caste thereto faire parcely, And oynons smaH mynced ; then caste there-to wyn, and a lituH vynegre or vergeous, pouder of peper, Canel, salt and saffron, and lete it stue on þe faire coles, And þen serue hit forthe ; if he have no wyne ne vynegre, take Ale, Mustard, and A quantite of vergeous, and do þis in þe stede of vyne or vinegre.

Capons Stwed. ¶ Take parcelly, Sauge, Isoppe, Rose Mary, and tyme, and breke hit bitwen thi hondes, and stoppe the Capon there-with ; colour hym

[1] fol. 4b.

with Safferoñ, and couche him in a ertheñ potte, or of brasse, and ley splentes vnderneth and al abouȝt the sides, that the Capoñ touche no thing*e* of the potte; strawe good herbes in þe potte, and put there-to a pottel of the best wyñ that thou may gete, and none other lico*u*r; hele [1] the potte with a close led, and stoppe hit aboute with dogh or bater, that no eier come oute; And set hit oñ þe faire charcole, and lete it seeth easly and longe tiH hit be ynowe. And if hit be añ ertheñ potte, þeñ set hit oñ þe fire whañ þou takest hit downe, and lete hit not touche þe grounde for breking; And whañ þe hete is ouer past, take oute the Capoñ with a prik; then make a sirripp*e* of wyne, Reysons of corauce, sugur and safferoñ, And boile hit a lituH; [2] medel pouder of Ginger with a litul of the same wyñ, and do þereto; then do awey the fatte of the sewe of the Capoñ, And do the Siryp*e* to þe sewe, and powr*e* hit oñ þe capoñ, and ser*u*e it forth.

Flathonys. ¶ Take mylke, and yolkes of egges, and ale, and drawe hem thorgh a strayno*u*r, with white sugur or blak; And melt faire butter, and put thereto salt, and make faire coffyns, and put hem into a Nowne [3] til þei be a lituH hard; þeñ take a pile, and a dissh fastned there-oñ, and fiH þe coffyns therewitH of the seid stuff*e* and lete hem bake a while.   And þeñ take hem oute, and ser*u*e hem forthe, and caste Sugur ynogh oñ hem.

Venysoñ ybake. ¶ Take hanches of Venysoñ, parboile it in faire water and salt; þeñ take faire paast, and ley there-oñ þe Venysoñ y-cutte in pieces as þou wolt have it, and cast vnder hit, and aboue hit, powder of ginger, or pep*er* and salt medyld*e* togidre, And sette hem in Añ oveñ, and lete hem bake til þey be ynogh.

Fruto*u*rs. ¶ Take yolkes of egges, drawe hem thorgh a streyno*u*r, caste there-to faire floure, berme and ale; stere it togidre til hit be thik.   Take pared appelles, cut hem thyñ like obleies, [4] ley hem in þe batur; þeñ put hem into a ffrying pañ, and fry hem in faire grece or buttur til þei beñ browne yelowe; then put hem in disshes, and strawe Sugur oñ hem ynogh, And ser*u*e hem forthe.

Longe Fruto*u*rs. ¶ Take Mylke And make faire croddes there-of in maner of chese al tendur, and take oute þe way clene; then put hit in a faire boH, And take yolkes of egges, and white, and menge floure, and caste thereto a good quantite, and drawe hit þorgh a streynoure into a faire vesseH; then put hit in a faire pañ, and fry hit [5] a lituH iu faire grece, but lete not boyle; then take it oute, and ley oñ a faire borde, and kutte it in faire smale peces

---

[1] cover.   [2] fol. 5.   [3] an oven.   [4] sacramental wafers.   [5] fol. 5*b*.

as thou list, And putte hem ayen into the panne til thei be browne; And then caste Sugur oñ hem, and serue hem forth.

Pety per̄nantes. ¶ Take faire floure, Sugur, Saffroñ, and salt, and make paast þer-of; then make small Coffyns, then cast in eche a coffyñ .iij. or iiij rawe yolkes of egges hole, and ij. gobettes or iij. of Mary couche þerin; þeñ take powder of ginger, Sugur, Reysons of Corans, and cast above; þeñ cover the coffyñ with a lyd of þe same paste; then bake hem in a oveñ, or elles fry hem iu faire grece fressh, And then serve hit forthe.

Auter peti per̄nantes. ¶ Take and make thi Coffyns as hit is a-for said; then take rawe yolkes of egges, trynde in sugur, pouder of Gynger, and resons of Corans, and mysed mary, but not to smalł, And caste alł this into a faire bolł, and medel alł to-gidre, and put hit in coffyns, and bake hem, or fry hem as þou diddest be þe toþer.

Custarde. ¶ Take Vele, and smyte hit in litulł peces, and wassh it clene; put hit into a faire potte with faire water, and lete hit boyle togidre; þeñ take parcelly, Sauge, Isoppe, Saucrey, wassh hem, hewe hem, And cast hem into flessh whan hit boileth; then take powder of peper, canel, Clowes, Maces, Saffroñ, salt, and lete hem boyle togidre, and a goode dele of wyne with alł, And whañ the flessh is boyled, take it vppe fro þe broth, And lete the broth kele. Whañ hit is colde, streyne yolkes and white of egges thorgh a streynour, and put hem to the broth, so many that the broth be styff ynowe, And make faire cofyns, and couche iij. or iiij. peces of the flessh in þe Coffyns; then take Dates, prunes, and kutte hem; cast thereto powder of Gynger and a litulł [1]Vergeous, and put to the broth, and salt; then lete the coffyñ and the flessh bake a litulł; And þen put the broth in the coffyns, And lete hem bake till they be ynogh.

Custard lumbarde. ¶ Take good creme,[2] and yolkes And white of egges, and broke hem thereto, and streyne hem alł þorgh a straynour till hit be so thik that it wolł bere him self; And take faire Mary, And Dates, cutte iu ij. or iij. and prunes, and put hem in faire coffyns of paast; And then put þe coffyñ in añ oveñ, And lete hem bake till thei be hard, And then drawe hem oute, and putte the licoure into þe Coffyns, And put hem into þe oveñ ayeñ, And lete hem bake till they be ynogh, but cast sugur and salt in þi licour whañ ye putte hit into þe coffyns; And if hit be in lentoñ, take creme of Almondes, And leve the egges And the Mary.

Tartus of flesh. ¶ Take fressh porke, hew it smalł, grynde it in a morter,

<hr />

[1] fol. 6.   [2] *The MS. has here* and ffoiles of parcelly *crossed through.*

and take it ⱱppe into a faire vesseH; And take yolkes and white of egges,
streyñ hem þorgh a streynour, and temper þe porke there-with; theñ take
pynys, reysons of coraunce, and fry hem in fressh grece, and cast thereto
pouder of peper, Gingere, CancH, Sugur, Safferoñ and salt, and do hit in a
coffyñ, and plante the coffyñ above with prunes, and kutte dates, and grete
reysynges, and smale birdes, and or elleȝ hard Yolkes of egges; and if þou
take birdes, fry hem a lituH in fressh grece, or thou putte hem into þe Coffyñ;
theñ endore hit with yolkes of egges and with saffroñ, and lete bake hit til
hit be ynogh, and so serue hit forth.

Lese fryes.[1] ¶ Take nessh chese, and pare it clene, and grinde hit in a
morter smaH, and drawe yolkes and white of egges thorgh a streynour, and
cast there-to, and grinde hem togidre; theñ cast thereto Sugur, [2]butter and
salt, and put al togidre in a coffyñ of faire paast, And lete bake ynowe, and
theñ serue it forthe.

Auter Tartus. ¶ Take faire nessh chese that is buttry, and par hit, grynde
hit in a morter; caste therto faire creme and grinde hit togidre; temper hit with
goode mylke, that hit be no thikker þeñ rawe creme, and cast thereto a litul
salt if nede be; And [3] thi chese be salte, caste thereto neuer a dele; colour hit
with saffroñ; theñ make a large coffyñ of faire paste, & lete the brinkes be
rered more þeñ an enche of hegh; lete þe coffyñ hardeñ in þe oveñ; þeñ take
it oute, put gobettes of butter in the bothom thereof, And caste the stuffe
there-to, and caste peces of buttur there-ⱱppoñ, and sette in þe oveñ with-oute
lydde, and lete bake ynowe, and theñ cast sugur thereoñ, and serue it forth.
And if þou wilt, lete him haue a lydde; but þeñ thi stuff most be as thikke
as Mortrewes.

Ðariolles. ¶ Take wyne and fressh broth, Clowes, Maces, Mary, powder of
Gynger, and Saffroñ, And lete al boyle togidre; And take Creme, (and if hit be
cloutes, drawe hem thorgh a streynour,) And yolkes of egges, and medle hem
togidre, and powre the licoure that þe mary was sodeñ in, thereto; And theñ
make faire cofyns of fyne paast, and putte the mary there-in, and myced dates
And streberies, if hit be in time of yere, and sette þe Coffyns in þe oveñ, And
lete bake a lituH while, And take hem oute, and putte the licour thereto, And
lete hem bake ynouH

Pies of Parys. ¶ Take and smyte faire buttes of porke and buttes of vele
togidre, and put hit in a faire potte, And putte thereto faire broth, And a
quantite of Wyne, And lete aH boile togidre til hit be ynogh; And þeñ take
hit fro the fire, and lete kele [a litel, and cast ther-to raw yolkes of eyreñ,

---

[1] D. Leche fryeȝ.   [2] fol. 6b.   [3] If.

and pouudre of gyngeuere, sugre and salt, and mynced dates, reysyns of
coreuce : make then coffyns of feyre past, and do it ther-ynne, and keuere
it & lete bake y-nogh.][1]

[2]Grete pyes. ¶ Take faire yonge beef, And suet of a fatte beste, or of Mottoñ,
and hak all this oñ a borde smaH ; And caste thereto pouder of peper and
salt; And whañ it is smaH heweñ, put hit in a bolle, And medle hem woH ;
theñ make a faire large Cofyñ, and couche soñ of this stuffur in// Theñ
take Capons, Hennes, Mallardes, Connyuges, and parboile hem cleue ; take
wodekokkes, teles, grete briddes, and ploñ hem in a boiling potte ; And
theñ couche al þis fowle in þe Coffyñ, And put in cuerych of hem a quantite
of pouder of peper and salt// Theñ take mary, harde yolkes of egges, Dates
cutte in ij. peces, reisons of coraunce, prunes, hole clowes, hole maces, CaneH,
and saffroñ.   But first, whan thou hast cowched aH thi foule, ley the remenaunt of thyue other stuffur of beef a-bougĥt hem, as þou thenkest goode;
and theñ strawe on hem this : dates, mary, and reysons, &c., And theñ close
thi Coffyñ witĥ a lydde of the same paast, Aud putte hit in þe oveñ, And
late hit bake ynogĥ ; but be ware, or thou close hit, that there come no saffroñ
nygĥ the brinkes there-of, for theñ hit wol neuer close.

Herbe-blade. ¶ Take buttes of Porke, and smyte hem in peces, and sette
hit oñ the fire, and setĥ it in faire water ; And whañ hit is sodeñ y-nogĥ, take
it oute, and baude hit, and pike oute þe bones, and hewe it smaH, and putte
hit in a faire boH.   And take Isop, Sauge, and parcelly a goode quantite ;
pike hit, and hewe hit smaH, And put hit in faire vessellez ; And take a litul of
þe brotĥ þat þe porke was sodeñ yñ, and drawe hit þorgh a streynour, and
caste to the erbeblade, and yef hit a boyle ; theñ take oute þe herbes witĥ a
Skymour fro the broth, And cast hem into þe porke in þe bolle ; And theñ
myce faire dates smaH, And caste hem there-to, And reysoñs of coraunce, and
pynes ; And draw rawe yolkes of egges thorgh a straynour, and caste thereto
Sugur, powder of Ginger, salt; colour hit witĥ a lituH saffroñ ; And truH
hit with [3]thi honde, al this togidur in þe bolle ; And þeñ make faire rownde
cofyns, and put hem in the oveñ, and hard hem a lituH, and take hem oute
ayeñ, and with a dissĥ in thi honde, fil hem full of the stuffe, and sette hem
ayeñ in the oveñ al opeñ, And let hem bake ynowe. And thenne serue hit fortĥ.

Chawdwyñ. ¶ Take Gysers, lyuers, and hertes of Swannes, or of wilde
gese ; And if þe guttes be fatte, slytte hem, and cast hem there-to, And boile
hem in faire water ; And theñ take hem vppe, And hew hem smale, and caste

into þe same broth ayene, but streyne hit þorgh a streynour firste; And caste
thereto pouder of peper and of canell, and salt, and vinegre, And lete boile;
And þeñ take þe blode of þe swañ, and fressh broth, and brede, and drawe
hem þorgh a streynour and cast thereto, And lete al boyle togidre; And
þeñ take pouder of Gynger, whañ hit is al-moost ynough, And caste [1] there-to,
And serue it forthe.

PikkyH *pour* **le Mallard.** ¶ Take oynons, and hewe hem smaH, and fry
hem in fressh grece, and caste hem into a potte, And fressh broth of beef,
Wyne, & powder of peper, canel, and dropping of the mallard/ And lete hem
boile togidur awhile; And take hit fro þe fyre, and caste thereto mustard a
litul, And pouder of ginger, And lete hit boile no more, and salt hit, And
serue it forthe with þe Mallard.

Sauce gamelyne. ¶ Take faire brede, and kutte it, and take vinegre and
wyne, & stepe þe brede therein, and drawe hit thorgh a streynour with
powder of canel, and drawe hit twies or thries til hit be smoth; and þeñ take
pouder of ginger, Sugur, and pouder of cloues, and cast þerto a litul saffroñ
and lete hit be thik ynogh, [2] and thenne serue hit forthe.

Sauce sermstele. [3] ¶ Take Milke and a litul floure, And caste hit in a potte,
And lete boile al togidur al thyñ; and whañ hit is wel boyled, take and
stampe garlek small, and caste there-to pouder of peper, and salt, And then
serue hit forthe.

Sauce oylepeu*er*. [4] ¶ Take faire browne brede, and tost hit, and stepe hit in ·
vinegre, and drawe it thorgh a streynour, and caste there-to garlek (butte
stampe it smaH first); And caste there-to pouder of peper, And salte, And
serue hit forth.

Sauce Verte. ¶ Take *p*ercely, Mintes, Betany, Peleter, and grinde hem
smale; And take faire brede, and stepe hit in vinegre, and drawe it thorgh a
streynour, and cast thereto pouder of peper, salt, and serue it forth.

Sauce Gynger. ¶ Take faire white brede, and stepe it in vinegre, and
drawe hit thorgh a streynour twies or thries, and caste there-to pouder of
ginger and salte; but lete it not be to thyñ, but soñ what stiff, And then
serue hit forthe.

Sauce SoreH. ¶ Take SoreH, gryñde hem smaH, And drawe hem thorgh a
Streynoure, and caste there-to Salt, and serue hit forth.

Sauce galentyne. ¶ Take faire crustes of browne brede stept in vinegre,
And cast thereto pouder of caneH, and lete hit stepe therewith, til hit be

---

[1] caste *repeated in* MS.   [2] fol. 8.   [3] D. Sauuce gauncelle.   [4] D. Sauuce alpeu*e*re.

browne; þeñ drawe hit thorgh a streynour ones or twyes, And caste there-to pouder of peper, And lete hit be soṁ-whatte stonding, And þeñ serue hit forthe.

Swañ rosted. [1]¶ Kutte a Swañ in the rove[2] of the mouthe toward the brayne enlonge, and lete him blede, and kepe the blode for chawdewyñ; or elles knytte a knot oñ his nek, And so late his nekke breke; then skald him. Drawe him and rost him eveñ as thou doest goce in all poyntes, and serue him forth with chawd-wyne.

Crane rosted. ¶ Lete a Crane blode in the mouthe as thou diddist a Swañ; fold vp his legges, kutte of his winges at þe ioynte next þe body, drawe him, Wynde the nekke abought the spit; putte the bill in his brest: his sauce is to be mynced with pouder of ginger, vynegre, & Mustard.

ffesaunte rosted. ¶ Lete a ffesaunte blode in þe mouthe as a crane, And lete him blede to dethe; pull him dry, kutte awey his hede and the necke by þe body, and the legges by the kne, and putte þe kneys in at the vente, and roste him: his sauce is Sugur and mustard.

Partrich rosted. ¶ Take a partrich, and sle him in þe nape of the hede with a fethur;[3] dight him, larde him, and roste him as þou doest a ffesaunte in the same wise, And serue him forth; then sauce him with wyne, pouder of ginger and salt, And sette hit in a dissh oñ the fuyre til hit boyle; then cast powder ginger, Canell, thereoñ, And kutte him so; or elles ete him with sugur and Mustard.

Partrich stwed. ¶ Take faire mighti broth of beef or of Muttoñ when hit is boyled ynow, and streyñ hit thorgh a streynour, and put hit into añ ertheñ potte, And take a good quantite of wyne, as hit were half a pynte, And take partrich, cloues, Maces, and hole peper, and cast in-to þe potte, and lete boile wel togidre; And whañ the partrich beñ ynogh, take the potte from the fuyre, and then take faire brede kutte in thyñ[4] browes, and couche hem in a faire chargour, and ley the partrich oñ loft; And take powder of Ginger, salt, and hard yolkes of egges mynced, and caste into the broth, and powre the broth vppoñ the partrich into the chargeour, and serue it forth, but late hit be colored with saffroñ.

Heroñ rosted. ¶ Take a Heroñ; lete him blode as a crane, And serue him in al poyntes as a crane, in scalding, drawing, and kuttyng the bone of the nekke a-wey, And lete the skyñ be oñ, &c.; roste him and sause him as þe Crane; breke awey the bone fro the kne to þe fote, And lete the skyñ be oñ.

Bytor rosted. ¶ Take a Bito*ur*, sle him in the mouthe, skalde him, s*er*ue him in all poyntes as þou doest a Crane, but lete him haue oñ his winges wheñ he is rosted, And serue him forthe.

Curlewe rosted. ¶ Take a Curlewe, sle him as a Crane, pul him dry, kutte of the winges by the body, drawe him, dight him as a Henne, And folde vp his legges as a crane ; lete his necke and his hede be oñ ; take awey the nether lippe and throte boll, and put his hede in at his shuldur, and roste him as a Crane, and no sauuce but salte.

Egrete rosted. ¶ Take añ Egrete, sle him as a Crane, skalde him and drawe him, and kutte his winges, and folde his legges as a crane, and roste him, And s*er*ue him fortħ ; and no sauce but salte.

Brewe rosted. ¶ Take a Brewe, sle him as þe Curlewe, skalde him, drawe him as a heñ, breke his legges at þe kne, and take awey the bone fro the kne to þe fote, as a heroñ ; And kutte the winges by the body, and his hede by the body, and put him oñ a spitte, And bynde his legges as a heroñ ; roste him, reyse his legges and his winges as a heroñ, And take no maner sauce butte salte.

[1]**Quayle rosted.** ¶ Take a Quayle, and sle him, And s*er*ue him as thou doest a partricħ in all Degre.   His Sauce is sauce gamelyne.

Pecok rosted. ¶ Take a Pecok, breke his necke, and kutte his throte, And fle him, þe skyñ and the ffethurs togidre, and the hede still to the skyñ of the nekke, And kepe the skyñ and the ffethurs hole togiders ; drawe him as an heñ, And kepe þe bone to þe necke hole, and roste him, And set the bone of the necke aboue the broche, as he was wonte to sitte a-lyve, And abowe the legges to þe body, as he was wonte to sitte a-lyve ; And whañ he is rosted ynowe, take him of, And lete him kele ; And þeñ wynde the skyñ witħ the fethurs and the taile abought the body, And s*er*ue him forthe as he were a-live ; or elleȝ pull him dry, And roste him, and s*er*ue him as þou doest a henne.

Sorcell rosted. ¶ Take a Sorcell or a tele, and breke his necke, and pul him dry, And draw him as a chekoñ, and kutte off his fete and winges by the body and þe nekke, and roste him, and reise his winges and his legges as a heroñ, if he be a Sorcell ; And no sauce but salt.

Plouer. ¶ Take a plouer, and breke his skoll, and pull him dry, And drawe him as a chekoñ, And kutte þe legges and the winges as a henne ; And no sauce but salt.

[1] fol. 9*b*.

Wodekok. ¶ Take a wodecok, and sle him as þe plouer; pul him dry, or elles breke his bakke, And lete the sculle be hole; drawe him, And kutte of his winges by the body, and turne vp the legges as þou doest of a crane; put his bill thorgh bothe his thighes; roste him, And reise his legges And his winges, as thou doest of all maner of other clouen fote fowle.

[1] **Snyte.**—Take a Snyte, and sle him as thou doste a wodecok; pulle him, late his necke be hole, save the wesing; put the bill in the shulder, and folde þe legges as a Crane; roste him, And dight him as the Wodecok.

Conyng. ¶ Take a Conyng, fle him, And draw him aboue and byneth, And parboile him, And larde him, and roste him, And late the hede be on; And vndo him, and sauce him with sauce, ginger, And vergeous, and powder of ginger, And thenne serue hit forth.

Conyng in Gravey. ¶ Take blanched Almondes, grinde hem with wyñ And gode broth of befe and Mutton, and draw hit thorgh a Streynour, and cast hit into a potte, and lete boile; and caste there-to pouder of ginger, clowes, Maces, and sugur// And then take a Conyng, and seth him ynogh in goode fressh broth, and choppe him, And take of the skyñ clene, and pike hem clene And cast hit to the Sirippe, And lete boyle ones, And serue forth.

Conyng or heñ in clene[2] broth. ¶ Take a Conyng or a heñ, and seth him ynowe in good fressh broth, and drawe þe same broth thr[o]gh a Streynour; And take half a pynte of white wyñ, and caste there-to; And then sette it ouer the fire, and then choppe the Conyng or the heñ, and take of the Skyñ, and pike hem clene, and caste thereto, And lete boile togidre; And whañ hit is boiled ynogh, caste there-to powder of ginger, vergeous, and salt also; And then thou shall serue it forth.

Conyng, heñ, or Mallard.[3] ¶ Take Conyng, Heñ, or Mallard, and roste him al-moste ynowe; or elles choppe hem, and fry hem in fressh grece; and fry oynons myced, and cast al togidre into a potte, and caste there-to fressh broth and half wyne; caste thereto Cloues, Maces, powder of Peper, Cancll; then stepe faire brede with the same broth and drawe hit thorgh [4] a streynour with vinegre. And whañ hit hath wel boiled, caste the licour thereto, and pouder ginger, and vinegre, and cesoñ hit vppe, And then thou shall serue hit forth.

Gelyne endobat. ¶ Take a heñ, and roste hir al-moost ynogh, and chop hir small in faire peces, and caste hem into a potte; and take fressh broth and halff wyne, and caste there-to Maces, Peper, Clowes, and cancll; and stepe

---

[1] fol. 10. Snipe.   [2] Douce MS. clere.   [3] D. adds en oyle.   [4] fol. 10b.

faire brede with the same broth and with vinegre, and drawe hit thorgh a streynour; and whan it hath wel boiled, caste thereto pouder of gin*ger* and vinegre, and seson hit vppe and ser*ue* it forth.

Gelyn*e* in broth*e*. ¶ Take rawe hennes, chop hem, caste hem into a potte; cast to fressh broth Wyne, *par*celly, oynons myced, powder of pep*er*, clowes, Maces, saffrou*n*, and salt; then stepe brede with vinegre and þe same broth, and draw hit thorgh a streynour, and cast it thereto, and lete boyle ynogh; And caste thereto pouder gin*ger*, and sesone hit vp, & se*rue* forth.

Rabette rosted. ¶ Take a Rabette, and sle him, And drawe him, And lete his hede be o*n*, as a Conyng; roste hi*m* as a Conyng, And ser*ue* him forth.

Kede rosted. ¶ Take a kydde, and slytte the skyñ in þe throte, And seke the veyne, and kut him, and lete him blede to deth; and fle him, And larde him, And trusse his legges in þe sides, and roste him, And reyse the shuldres and legges, and sauce hit with vinegre and salte.

Venyso*u*n rosted. ¶ Take faire ffelettes of venesoun, and pike awey the skyñ and þe bo*n*e, and *par*boile hem, and roste hem oñ a spitte; And sauce there-to, And ser*ue* hit forth.

Vele rosted. ¶ Take faire brestes of vele, And parboyle hem, And larde hem, And [1]roste hem, And then serue hem forth.

Chik farsed. ¶ Take a faire chek, and skald him, and broke the skyñ (as sone as he is scalded) in the necke behinde, and blowe him, And cast him in faire wat*er*, and wassh him; and þeñ kutte of þe hede and nek, and lete þe ffete be oñ al hole, and draw him clene; and þeñ pike faire *par*celly, and parboile hit; And þeñ take hard yolkes of eyroñ, and hewe hem and þe *par*celly togidre, and fressh grece, and caste there-to pouder of gin*ger*, pep*er*, a litel saffroñ and salt, And put al in-to þe Chike, and put hit oñ a Spitte; And thenne late him roste, and ser*ue* forth.

Chike endored. ¶ Take a chike, and drawe him, and roste him, And lete the fete be oñ, and take awey the hede; then make batur of yolkes of eyroñ and floure, and caste there-to pouder of ginger, and pep*er*, saffroñ and salt, and pouder hit faire til hit be rosted ynogh.

Goce or Capoñ farced. ¶ Take *par*ciH, Swynes grece, or suet of shepe, and *par*boyle hem in faire wat*er* and fressh boyling broth; And þeñ take yolkes of eyroñ hard y-sodde, and hew hem smale, with the herbes and the salte; and caste thereto pouder of Ginger, Peper, CaneH, and salte, and Grapes in tyme of yere; And in oþer tyme, take oynons, and boile hem; and whañ they

[1] fol. 11.

G

beñ yboiled ynowe with þe herbes and with þe suet, al þes togidre, þeñ put aH in þe goos, or in þe Capoñ; And theñ late him roste ynogħ.

Pigge ffarced. ℂ Take rawe egges, and drawe hem þorgh a streynour, And þeñ grate faire brede; And take saffroñ, salt, pouder ginger, And suet of Shepe, And do medle al togidre into a faire vesseH, and put hit in þe pigge wombe Whañ he is oñ þe brocche, And þeñ sowe the hole togidre; or take a prik, and prik him togidur, And lete him roste.

[1] **ffelettes of Porke endored.** ℂ Take ffelettes of porke, and roste hem faire, And endore hem with þe same batur as þou doest a cheke as he turneth aboute the spitte, And serue him forth.

ffelettes in galentyne. ℂ Take faire porke of þe fore quarter, and take of the skyñ, and put þe pork on a faire spitte, and roste it half ynogħ; and take hit of, and smyte hit in peces, and cast hit in a faire potte; and þeñ take oynons, and shred and pul hem, not to smaH, and fry hem in a pañ with faire grece, And theñ caste hem to þe porke into þe potte; And theñ take good broth of beef or Mottoñ, and cast thereto, and set hit oñ þe fire, and caste to pouder of Peper, Canel, Cloues & Maces, and lete boile wel togidur; and þeñ take faire brede and vinegre, and stepe the brede with a lituH of þe same broth, and streyne hit thorgħ a streynour, and blode with aH; or elles take Saundres and colour hit therewith, and late hem boile togidur, and cast thereto Saffroñ and salt, and serue hit forth.

Losinges de chare. ℂ Take faire buttes of porke, and hewe hem, and grynde hem, and caste there-to yolkes of eyreñ rawe, and take it vppe into a faire vesseH; and take reysons of Corance, and myced dates, and pouder ginger, peper, saffroñ, and sugur, and medle al this to-gidre; and make faire paast of sugur, saffroñ, and salte, and temper therein; And make thereof ij. faire cakes, and ley the stuff therein al abrode oñ þe cakes aH flatte. And þeñ take anoþer Cake, and ley him al abrode thereoñ, and þeñ kutte þe Cakes thorgħ with a knyfe, in maner of losinges; And theñ make faire bater of rawe yolkes of eroñ, sugur and salt, and close þe sides of þe losinges therewith, and theñ fry hem in fressħ grece ynow, And so serue hem forthe.

Tripe de Muttoñ. ℂ Take a pauche of a shepe, and make it clene, and caste hit in a potte [1]of boyling water, and skyme hit clene, and gader al awey the grece, and lete hem boile til þei be al tendur; then take hem vppe oñ a faire borde, and kutte hem in smale peces of ij peny brede, and caste hem yñ añ ertheñ potte with stronge broth of bef or Muttoñ; take ffoyles of parcelly,

[1] fol. 11b.   [1] fol. 12.

and hewe hem smaH, and cast hem to, And lete boyle togidre til they beñ
tendur/ And þeñ take pouder of ginger, and a quantite of vergeous, and take
saffroñ and salt and caste there-to, and lete hem boile togidre til þey be ynogh.

Allowes de Muttoñ. ¶ Take faire Muttoñ of the Buttes, and kutte hit in
þe maner of stekes; And þeñ take faire rawe parcelly, and oynons shred
smale, yolkes of croñ soddeñ hard, and mary or suet; hewe all þes smale
togidre, and theñ caste thereto pouder of ginger, and saffroñ, and stere hem
togidre with thi honde, and ley hem vppe-oñ þe stekes al abrode; and cast
there-to salt, and rolle hem togidre, and put hem oñ a spitte, and roste hem
till þei be ynogh.

Browne fryes.[1] ¶ Take browne brede, and kut hit thyñ; And theñ take
yolkes of eyreñ, and soñ with[2] of the white; and take meyned floure, and
drawe the eireñ and the floure thorgh a streynour; and take sugur a gode
quantite, and a litul saffroñ and salt, And cast thereto: and take a faire
panne with fressh grece; And whañ þe grece is hote, take downe and putte it
in þe batur, and turne hit wel therein, and þeñ put hit in þe pañ with the
grece, And lete hem fry togidre a lituH while; And theñ take hem vpp, and
caste sugur thereoñ, and so serue hit hote.

Payñ purdeuz. ¶ Take faire yolkes of eyreñ, and try hem fro the white,
and drawe hem þorgh a streynour; and then take salte, and caste thereto;
And then take manged brede[3] or payñmañ, and kutte hit in leches; and þeñ
take faire buttur, and clarefy hit, or elles take fressh grece and put hit yñ [4] a
faire pañ, and make hit hote; And then wete þe brede weH there in þe yolkes
of eyreñ, and then ley hit oñ the batur in þe pañ, whañ þe buttur is al hote;
And then whañ hit is fried ynowe, take sugur ynowe, and caste there-to
whañ hit is in þe dissh, And so serue hit forth.

Perre. ¶ Take grene pesyñ, and boile hem in a potte; And whañ they beñ
y-broke, drawe the broth a good quantite þorgh a streynour into a potte, And
sitte hit oñ the fire; and take oynons and parcelly, and hewe hem smaH
togidre, And caste hem thereto; And take pouder of CaneH and peper, and
caste thereto, and lete boile; And take vynegur and pouder of ginger, and
caste thereto; And then take Saffroñ and salte, a lituH quantite, and caste
thereto; And take faire peces of payumain, or elles of such tendur brede, and
kutte hit yñ fere mosselles, and caste there-to; And þeñ serue hit so f rth.

Malasade.[5] ¶ Take yolkes and white [of] eireñ togidre, And drawe hem

---

[1] The recipe on p. 43 makes *Brawn* of this dish.
[2] Some of the white therewith. See p. 43, Recipe xlv.
[3] Douce MS. maynche brede. Manchet.
[4] fol. 12b.   [5] So in Douce MS.; *Malafade* in Harl.

thorgh a streynoure; and þen take a litul butter, and caste hit in a faire frying
panne; And whan the butter is hote, take þe eiren that ben y-drawe, and caste
there-to. And þen take a Saucer, and gadur the eyren togidre in the panne,
in the brede of a pewtre dissh; And then couche faire [pecys][1] of brede
downward in þe pan; and take it vp oute of the pan, And caste faire
white Sugur thereto, and serue it forth. And to[2] euery malesade, take the
mowntayne[3] of xij. eyren And mo.

Blaunde sorre. ℂ Take almondes, and blanche hem, and stampe hem in a
morter, and temper hem with fressh lene broth of a Capon, or beof, and wyne;
And if hit be in lenton or in a fissh day, take faire broth of fressh fissh and
wyne, And boyle hem to-gidre a good while, and take hit vppe in a faire
lynnen cloth that is clene wasshen, and þe water y-wronge oute there-of;
And drawe vnder the cloth, with a ladell, al the water that ye may, euen as
ye [4] make colde creme; and then take it oute of the clothe, and cast hit in a
faire potte, and lete boile; and then take brawne of a capon and tese hit small,
and bray hit in a morter/ (or elles in a fissh day, take a codlyng or a haddok),
and temper hit with almond melke, and cast sugur ynogh thereto; and then
caste hit in the potte, And lete hit boile togidur a goode while; and þen take
hit oute of the potte al hote, and dresse hit into a dissh as ye doeth a colde
creme; And sette ther-on rede Anneys in confite, and serue hit forth; or elles
take faire almondes yblanched, & set þeron/

Hagas de almondes. ℂ Take faire yolkes of eyren, and the White, and
drawe hem thorgh a Streynour, and take faire parcelly, and parboyle hit in a
potte, & parboylingge broþe; And then take yolkes of yren, sodde hard, and
hewe the yolkes and the parcely small togidre; And [take][5] sugur, pouder of
Gynger, and salte, & cast to yolkes and parcelly; And take mary, and put hit
in a streynour, And lete hong[6] yn to þe boyling potte, and parboile; and take
hit vppe, and lette hit kele, And kutte hit then in smale peces; And then take
the drawen eyren, and putte hem in a pan al a-brode, (And vnneth eny grece
in þe pan,) and couche the yolkes and the parcelly there-on in þe pan.   And
then couche the peces of þe mary thereon; And then folde vp þe kake byneth
euery corner, to eche corner foure square al flatte, And turne hit on the pan;
And lete hit lye awhile, And then take it vp, and serue hit forth.

Hanoney. ℂ Take eyren, and drawe the yolkes and white thorgh a

---

[1] Added from Douce MS. : Harl. MS. reads *faire of a brede*.
[2] MS. do.   MS. has *malesade* here, but *Malafade* in the heading.   [3] amount, number.
[4] fol. 13.   [5] Added from Douce MS.   [6] Douce MS. : Harl. MS. *hold*.

streynour; And take oynons, And Shrede hem smaH; And take faire butter or grece, and vnneth ouere-couer the pañ therewith; And fry the oynons togidre; then late hem fry to-gidre a lite while; And take hem vppe, And serue hem forthe so, al to-broke yñ a dissh.

Blamanger. ¶ Take faire Almondes, and blanche hem, And grynde hem with sugour [1] water into faire mylke; and take ryse, and seth. And whañ they beth wel y-sodde, take hem vppe, and caste hem to the almondes mylke, and lete hem boile togidre til thei be thikk; And then take the brawne of a Capoñ, and tese hit smaH, And caste thereto; and then take Sugur and salt, and caste thereto, and serue hit forth in maner of mortrewes.

Buknade. ¶ Take veel, keed, or heñ, and boyle hem in faire water or elles in good fressh broth, and smyte hem in peces, and pike hem clene; And drawe the same broth thorgh a streynour, And cast there-to parcelly, Isoppe, Sauge, Maces and clowes, And lete boyle til þe flessh be ynogh; and þeñ set hit fro the fire, and aley hit vp with rawe yolkes of eyreñ, and caste thereto pouder ginger, and vergeous, & a litel saffroñ and salte, and cesoñ hit vppe and serue it forth.

Auter maner buknade. ¶ Take rawe Almondes, and blanche hem, and grynde hem, and draw hem thorgh a streynour with fressh broth and wyne into good stiff mylke; And then take veel, kede, or heñ, and parboile hem in fressh broth, and pike hem clene, and cast him thereto; take Clowes, maces, and herbes, and lete hem boile ynowe; And then caste a lituH Sugur, pouder ginger, and salt, and serue him forth.

Brest de mottoñ in sauce. ¶ Take faire brestes of Muttoñ rosted, and chopp hem; And then take Vergeous, and chaaf hit in a VesseH ouer the fire, and caste there-to powder ginger; and then caste the chopped brest in a dissh, And caste the sauce al hote there-oñ, And serue hit forth.

Rissħewes de Mary. ¶ Take faire floure, and rawe yolkes of eyreñ, sugur, salt, powder ginger, and saffroñ, and make faire Cakes. And then take Mary, Sugur, powder ginger, and ley hit oñ the kake, and folde him togidre; And then kutte hit in maner of risshewes, And fry hit in fressh grece, And then serue hit forth.

Lethe [3] lory. ¶ Take mylke, and caste it in a potte, And caste there-to salt and saffroñ; and þeñ take and hewe faire buttes of Calvis or porke al smalle and caste thereto. And take the white and yolkes of eyreñ, And drawe hem thorgh a streynour; And whañ the licour is at þe boyling, caste there-to the eyreñ, And a lituH Ale, And styrre till hit crudde; And if thou wilt haue hit farced, take mylke, and make hit scalding hote, And cast there-to rawe yolkes of eyreñ, sugur, powder ginger, Peper, clowes, and maces, And lete hit not fully boyle; And theñ take a faire lynneñ clothe, and presse the cruddes there-oñ, and theñ leche it; And ley þe leches .ij. or iij. in a dissħ, And cast saffroñ there-oñ in the dissħ, And so serue hit forthħ al hote.

Tansey. ⁋ Take faire Tansey, and grinde it in a morter; And take eyreñ, yolkes and white, And drawe hem thorgħ a streynour, and streyne also þe Iuse of þe Tansey thorgħ a streynour; and medle the egges and the Iuse togidre; And take faire grece, and cast hit in a pañ, and sette ouer þe fyre til hit mylte; and caste þe stuffe thereoñ, and gader hit togidre witħ a saweer or a dissħ, as þou wilt haue hit more or lasse; And turne hit in þe panne onys or twies, And so serue it forth hote, yleched.

Froyse. ⁋ Take egges, and drawe the yolkes and the white thorgh a Streynour; And theñ take faire beef or veel, and seth hit til hit be yuogh; and þeñ hewe hit colde or hote, al smaH, And medle the rawe beef or veel and the egges togidre, and caste there-to saffroñ, salt, And powder of peper, And medle al togidre. And theñ take a fryng pañ, and sette ouer the fire, and caste there-in fressħ grece, and make hit hote; And theñ cast the stuff there-oñ and stirre hit weH in the pañ till hit come togidre; And whañ hit is coñ weH togidre, caste there-oñ in þe pañ a [1] dissħ, and presse hit togidre, And turne hit, if hit be nede, fore clevyng in the turnyng, caste into þe pañ more grece, but turne hit ones or ij; [2] And take hit vppe fro the fire, And leche it in faire peces, & serue forth.

Gely. ¶ Take Calues fete, and scalde hem faire, and ley hem in faire water, and late hem wex white; Also take hoȝos of fele,[3] and ley hem in faire water fore to soke oute þe blode; And þeñ take hem oute of þe water, and ley hem in a faire lynneñ clothe, and lete the water reñ oute; And þeñ take a faire scoured potte, and put al thes hoȝos and calues fete þerin; And þeñ take good white wyñ, that woH hold colloure, or elles fyne claret wyne, and caste there-to a porciou, and none oþer licoure, that the flessħ be ouer-wose[4] with al; and sette hit ouer the fire, and boile hit, and skem hit clene. Whañ hit is boylled tender ynowe, take vppe the flessħ in a faire bolle, And saue wel þe licoure; and loke that þou haue faire sides of pigges, And faire smale chekynes scalded, and drawe hem, ([and the] legges and [the fete] on),[5] and wassħ

---

[1] fol. 14b.   [2] twies, twice.   [3] Douce MS.; houghys of veel.
[4] Douce MS. reads, nere wese with-alle.
[5] Thus Douce MS.: Harl. MS. hem legges and sette on.

faire, and caste hem in þe same first broth, And set hit ayeñ ouer the fire, and skym̃ hit clene, and lete a mañ euere-more kepe hit, and blow of þe grauey; And in case that þe licour waste awey, cast more of the same wyne þere-to; And put þi honde there-to, And, if thi honde be clammy, Hit is a signe þat it is gode; and lete not þe flessħ be so moche ysod that hit may bere no kuttyng; And theñ take hit vppe, and ley hit oñ a faire clothe, and set oute the licoure fro the fire; And put a fewe coles vnder þe vesseħ þat þe lycoure is yñ; and take salt, pouder of peper, and good quantite of saffroñ, (that hit haue faire Ambur colour,) and a good quantite of vinegre; And loke that hit be sauery of the salt and of the vinegre, & faire of colour of saffroñ; And put hit in a faire lyneñ clothe, And sette vnder-neth a faire dissħ, and late hit reñ thorgh the clotħ so oft þat hit reñ clene[1]; And if þou seest that hit hath to lituħ of the [2]vinegre, or salt, or saffroñ, caste thereto more, after thi discrecioñ); And theñ kut faire sidde ribbes of þe sides of pigges, and ley hem oñ a chargeour or oñ a dissħ,[2] And set hit faire oñ a colde place, and powre þe gely þeroñ; And theñ take faire blanched almondes, and caste auone thereoñ er hit kele, and foilles of tried pared ginger; and lete stonde to kele.

[**Guisseħ**[3]]. [4]¶ Take faire capoñ brotħ, or of beef, And sette hit ouer the fire, and caste þerto myced sauge, parcelly and saffroñ, And lete boile; And streyñ the white and þe yolke of egges thorgħ a streynour, and caste there-to faire grated brede, and medle hit togidre with thi honde, And caste the stuff to the brotħ into þe pañ; And stirre it faire and softe til hit come togidre, and crudded; And þeñ serue it forth hote.

Peris in Syrippe. ¶ Take Wardons, and cast hem in a faire potte, And boile hem til þei beñ tendre; and take hem vppe, and pare hem in ij. or in iij. And take powder of Caneħ, a good quantite, and cast hit in good red wyne, And cast sugur thereto, and put hit in añ ertheñ potte, And lete boile; And theñ cast the peris thereto, And late hem boile togidre awhile; take powder of ginger, And a liteħ saffroñ to colloure hit with, And loke that hit be poynante/ And also Doucet/

Peris in compost. ¶ Take Wyne, caneħ, And a grete dele of white Sugur, And sette hit ouer the fire, And hete hit but a lituħ, and noȝt boyle; And

---

[1] Douce MS. *clere*.

[2] Douce MS. adds [& pull the loynes of the chekyne iche from othere, and take awey the skyn, and pulle hem [in] quartres, and ley a quarter of a chikyne and a ribbe of the pygge to-gedrys on a dissh.]

[3] Taken from Douce MS.   [4] fol. 15.

drawe hit thorgħ a streynour; And theñ take [1] faire dates, and ɣ-take oute
the stones, and leche hem in faire gobettes al thyñ, and cast there-to; And
theñ take pere Wardones, and pare hem, And seth hem, And leche hem in
faire gobettes, and pike oute the core, and cast hem to the Syryppe; And take
a lituħ Saundres, and caste there-to in the boylyng, And loke that hit stonde
weħ, with Gynger, Sugur, And weħ aley hit with caneħ, and cast [salt] [2]
thereto, and lete boyle; And theñ caste it oute in a treyñ [3] vesseħ, And lete
kele; And theñ pare clene rasinges [4] of ginger, & temper hem ij. or iij. daies,
in wyne, And after, ley hem in clarefied hony colde, aħ a day or a nigħt;
And þen take the rasons [4] oute of the hony, And caste hem to the peres in
composte; And theñ serue hit forth with sirippe, aħ colde, And nougħt hote.

Chare de Wardone. ¶ Take peer Wardons, and seth hem in wine or water;
And theñ take hem vppe, and grinde hem in a morter, and drawe hem thorgh
a streynoure with the licour; [5] And put hem in a potte with Sugur, or elle₃
with clarefiede hony and caneħ ynowe, And lete hem boile; And theñ take
hit from the fire, And lete kele, and caste there-to rawe yolkes of eyreñ, til hit
be thik, and caste thereto powder of ginger ynowe; And serue hit forth in
maner of Ryse. And if hit be in lentoñ tyme, leve the yolkes of eyreñ, And
lete the remnaunt boyle so longe. til it be so thikk as thougħ hit were ɣ-
tempered with yolkes of eyreñ, in maner as A mañ setheþ charge de quyns;
And theñ serue hit forth in maner of Rys.

Mawmene. ¶ Take vernage, or oþer strenger wyne of the best that a mañ
may finde, and put hit in a potte, and cast there-to a gode quantite of powder
Caneħ, And sette hit ouer the fire, And ɣif hit a hete; And theñ wring oute
softe thorgħ a streynour, that þe draff go not oute, And put in a faire potte;
take and pike newe faire pynes, And wassħ hem clene in wyne, And caste
of hem a grete quantite þere-to; And take white sugur ynowe, as moche as
thi licour is, And cast there-to; and take confeccions or charge [6] de quyns, a
goode quantite, and cast thereto; and drawe a few saundres with stronge
wyne thorgħ a Streynour, and cast there to; And put al in a potte; And cast
there-to a good quantite of Clowes, and sette hit ouer the fire, & gif hit a
boyling; And take Almondes, [7] and drawe hem with migħti wyne thorgħ a
streynour; And at the first boiling, [9] a-ley hit vp, & yeve [8] hit a boyle; and [9] ley
hit vp witħ ale, and gif hit a boyle, and sette hit fro the fire; and caste

---

[1] Douce MS.　　[2] Douce MS.　　[3] fol. 15b. MS. repeats 'vesselle,' treyne is treen, wooden.
[4] shavings, parings.　　[5] Douce MS. with-out eny licour.
[6] ? MS.; for chare.　　[7] D. amydons.　　[8] fol. 16.　　[9]-[9] D. omits from a-ley . . . and.

thereto tesid brawne of Fesaunte, partrich, or capoñ, a good quantite, and
cesoñ hit vppe with pouder of ginger ynogh, and a lituH saffroñ and salt;
And if hit be stronge,[1] aley hit with vinegre of[2] swete wyñ, and dresse hit
flatte with the bak of a Saucer or A ladeH; And as thou dressest hit with
the saucer in vinegre[3] or mighty wyne, wete the saucer or ladeH fore cleving,
[and loke][4] that hit haue sugur right ynogH, And serve hit forth.

Longe Wortes de Pesone. ¶ Take grene pesyñ, and wassH hem clene, And
cast hem in a potte, and boyle hem til they broke; and then take hem vppe
fro the fire, and putte hem in the broth in añ other vesseH; And lete hem
kele; And drawe hem thorgH a Streynour into a faire potte. And then take
oynoñes in ij. or iij. peces; And take holo wortes, and boyle hem in fayre
water; And then take hem vppe, And ley hem oñ the faire borde, And kutte
hem in .iij. or in .iiij. peces; And caste hem and the oynons into þat potte
with the draweñ pesoñ, and late hem boile togidre til they be aH tendur,
And then take faire oile and fray, or elleꝫ fressh broth of some maner fissH,
(if þou maist, oyle a quantite), [5]And caste thereto saffroñ, and salt a quantite.
And lete hem boyle wel togidre til they beñ ynogH; and stere hem weH
euermore, And serue hem forthe.

Elys in Sorre. ¶ Take eles, and fle hem, and choppe hem in faire colpons,
And wassH hem clene, and putte hem in a faire potte; and then take parcelly,
oynons, and shrede togidre to the eles; And then take pouder of peper, &[5]
broth of fissH, and set hit ouer the fire, and lete hem boyle togidre; And þeñ
take a lofe of brede, and alay the brede in the þe same broth, And drawe hit
thorgh a streynour; And whañ the eles beñ almoost y-sodde ynowe, caste
there-to;[7] And lete hem boile togidre; and take hem vp fro þe fire, aud cast
þer-to salte, vinegre, And serue hit forth.

[6]**Ballok broth.** ¶ Take elys, and fle hem, and kutte hem in colpons, and
caste hem into a potte with faire water/ and then take parcelly, and oynons,
and shrede hem, not to smale; And take Clowes, Maces, pouder of Peper,
pouder of CaneH, And a gode porcioñ of wyne, and cast thereto, And lete
hem boyle; And whañ þe eles beH wel y-boiled, take faire stokfissH, and do

---

[1] Douce MS. *to stondyng.*   [2] Douce MS. *vernage or.*
[3] Douce MS. *vernage.*   [4] Added from Douce MS.
[5] Douce MS. *reads here*: other elles fressh broth of some maner of fressh fisshe (yffe thou
have none oile) a quantite.
[6] Douce MS. *adds*: canelle, & clowes and maces, & cast ther-to, and take fressh, *between*
& *and* broth.
[7] Douce MS. *adds*: and alay hit ther-with, & cast wyne ther-to and lete hem buille to-
gederys: & then take hem vppe fro the fyre and cast ther-to wyne, &c.   [8] fol. 16b.

a-wey þe skyñ, and caste thereto, And lete boyle. And whañ the eles beñ
weH y-boyled, take faire berme, and put þerto, And lete boyle awhile; and
þeñ take Saffroñ and salt, and a litel vinegre, and cast thereto ; And lete
serue hit forthe fore gode potage.

Soppes Dorre. ¶ Take rawe Almondes, And grynde hem in A morter, And
temper hem with wyñ and drawe hem thorgh a streynour; And lete hem
boyle, And cast there-to Saffroñ, Sugur, and salt; And then take a paynmain,
And kut him and tost him, And wete him in wyne, And ley hem in a dissħ,
and caste the siryppe thereon, and make a dregge [1] of pouder ginger, sugur,
CaneH, Clowes, and maces, And cast thereon ; And whañ hit is I-Dressed,
serue it forth fore a good potage.

Soppes pour Chamberleyne. ¶ Take wyne, CaneH, powder ginger, sugur/
of eche a porcioñ ; And cast aH in a Streynour, And honge hit oñ a pyñ, And
late hit reñ thorgh a streynour twies or thries, til hit reñ clere ; And then
take paynmain, And kutte hit in a maner of Browes, And tost hit, And ley
hit in a dissħ, and caste blanche pouder there-oñ ynogħ ; And then cast the
same licour vppoñ þe Soppes, and serue hit forthe fore a good potage.

Muscules in brotħ. ¶ Take Muscules, And sitħ [2] hem, And pike hem oute
of the sheH ; And drawe the brotħ thorgħ a streynour into a faire vesseH,
And sette hit oñ the fire ; And then take faire brede, and stepe hit witħ þe
same [3] brotħ, and draw hit thorgħ a streynour, And cast in-to a potte witħ þe
sewe ; and menge [4] oynons, wyñ, and pouder peper, and lete boyle ; & cast
there-to the Musculis and pouder ginger, and saffroñ, and salte ; And then
serue ye hit forthe.

Muscules in Shelle. ¶ Take and pike faire musculis, And cast hem in a
potte ; and caste hem to, myced oynons, And a good quantite of peper and
wyne, And a lite vynegre ; And assone as thei bigynnetħ to gape, take hem
from þe fire, and serue hit forthe with the same brotħ in a dissħ al hote.

Mortrewes of Pesyñ. ¶ Take a Gurnard, or elles a Codling, (the lyuer And
þe Spawne with-in him), And setħ him ynowe in faire water; and pike oute
the bones, and grinde the fissħ in a morter, and temper hit witħ almond
mylke, and caste-to grated brede ; and þeñ take hit vppe, and put hit in a
faire potte, and lete boyle ; And caste thereto sugur, Safferoñ, and salte ; and
serue hit in a dissħ in maner of mortrewes of flessħ, And caste powder of
Ginger there-oñ.

Blanche porrey. ¶ Take blanche almondes, And grinde hem, and drawe

---

[1] dredge. Douce MS. dragge.   [2] seethe, boil.   [3] fol. 17.
[4] Douce MS. *mynced*; see next recipe.

hem wit*h* sug*ur* water thorgħ a streynou*r* into a good stuff mylke into a
potte ; and þeñ take þe white of lekes, and hew hem smaħ, and grynde hem
in a mort*er* witħ brede ; and þeñ cast al to þe mylke into þe potte, and caste
þerto sugur and salt, and lete boyle ; And setħ feyre poudrid eles in faire
water ynowe, and broile hem oñ a gredreñ ; and kut hem in faire longe peces,
and ley two or thre in a dissħ togidre as ye do reneson witħ ffurmenty,
And *ser*ue it fortħe.

CaudeH ffery. ¶ Take rawe yolkes of eyreñ and trie hem, and bake hem ;
and take good wyne, and warme hit ouer the fire in a potte, And cast there-
to the yolkes, and stere hit weH, butte lete hit not boyle til hit thikke ; [1] and
theñ caste there-to sugur and salt, and *ser*ue hit fortħ as mortrewes.

Prenade.[2]—Take wyñ, and put hit in a potte, and clarefied honey,
sawndres, pouder of pep*er*, Canel, Clowes, Maces, Saffroñ, pynes, myced dates,
& reysons, And cast thereto a litul vinegre, and sette hit ouer the fire, and
lete hit boyle ; and setħ figges in wyñ and grynde hem, and draw hem
thorgh a streynou*r*, and cast thereto, and let boile al togidre. And þeñ take
floure, saffroñ, sugur, and faire water, and make faire kakes, and late hem be
thyñ ynogħ ; And þeñ kutte hem like losing*es* ; And þeñ caste hem in faire
oyle, and fry hem a litul while ; And theñ take hem vp oute of the pañ, and
caste hem to þe wesseH with the sirippe, altogidre, in a dissħ ; And therefore
thi sirip*e* most be reunyng ynow, and noȝt to stiff ; and so *ser*ue it forth fore
a good potage, in faire disshes aH hote.

Froyte de almondes.[3] ¶ Take blak sugur and colde water, and caste the
sugur and þe water in a potte ; and lete hem boile togidre, and salt, and skeme
hem clene, and let hit kele ; And þeñ take Almondes, and blanche hem clene,
and stampe hem in a mort*er* al smal, and drawe hem thik ynowe thorgh a
streynou*r* with sugur water, into a faire vesseH. And if hit so be þat the
mylke be not swete, take white sug*ur* and cast thereto ; And *ser*ue hit fortħ in
maner of potage, And namly in lentoñ tyme.

Fried creme de almondes. ¶ Take Almondes, and blanche hem, and
wassħ hem in faire water, and bray hem smaH in a morter with faire water ;
And theñ take hem and þe water togidre soñ-what thik, and drawe hem
þorgh a streynou*r* into a faire potte, And set hem ouer the fire, and lete hem
boyle ones ; And þeñ take hem downe, and cast ther*e*to Salte, and lete stonde
a forlonge wey ór .ij. And cast a lituH vinegre þerto ; And þeñ cast hit oñ a
faire lynneñ clotħ that [4] is faire wassħ, and þe water y-wronge oute there-of ;

---

[1] fol. 17*b*.   [2] Called *Brewes* in D.   [3] Douce MS. *Froydelet dalmandes*.   [4] fol. 18.

and cast hit aH abrode with the laduH, and lete men hold the cloth al abrode; and þen take a ladiH, and draw vndur þe cloth, and draw awey þe water aH that a man may. And þen gadur al þe creme togidur in þe clothe; And þen take þe cloth with the creme, and hange hit vppon a pyn, and lete þe water droppe oute two or thre houres or more; And then take hit of þe cloth, and putte hit in a boH of tre, And caste Sugur ynogh þereto and a litul salt. And if hit wex to thik, take swete wyne, and temper hit with ale; And þen take reysons of coraunce, clene y-wassh, and put hem there-in, that þey be not seyn; And whan hit is dressed in maner of mortrewes, take rede anneys in confite, or elles levis of Burage,[1] and set þere-on in a dissh.

Creme boiled. ¶ Take mylke, and boile hit; And þen take yolkes of eyren, and try hem fro the white, and drawe hem thorgh a streynour, and cast hem into þe mylke; and then sette hit on þe fire, and hete hit hote, and lete not boyle; and stirre it wel til hit be som-what thik; And caste thereto sugur and salte; and kut þen faire paynmain soppes, and caste the soppes there-on, And serue it in maner of potage.

Letlardes. ¶ Take mylke scalding hote; And take eyren, the yolkes and the white, and drawe hem thorgh a streynour, and caste to þe mylke; And þen drawe þe iuce of herbes, which that þou wiH, so þat þey ben goode, and drawe hem thorgh a streynour. And whan the mylke bigynneth to crudde, caste þe luce thereto, if þou wilt haue it grene; And if þou wilt haue it rede, take Saundres, and cast to þe mylke whan it croddeth, and leue þe herbes; And if þou wilt haue hit yelowe, take Saffron, and caste to þe mylke whan hit cruddeth, and leve þe Saundres; And if þou wilt haue it of al þes colours, take a potte with mylke & luse of herbes, and anoþer potte with mylke and saffron; And anoþer [2]potte with mylke and saundres, and put hem al in a lynnen clope, and presse hem al togidur; And if þou wilt haue it of one colour, take but one cloth,[3] and streyne it in a cloth in þe same maner, and bete on þe clothe with a ladeH or a Skymour, to make sad or[4] flatte; and leche it faire with a knyfe, and fry the leches in a pan with a lituH fressh grece; And take a lituH, and put hit in a dissh, and serue it forth.

Leche lumbarde. ¶ Take Dates, and do awey þe stones; and seth hem in swete wyne; and take hem vppe, and grinde hem in a morter, and drawe hem þorgh a streynour with a lituH swete wyne and sugur; and caste hem in a potte, and lete boyle til it be stiff; and þen take hem vppe, and ley hem vp apon a borde; and then take pouder ginger, CaneH, and wyn, and melle al

---

[1] D. adds *flowres.*   [2] fol. 18b.   [3] Douce MS. *of these.*   [4] Douce MS. *and.*

togidre in thi honde, and make it so stiff that hit woH be leched; And if hit be not stiff ynowe, take hard yolkes of eyreñ and creme thereoñ, or elles grated brede, and make it thik yuogh; take Clarey, and caste thereto iu maner of sirippe, whañ þou shaH serue hit forthe.

Auter leche lumbard. ¶ Take faire hony, and clarefy it in þe fire til hit[1] be stiff ynowe; and theñ take hit vppe and ley hit oñ a borde; and take faire grated brede and pouder of peper, and meH al togidre witħ thi honde, til hit be so stiff that hit wol be leched; and leche hit. And theñ take wyne, pouder of Gynger, CaneH, and a litel clarefied hony, and lete reñ thorgħ a streynour, and cast þe sirip there·oñ, whañ that thou shaH serue hit in stede of Clarre.

Cryspes. ¶ Take white of eyreñ, Milke, and fyne floure, and bete hit togidre, and drawe hit thorgħ a streynour, so that hit be rennyng, and noght to stiff; and caste there·to sugur and salt. And theñ take a chaffur ful of fressħ grece boyling; and þeñ put thi honde in the batur[2] and lete the bater reñ thorgħ thi fingers iuto þe chaffur; And whan it is reñ togidre in the chaffre, and is ynowe, take a Skymour, and take hit oute of the chaffur, and putte oute al the grece, And lete reñ; And putte hit in a faire dissħ, and cast sugur thereoñ ynow, and serue it fortħ.

Poterous.[3] ¶ Take a shoueH of yreñ, and hete him brennyng hote in þe fire; and þeñ take him oute of the fire, and fil him fuH of salt; And then make a coffyw, and putte in the salt al holowe, þe shappe of a treyñ dissħ; and sette þe pañ and þe salt ouer the fire ayeñ, til þe salt be brennyng hote; and theñ cast the white and þe yolkes of rawe eyreñ iu·to þe hole of salt, and lete stonde in þe fire til hit be half hard; And theñ put a dissħ half of salt; And þeñ take a dressing knyfe, and put vnder þe salt[4] and þe pañ, and heve hit vppe fro the fire, that þe coffyñ witħ the eyreñ broke not; And þeñ sette hit in þe dissħ with the salt, and serue it fortħ.

Risshewes. ¶ Take figges, and grinde hem aH rawe in a morter, and cast a lituH fraied oyle there·to; And þeñ take hem vppe yñ a vesseH, and caste there·to pynes, reysyns of corañce, myced dates, sugur, Saffroñ, pouder ginger, and salt: And þeñ make Cakes of floure, Sugur, salt, and rolle þe stuff in thi honde, and couche it in þe Cakes, and folde hem togidur as risshewes, And fry hem in oyle, and serue hem fortħ.

---

[1] Douce MS. *adds after* hit: 'wex hard: & take hard yolkes of eyreue & cryme hem a grett quantite ther-to, till it,' &c.   [2] fol. 19.   [3] Harl. MS. Poterons.

[4] MS. repeats 'And then take a dressing knyfe, and putte vnder the salt.'

Potage de egges.[1] ¶ Take faire water and cast in a faire fryiug pañ, or elle; in an oþer vesseH, til hit boyle, and skeme it weH ; And then broke faire rawe egges, and caste hem in þe water, And lete þe water stonde stil ouer þe fire, and lete the egges boyle harder or nessher as þou wilt.

Taylours. ¶ Take almondes, and grynde hem raw in a morter, and temper hit [2]witH wyne and a litul water; And drawe hit þorgh a streynour into a goode stiff mylke into a potte ; and caste thereto reysons of coraunce, and grete reysons, myced Dates, Clowes, Maces, Pouder of Peper, Canel, saffron a good quantite, and salt; and sette hem ouere the fire, And lete al boyle togidre awhile ; And alay hit vp with floure of Ryse, or elles grated brede, and cast there-to sugur and salt, And serue hit forth in maner of mortrewes, and caste there-oñ pouder ginger in þe dissH.

Malmens bastard. ¶ Take a poteH of clarefied houy, and a pounde of pynes,[3] and I. pounde of Reysons of coraunce, Saundres, pouder caneH, And ij. galons of wyne or ale, and pouder peper, and cast al in a potte, And skeme hit clene ; And þeñ take iij. li. pouude[4] Almondes,[5] and stepe to-gidre, And drawe hem þorgh a streynour; And whañ the potte boyleth, cast þe licour to, & aley hit vp al stonding; And þeñ take pouder ginger, salt in[6] saffrou, aud cesoñ hit vppe, and serue hit forth in a dissh al hote, and salt; And cast pouder ginger thereon in þe dissh, and serue it forth.

Gyngautrey.[7] ¶ Take paunches and lyuers of a codlyng, or haddok, or elles kelyng, and seth hem in faire water; And take hem vppe oñ a faire borde, & myce the panches smaH; And þeñ take fressH broth of fressH Salmoñ, or of eles, or of turbut, and cast þe myced paunches there-to, And pouder of peper, and lete boyle ; And then take the broth that þe paunches aud lyuers were y-sodde in, And stepe there-in faire brede, and drawe hit thorgh a streynour ; And þeñ myce þe lyuers in faire peces; And whañ the paunche hath wel y-boyled in þe licour, caste þe lyuers thereto, and lete boyle a while; And serue hit forth hote for gode potage ; and late hit be soñ-dele rennynge.

ffygey. ¶ Take figges, and caste hem in a potte, And cast there-to wyne or Ale, [8]and lete hem boile, And take hem vppe, and bray hem in a morter ; And þeñ take brede, and stepe in þe same licour, and cast thereto, And drawe hem þorgh a streynour, and caste hit in a faire potte with wyne or ale ; and

---

[1] D. *Poched egges*.   [2] fol. 19b.   [3] D. pepyr pynes.   [4] 3 pounds of pounded.
[5] Amydoues, Douce MS. *which adds*, a galone of wyue, & a gode quantite of vynegre & lete.   [6] Douce MS. *and*.   [7] Harl. MS. Gyngautrey.
[8] Douce MS. *adds*: cast the liour ther-to and lete buille awhile, & then ; *the liour being the* brede aud broth.   [9] fol. 20.

þen take figes, and kutte hem smale, pynes, saundres, pouder of peper, a lituH saffroñ and salt, and cast þer-to, and serue hit stonding.

Chaudewyne. ¶ Take þe Guttes of fressh Samoñ, and do awey the gaH; and slytte hem, and caste hem in a potte, and boyle hem in water right weH; And ley hem vpoñ a borde, and hewe hem; And þen stepe brede in þe same licour, And cast soñ of the samoñ broth thereto, And drawe aH thorgh a streynour; and theñ caste the heweñ guttes and þe draweñ brede in a potte, and a lituH wyñ, pouder of CaneH, or saffroñ, And lete boyle togidre; And cast there-to pouder of peper, Vinegre, and salt; And lete hit be rennyng.

Rapes. ¶ Take half figges and half reysons, and boile hem in wyñ, and take hem vp, and bray hem in a morter, And drawe hem with þe same licour thorgh a streynour, so thik that hit be stonding; And theñ take resons of corance, Pynes, Clowes, Maces, sugur of Cipris, and cast þereto, and put hit in a faire potte; And theñ take a fewe Saundres, pouder peper, CaneH, and a lituH Saffroñ; And if hit be not stonding ynogh, take a lituH floure of Amidons, And drawe hit with wyñ thorgh a streynour, And cast there-to salt, and serue it forth stondyng.

IussheH. ¶ Take the Hfry of a pyke, and cast hit rawe in a morter, and cast there-to myced[1] brede grated, and bray hem asmaH as þou maist; And if hit be to stonding, caste there-to a lituH mylke of Almondes, And bray hit togidre, and strek[2] hit togidre with thi honde; And cast there-to a lituH saffroñ with Sugur and salt, And put aH in a treeñ boH, and truH[3] hit to-gidre with thi honde; And loke þat hit be noȝt to thik, but as [4]a mañ may powre it oute of þe boH; And þeñ take a pañ, and caste thereto faire grauey of a pike, or of a fressh samoñ, and drawe hit thorgh a streynour, and sette it ouer the fire; and take faire parcely and Sauge, and caste there-to, and lete hit boile, and caste there-to a lituH saffroñ and salt; And whañ hit hath boyled a while, sterre hit fast, and caste the stuff thereto, and ster hit euermore. And whañ hit is al oute of the bolle, [cast it][5] a liteH and a liteH into þe pañ, stere it softer and softer til hit be roñ to-gidre; And þeñ take a ladeH or a skymmour, and drawe hit togidre soft til hit come to-gidre, And take hit fro þe fire, and sette þe vesseH oñ a fewe colys, and lete hit wax stiff be his owne accorde, and theñ serue it forth with a skymour, like as þou wolt serue IusseH, aH hote.

Gele of pesoñ. ¶ Take a pike newe right y-drawe,[6] and smyte him in faire

---

[1] MS. myced myced. D. *maynchete.*   [2] Douce MS. *strike.*
[3] ? twille, as Douce MS.   [4] fol. 20b.   [5] Added from Douce MS.
[6] Douce MS.: Draw new pikes and new righ, and smyte hem.

peces, and sethe him in same licour as þou doest Gele of flessħ/ And whañ hit
is ynoȝħ, take hit vppe; And þeñ take perches, tenches, elys, & kutte hem
in faire peces, and wassħ hem, and put hem in the same licour; and loke that
thou haue fissħ ynogħ, that the licoure may be stiff ynowe; And in caas þat
þou faile fissħ, that þou hast not ynogħ to make gely, take faire soundes of
watered stokfissħ, or elles of ffresħ Milleweħ, or elles of kelyng,[1] and cast
thereto; and sette ouer þe fire, and lete it boyle; and þat woħ help hit to gele;
and skem clene þe grave; And whañ hit is ynogħ, lete noȝt the fissħ breke,
but take vppe the fissħ hole, and set the licour fro the fire, and put coles
vndernetħ the vesseħ as þou doest afore to the oþer gele of flessħ, with
vinegre, pouder of peper, saffroñ & salt; And þeñ take a pike, perche, and
tenche, and pul of the skyñ, And put a pece of one and a pece of anoþer in a
faire dissħ, as þou dost oþer gele of flessħ, And poure the licour there-oñ, as þou
doest oþer gele of flessħ; and cast there-oñ almondes blanched, and foyles of
tried [2]ginger pared, and set hit in a colde place, and lete hit gele.

Caudeħ. ¶ Take faire tryed yolkes of eyreñ, and cast in a potte; and take
good ale, or elles good wyñ, a quantite, and sette it ouer þe fire/ And whañ
hit is at boyling, take it fro the fire, and caste þere-to saffroñ, salt, Sugur;
and cesoñ hit vppe, and serue hit forth hote.

Oyle soppes. ¶ Take a good quantite of oynons, and myce hem, noȝt to
smale, & setħ hem in faire water, And take hem vppe; and theñ take a
good quantite of stale ale, as .iij. galons, And there-to take a pynte of goode
oyle that is fraied, and cast the oynons there-to, And lete al boyle togidre a
grete [while];[3] and caste there-to Saffroñ and salt, And þen put brede, in
maner of brewes, and cast the licour there-oñ, and serue hit fortħ hote.

Caudeħ de Almondes. ¶ Take rawe almondes, and grinde hem, And
temper hem with goode ale and a litul water; and drawe hem thorgh a
streynour into a faire potte, and lete hit boyle awhile; And cast there-to
saffroñ, Sugur and salt, and serue hit forth hote.

[4]**Cheaut de Almondes.** ¶ Take almondes, and blanche hem, and grynde hem
with faire water, and drawe hem thorgħ a streynour, and sette hem oñ the
fire, and lete hem boyle ones; and cast there-to sugur and salt, And serue it
fortħ hote.

Lente ffrutours. ¶ Take goode floure, Ale yeest,[5] saffroñ, and salt, and bete
al to-gidre as thik as oþer maner frutours of flessħ; and þeñ take Appels, and

---

[1] D. kodelyng.   [2] fol. 21.   [3] Douce MS. wile.
[4] Chaudlet Douce MS.   [5] D. however reads Ale and yeest.

pare hem, and kut hem in maner of ffrutours, and wete hem in þe batur vp
and downe, and fry hem in oyle, and cast hem in a dissħ, and cast sugur
þeroñ ynowe, and serue hem forth hote.

[**Lesenges Fries.**¹] ¶ Take floure, water, saffroñ, sugur, and salt, and
make fyne paast þer-of, ²and faire thyñ kakes; and kutte hem like losenges,
and fry hem in fyne oile, and serue hem forthe hote in a dissħ in lenteñ tyme.

[**Risschewes de frute.**³] ¶ Take ffigges, and grinde hem in a morter al smal
with a liteħ oyle, and grynde witħ hem, clowes, and maces; and theñ take
hem vppe in-to a dissħ, and caste thereto pynes, saundres, reisons of coraunce,
myced dates, pouder of Peper, Caneħ, Saffroñ, and salt; And theñ make fyne
paast of floure, water, sugur, saffroñ, and salt, And make there-of faire kakes;
and theñ rolle the stuff in thi honde, and couche hit in þe kakes; kutte hem,
and so folde hem [togedrys]⁴ as risshewes, And fry hem in goode Oyle, And
serue hem forthe hote.

[**Trayne roste.**⁵] ¶ Take Dates and figges, and kutte hem in a peny
brede; And þeñ take grete reysons and blanched almondes, and prik hem
thorgh with a nedel into a threde of a mannys lengtħ, and one of one frute
and a-noþer of a-noþer frute; and þeñ bynde the threde with the frute
A-bought a rownde spete, endelonge þe spete, in maner of an hasselet; And
theñ take a quarte of wyne or Ale, and fyne floure,⁶ And make batur thereof,
and cast thereto pouder ginger, sugur, & saffroñ,⁷ pouder of Clowes, salt;
And make þe batur not fully rennyng, and noþer stonding, but in þe mene,
that hit may cleue, and⁶ than rost the⁸ treyne abought the fire in þe spete; And
þeñ cast the batur oñ the treyne as he turnetħ abough[t] the fire, so longe
til þe frute be hidde in the batur; as þou castest þe batur there-on, hold a
vesseħ vndere-nethe, for⁹ spilling of þe batur/ And whan hit is y-rosted weħ,
hit wol seme a hasselet; And theñ take hit vppe fro þe spit al hole, And kut
hit in faire peces of a Spañ lengtħ, And [serue]¹⁰ of hit a pece or two in a
dissħ al hote.

Quynces or Wardones in paast. ¶ Take and make rounde coffyns of
paast; and take rawe quynces, and [pare]¹¹ ¹²hem witħ a kuyfe, and take
oute clene the core; And take Sugur ynogħ, and a lituħ pouder ginger and
stoppe the hole fuħ. And þeñ couche ij. or iij. quynces or wardons in a
Coffyn, and keuer hem, And lete hem bake; or elles take clarefied hony instede of sugur, if thou maist none sugur; And if þou takest [hony],¹³ put

---

¹ Douce MS.   ² fol. 21b.   ³ Douce MS.   ⁴ Douce MS.
⁵ Douce MS.   ⁶ D. MS.; sugur, Harl. ⁷ Douce MS. ⁶⁻⁸ D. MS.; that rost, Harl.
⁹ against, to stop. ¹⁰ Douce MS. ¹¹ added from D. MS. ¹² fol. 22. ¹³ Douce MS.

thereto a lituH pouder pep*er*, and ginger, and put hit in þe same maner in the quynces or wardons, and late hem bake ynogħ.

¹Rastons. ¶ Take fyne floure, and white of eyreñ, and a litul of the yolkes ; And theñ take warme berm̄, and put al thes togidre, and bete hem togidr*e* with thi honde so longe til hit be² short and thik ynogħ. And caste sug*ur* ynowe thereto ; And þeñ lete rest a while ; And theñ cast hit in a faire place in añ oveñ, and lete bake ynogħ ; And þeñ kut hit with a knyfe rownde aboue in maner of a crowne, and kepe þe crust þat þou kuttest, and pile³ all þe cremes⁴ within togidre ; and pike hem smaH with thi knyfe, and saue the sides and al þe cruste hole w*ith*oute ; And þeñ cast thi clarefied butter, and medle þe creme⁵ and þe butt*ur* togidre, And couer hit ayeñ with þe cruste that þou kuttest awey ; and theñ put hit in the oveñ ayeñ a lituH tyme, and take it oute, and serue hit forthe aH hote.

Tart de ffruyte. ¶ Take figges, and seth hem in wyne, and grinde hem smale, And take hem vpp*e* into a vesseH ; And take pouder pep*er*, CaneH, Clowes, Maces, pouder ging*er*, pynes,⁶ gr*e*te reysons of coraun*ce*, saffroñ, and salte, and cast thereto ; and þeñ make faire lowe coffyns, and couche þis stuff ther*e*-in, And plonte pynes aboue ; and kut dates and fressħ salmoñ in faire peces, or elles fressħ eles, and p*ar*boyle hem a lituH in wyne, and couche thereoñ ; And couche⁷ the coffyns faire with þe same paaste, and endore the coffyñ withoute w*ith* saffro*n* & almond mylke ; and set hem in þe oveñ and lete bake.

[**Chewettes**]. ¶ ⁸Take and make faire paste of floure, water, saffroñ, and salt ; And make rownde cofyns þere-of ; and þeñ make stuff as þou doest for rissħeshewes, and put þe stuff in þe Coffyns, and couer the coffyns with þe same paaste, and fry hem in goode oyle as þou doest rissħshewes, and s*er*ue hem forthe hote in the same maner.

Lamprey I-bake. ¶ Take and make a faire rounde coffyñ of paast ; and þeñ take a fressħ lamprey, and lete him blode .ij. fingers within þe naueH, And lete him blode in a vesseH, and lete him dy in þe same blode ; And theñ take browne brede, and kut hit, and stepe hit in vinegr*e*, and drawe hit þorgħ a streynou*r* ; and þeñ take þe same blode, and pouder of CaneH, And cast there-to, til hit be browne ; And theñ cast thereto a litul pouder of pep*er* and salt, and a lituH wyne, that hit be not to stronge with vynegre ; And theñ skald the lamprey, and pare him clene, and couche him rounde in

---

¹ Douce MS.; *Bastons*, Harl.   ² Douce MS.   ³ Douce MS.: *pike* Harl.
⁴ Douce MS. *cremes*.   ⁵ Douce MS. *crommes*.   ⁶ D. *adds*: reysyns fried in oyle.
⁷ Douce MS. keu*e*re.   ⁸ fol. 22*b*.

a coffyn; and þen caste al þe sewe rownde abought vppon him in the coffyn
til hit be couered; And then couer þe coffyn, and hele hit with a lydde aboue,
saue a litul hole; and at the hole blowe in the coffyn with thi mouthe
a good blast of wynde; and sodenly stoppe the hole, that the wynde abide
withiu þe coffyn, to ryse up þe cofyn that he faH not a-downe. And whañ
hit is a litul y-harded in þe oven, prik the coffyn with a pyn, for[1] brestyng[2]
of þe coffyn; And lete bake ynowe, And serue it forthe colde.   And whañ
the lamprey is ytake oute of þe coffyn, and I-ete,[3] take the sirippe oute of
þe coffyn, and put hit in a chargeour, and caste wyne there-to, And pouder
of ginger, And lete boyle ouer þe fire; And take paynmain, and kutte hit
and wete hit yn, And ley þe soppes yn the coffyn of þe lamprey, And cast
the sirippe aboue, and ete it so/

Sauce pour lamprey. ¶ Take a quyk lamprey, And lete him blode at þe
nauell, And lete him blode in an erthen potte; And scalde him with hey, and
wassh him [4]clene, and put him [on a spitte;][5] and sette the vessell with þe
blode vnder þe lamprey while he rosteth, And kepe the licoure þat droppeth
oute of him; And then take oynons, and myce hem smaH, And put hem yn a
vessell with wyne or water, And let hem parboyle right well; And then take
awey the water, and put hem in a faire vessell; And þen take pouder of CaneH
and wyne, And drawe hem thorgh a streynour, and cast [hit to][6] the oynons,
and set ouer the fire, and lete hem boyle; And cast a lituH vinegre and
parcely there-to, and a litul peper; And þen take þe blode and þe dropping
of þe lamprey, and cast thereto [& lete buille to-gedrys tiH it be a liteH
thykke, & cast therto][7] pouder ginger, vynegre, salt, and a lituH saffron;
And whañ þe lamprey is[8] rosted ynowe, ley him in a faire chargeour, And
caste aH the sauce apon him, And so serue him forth.

Lamprey poudred. ¶ Take a lamprey poudred, and stryke away the salt
with thi honde; take awey the bone fro þe þrote into þe tayle by the bely
side, And ley him in water a day and a nyght, and scald him in water with
strawe or hey, to stripe him with-aH; And then wassh him clene, and cast
him in faire water colde, and seth him, and cast x. or xij. oynons hole vn-
pullud, and lete hem seth togidre, and skem it; And þen take vp the lamprey
and þe oynons fro þe water, and ley hem in a dissh tiH they ben colde aH;
and serue hem forthe colde with sauce Galentyne; and myce the oynons in[9]
the sauce, & ete hem so.

---

[1] against, to stop.　　[2] Douce MS.; *brennyng*, Harl.　　[3] eaten.　　[4] fol. 23.
[5] Douce MS.; Harl. MS. *in a faire brothe.*　　[6] added from Douce MS.
[7] added from Douce MS.　　[8] Harl. MS. *is ro.*　　[9] Douce MS.; *and* Harl.

Stokfissh in sauce. ¶ Take faire broth of elys, or pike, or elles of fressh samond, And streyn hit thorgh a streynour; and take faire parcelly, And hewe hem smaH, And putte the broth and þe parcelly into añ ertheñ potte, And cast þerto pouder ginger, and a litul vergeous, And lete hem boyle to-gidre; and þeñ take faire soddeɴ stokfissh, aud ley hit in hote water; and whañ þou wilt serue it forth, take þe fissh fro þe water, and ley hit in a dissh, And caste the sauce al hote there-oñ, aud serue it forth.

Lamprons in Galentyne. ¶ Take brede, and stepe it in wyne and vynegre, and cast there-to CaneH, [1] and drawe it thorgh a streynour; and do it in a potte, and cast pouder of peper thereto; And take smale oynons, and myce hem, and fry hem in oyle, & cast there-to a fewe saundres, and lete hem boyle a litul; And theñ take lamprons, and scalde hem with hey in hote water, and seth hem; and þeñ b[r]oyle [2] hem oñ a faire gredreñ, and þeñ couche hem iu a dissh and cast the sauce oñ hem, And theñ serue it forth.

Lamprons ybake. ¶ Take lamprons, and scalde hem with hey; and make faire paaste, and couche ij. or iij. lamprons thereoñ, with pouder ginger, salt and peper, and lete bake; And leche samoñ in faire brode peces, and bake hem in þe same maner.

Oystres in grauey. ¶ Take almondes, and blanche hem, and grinde hem, and drawe hem þorgh a streynour with wyne, and with goode fressh broth into gode mylke, and sette hit oñ þe fire and lete boyle; and cast þereto Maces, clowes, Sugur, pouder of Ginger, and faire parboyled oynons myced; And þeñ take faire oystres, and parboile hem togidre in faire water; And then caste hem there-to, And lete hem boyle togidre til þey beñ ynowe; and serue hem forth for gode potage.

Oystres in cevey. ¶ Take oystres and sheH hem and put hem in a vesseH, (and þe water that is withiñ þe oystres with-aH;) And cast þerto a litul wyne, And sette hem over the fire, and parboyle hem; And þeñ take faire þe oystres vppe of the broth, and put hem in a faire potte; And take þe same broth, and drawe hit thorgh a streynour, and cast hit in-to þe oystres, And sette hit ouer the fire; And take a lituH Of þe same broth ayeñ; and a lituH wyne, and put hit yñ a faire vesseH, and put þere-to browne crustes and pouder caneH, and draw hit thorgh a streynour; aud myce oynons smaH, aud fry hem in oyle or in butter, and caste hem there-to, and sette ouer the fire. And whañ þe oystres boyleth, caste the licoure [3] there-to, and ceson hit vppe with pouder of peper, salt, and a litel saffroɴ, and cast there-to a litul vinegre, þat hit be

---

¹ fol. 23b.   ² Douce MS. *bouille*.   ³ fol. 24.

poynaut there-of in þo sesenyng and browne also; And serue hit forth for a
gode potage.

Pike in galentyne. ¶ Take a pike and seth him ynowe in gode sauce; And
þeñ couche him in a vesseH, that he may be y-caried yñ, if þou wilt// And
what tyme he is colde, take brede, and stepe hit in wyne and vinegre, and cast
there-to caneH, and drawe hit þorgħ a streynour, And do hit in a potte, And
caste there-to pouder peper; And take smale oynons, and myce hem, And
fry hem in oyle, and cast there-to a fewe saundres, and lete boyle awhile;
And cast aH this hote vppoñ þe pike, and cary him forth.

Pike boyled. ¶ Take and make sauce of faire water, salt, and a lituH Ale
and parcelly; and þeñ take a pike, and nape him, and drawe him in þe bely,
And slytte him thorgħ the bely, bak, and hede and taile, with a knyfe in to [1]
peces; and smyte þe sides in quarters, and wassħ hem clene; And if thou
wilt have him rownde, schoche him by þe hede in þe backe, And drawe
him there,[2] And skoche him in two or iij. peces [3] in þe bak, but noȝt thorgh;
And slyt the pouuche,[4] And kepe the fey or the lyuer, and kutte awey the
gaH. And whañ þe sauce biginneth to boyle, skeñ hit, And wassħ þe pike,
and cast him þere-in, And caste þe pouche and fey there-to, And lete hem
boyle togidre; And þeñ make the sauce thus: myce the pouche and fey,
[in] [5] a litul gravey of þe pike, And cast þere-to pouder of ginger, vergeous,
mustarde, and salt, And serue him forth hote.

Pike in brase. ¶ Take CaneH, a quarte of wyne, and a lituH vinegre,
And stepe there-yñ tendur brede; and thrawe it þorgh a streynour, And lete
boyle with pouder of peper; And take the pike, and roste him splat oñ a
gredire ynogħ; And cast to þe sauce þen, [with] pouder of ginger and sugur;
And ley the pike in A [6] charger, the wombe side vpward; and theñ caste the
sauce there-oñ al hote, and so serue him forth.

Auter pike in Galentyne. ¶ Take browne brede, and stepe it in a quarte
of vinegre, and a pece [7] of wyne for a pike, and quarteren of pouder caneH,
and drawe it thorgħ a streynour skilfully thik, and cast it in a potte, and lete
boyle; and cast there-to pouder peper, or ginger, or of clowes, and lete kele.
And þeñ take a pike, and seth him in good sauce, and take him vp, and lete
him kele a litul; and ley him in a boH for to cary him yñ; and cast þe sauce
vnder him and aboue him, that he be al y-hidde in þe sauce; and cary him
wheþer euer þou wolt.

---

[1] *i.e.* two.   [2] MS. there &.   [3] Douce MS. *placys.*   [4] i.e. *poche* of a fish, see below.
[5] Douce MS., *and* Harl.   [6] fol. 24*b*.   [7] Douce MS. *pynt.*

Salmoñ fressħ boiled. ¶ Take a fressħ Salmoñ, and drawe him in þe bely; and chyne him as a swyne, and leche him flatte with a knyfe; and kutte the chyne in ij. or in .iij. peces, and roste him oñ a faire gredryñ; & make faire sauce of water, parcelly, and salt. And whañ hit begynneth to boyle, skeñ it clene, and cast þe peces of salmoñ þere-to, and lete hem sethe; and þeñ take hem vppe, and lete hem kele, and ley a pece or ij. in a dissħ; and wete faire foiles of parcely in vinegre, and caste hem vppoñ þe salmoñ in the dissħ; And þeñ ye shaH serue hit forthe colde.

Samoñ roste in Sauce. ¶ Take a Salmond, and cut him rounde, chyne and aH, and roste the peces oñ a gredire; And take wyne, and pouder of CaneH, and drawe it þorgħ a streynour; And take smale myced oynons, and caste þere-to, and lete hem boyle; And þeñ take vynegre, or vergeous, and pouder ginger, and cast there-to; And þeñ ley the samoñ in a dissħ, and cast þe sirip þeroñ al hote, & serue it forth.

Troute boyled. ¶ Take a troute, and nape him; And make faire sauce of water, parcely, [1]and salt, and whañ hit bigynneth to boile, skeme hit clene; and drawe him in þe bely; and if þou wilt haue him rounde, kut him in þe bakke in two or þre places, but noȝt þorgħ, And drawe him in þe sket[2] next the hede, as thou doest a rounde pike; and þe sauce is verge sauce; or eHes setħ þe pouche as þe dost þe pouche of a pike, and myce hem witħ þe grauey, and pouder of ginger; and serue him forth colde, and cast þe foiles of parcelly, y-wet in vinegre, oñ him in a dissħ.

Crabbe or Lopster boiled. ¶ Take a crabbe or a lopster, and stop him in þe vente witħ oñ of hire clees, and setħ him in water, and no salt; or elles stoppe him in þe same maner, and cast him in añ oveñ, and bake him, and serue him forth colde. And his sauce is vinegre.

Perche boiled. ¶ Take a perche, and drawe him in þe throte, and make to him sauce of water and salt; And whañ hit bigynneth to boile, skeme hit and caste þe perche there-in, and setħ him; and take him vppe, and pul him, and serue him forth colde, and cast vppoñ him foiles of parcelly. and þe sau[c]e is vinegre or vergeous.[3]

ffloundres boiled. ¶ Take floundres, and drawe hem in the side by the hede, and setħ[4] hem, & make sauce of water and salt, and a good quantite of ale; And whañ hit biginneth to boile, skeme it, and caste hem there-to; And lete hem sethe, and serue hem fortħ hote; and no sauce but salt, or as a mañ luste.

---

[1] fol. 25. [2] Douce MS. skoch. [3] Douce MS. vert sauce. [4] Douce MS. scocch.

Shrympes. ¶ Take Shrympes, and seth hem in water and a lituH salt, and lete hem boile ones or a lituH more. And serue hem forthe colde; And no maner sauce but vinegre.

Breme or Roche boiled. ¶ Take a Breme or a roche, and scalde him in water, and drawe him þe side by þe hede, and scocche[1] him [in] þe side in two or thre places, but not [2]thorgh, and seth him in water, ale, and salt, and serue him forth hote; the sauce is vergyussauce or sauce ginger.

Breme rost ensauce. ¶ Take a breme, and scald him, (but noȝt to moche,) and drawe him in þe bely, and pryk him þorgh þe chyne bon ij. or iij.[3] with a knyfe, and roste him on a gredire. And take wyne, and boile hit, and cast there-to pouder ginger, vergeous, and salt, and cast on þe breme in a dissh, and serue him forth hote.

Plaise boiled. ¶ Take a playse, and drawe him in the side by the hede; And make sauce of water, parcelly, salt, And a litul ale; And whan hit bigynneth to boyle, skeme hit clene, and caste hit there-to, and lete seth/ And sauce to him is mustard and ale and salt; And serue it forthe hote/ or elles take a plays, and drawe him, pryke him with a knyfe for breking, as he frieth; And fry him in hote oile, or elles in clarefied buttur.

Ray boiled. ¶ Take a Ray, and draw him in þe bely, and kutte him in peces, and seth him in water, and no salt, and serue him forth colde. And his sauce is vergeous, or lyuer with mustarde; And boyle þe lyuer with him, And serue him forthe.

Sole, boiled, rost, or fryed. ¶ Take a sole, and do awey þe hede, and drawe him as a plais, and fle him; And make sauce of water, parcelly and salt; And whan hit bygynneth to boile, skeme it clene, and lete boyle ynogh. And if þou wilt haue him in sauce, take him whan he is y-sodde; or elles take him rawe and drawe him, and scale him with a knyfe, And ley him vppon a gredryn, and broile him. And take wyne and pouder of CaneH, and lete boyle a while, And caste there-to pouder ginger, And vergeous; and caste þe sauce on þe sole in þe dissh, And serue him forthe hote. Or elles take a sole, and do a-wey þe hede; drawe him, and scalde him, and pryk him with a knyfe in diuerse places for [4] brekyng of þe skyn; And fry it in oyle, or elles in pured buttur.

Gurnard rosted or boyled. ¶ Take a Gurnard, and drawe him in þe bely and sauce[5] the powche with-yn hole; and make sauce of water and salt; And whan hit bigynneth to boile, skeme it clene, And cast the Gurnard thereto,

---

[1] Harl. *scorche*; Douce MS. *scocche*.   [2] fol. 25b.   [3] twies or thries.
[4] fol. 26.   [5] Douce MS. : Harl. *sauce*.

And seth him, and[1] sauce/ to him is sauce of ginger, or vergyussauce, and serue him colde.

Anoþer. ¶ Take a gurnard rawe, and slytte him endelonge the bak, þorgħ þe hede and tayle, and splatte him, and kepe the lyuer; And take þe rawe lyuer, and brede, and fissħ brotħ, Wyne, and vinegre, And drawe hem thorgħ a streynour, and lete boyle; and þeñ cast there-to pouder ginger, saffroñ, and salt. And þeñ roste the gurnard, and splatte him oñ a gredire, and [2]ley hym in a dissh.[2] And þeñ cast þe sauce oñ hym in þe dissh, and serue him forthe hote.

Menese or loche boiled. ¶ Take Menyse or loche, and pike hem faire; And make sauce of a gode quantite of ale and parcelly. And whañ hit biginnetħ nye to boyle, skeme it clene, and cast þe fissħ thereto; and lete setħ. And if a mañ wol, cast a litul saffroñ thereto : and sauce is vergesauce[3]; And theñ ye shaħ serue him forth hote.

Haddok or codlyng. ¶ Take añ haddok or codlyng, and drawe him in þe bely. And make sauce of water and salt; And whañ hit bigynnetħ to boyle, skeme hit clene, and caste the fissħ thereto, And setħ hit in his sauce. His sauce is garlek or verge-sauce; and serve him hote.

Barbeħ boyled. ¶ Take a barbeħ, and kutte him, and [4]draw him rounde; And pike[4] in þe nape of the hede and setħ him in water and salt, Ale, and parcely. And whañ hit bygynnetħ to boile, skeme hit clene, and caste the barbel there-to, And setħ him. And his sauce is garlek or vergesauce, [5]And þeñ serue him fortħ.

Millet boyled. ¶ Take a Millet, and scale him, and drawe him in þe bely, and wassħ him clene; and þeñ take a pynte of wyne, and pouder caneħ, And boile hem ouer the fire. And whañ hit is yboiled ynowe, caste there-to pouder ginger and a litel vergeous; and caste the same licour vppoñ him in the dissħ, and serue him forth hote; other elles scale him and drawe him, and fry him in good oyle.

Sturgeoñ boiled. ¶ Take a Sturgeoñ, and kut of the vyñ fro the tayle to þe hede, oñ þe bakke; and chyne him and boyle him. And whañ hit boiletħ, skeme it, and caste parcelly there-to, And lete hem boyle ynowe, And then take him vppe, And serue him fortħ colde witħ leves of parcelly wet in vinegre, and caste there-oñ in þe dissħ; And sauce þer-to is vinegre.

Sturgeoñ in brotħ. ¶ Take fressħ sturgeon, and chop it, and parboile it in

---

[1] MS. *in.*
[2]-[2] Douce MS.; Harl. *reste him.*
[3] Douce MS. *vert sauce.*
[4]-[4] Douce MS. *draw hym as a rounde pike.*
[5] fol. 26b.

water; and take hit fro the fire, and streyne it [1] þorgħ a streynour into a potte ; and pike clene the fissħ thereto ; and cast there-to pouder peper, clowes, Maces, and caneħ, and faire brede, and stope hit with the same licour, and streyne hit thorgħ a streynour, and caste there-to ; And lete boyle togidre ; And caste thereto Saffroñ, pouder ginger, salt, And vinegre ; And theñ ye shaħ serue it forth.

Sturgeoñ pour porpeys. ¶ Take a Sturgeoñ, Turbut, or porpeys, and kut hit in faire peces to bake ; And theñ make faire kakes of faire paast, And take pouder of peper, pouder of Ginger, Caneħ, aud salt, And medle þes poudres and salt togiders ; And take and ley a pece of the fissħ oñ a kake/ and ley þe pouders vnderneth þe fissħ, and aboue ynowe ; And þeñ wete the sides of þe paast witħ faire colde water, and close the sides to-gidre, and sette hem in añ oveñ, and bake hem ynowe.

[2] **ffirmenty witħ porpeys.** ¶ Take faire almondes, and wassħ hem clene, and bray hem in a morter, and drawe hem witħ water thorgħ a streynour into mylke, and caste hit in a vesseħ. And theñ take wete, and bray it in a morter, that al þe hole hoħ be awey, and boyle hit in faire water til hit be wel ybroke and boyled ynowe. And þeñ take hit fro the fire, and caste thereto þe mylke and lete boyle. And whan hit is yboyled ynowe, and thik, caste there-to Sugur, Saffroñ, and salt ; and þeñ take a porpeys, and chyne him as a Samoñ, And setħ him in faire water. And whañ hit is ynowe, baude hit, and leche hit in faire peces, aud serue hit forth witħ firmanty, and cast there-oñ hote water [3] in þe dissħ.

Tenche in brase. ¶ Take a tenche, and nape him, and slyt him in þe bak thorgħ the hede and taile, And drawe him ; and þeñ make sauce of water and salt. And whañ hit bigynnetħ to boyle, skeme it clene, and cast þe tenche therein, and setħ him ; And take him vppe, and pul of the skyñ, And ley him flatte, and þe boly vpwardes in a dissħ. And þen take percelly and oynons And hewe hem smaħ to-giders ; And cast þere-to pouder of Ginger, and cast hit in vinegre ; And caste aħ oñ þe tenche iu þe dissħ, and serue him forthe colde.

Another diting of a tenche. ¶ Take a quarte of wyne and a litul vinegre, And tendure brede, And stope aħ togidre, and drawe hit thorgħ a streynour ; and lete hit boyle ; And caste there-to pouder peper ; And take a tenche, and splat him, and reste him oñ a gredire, and cast his sauce vppoñ him in the dissħ ; And þeñ serue hit forthe hote.

Turbut boyled. ¶ Take a Turbut, and drawe him in the side as a plays by

[1] i.e. *the broth*, as Douce MS reads.   [2] fol. 27.   [3] Douce MS. *broth*.

the hede; and þeñ chyne him, and kut him in brode peces; And þeñ make
Sauce of the water and salt; And when hit bigynneth to boyle, skeme hit
clene and [1] wassh the peces clene, and caste hem thereto, and lete hem boyle
ynowe. And þeñ take hem vppe, and let hem kele, And ley a pece or two in
A dissh, and caste the levys of parcelly wette in vinegre there-oñ, And serue
forth; And his sauce is verge-sauce.

Turbut roste ensauce. ¶ Take a Turbut, and kut of þe vynnes in maner
of a hastelette, and broche him oñ a rounde broche, and roste him; And whañ
hit is half y-rosted, cast thereoñ smale salt as he rosteth. And take also as
he rosteth, vergeous, or vinegre, wyne, pouder of Gynger, and a lituH caneH,
and cast thereoñ as he rosteth, And holde a dissh vnderneth, fore spilling of
the licour; And whañ hit is rosted ynowe, hete þe same sauce ouer the fire,
And caste hit in a dissh to þe fissh aH hote, And serue it forth.

Tripe de Turbut. ¶ Take the mawes of a Turbot, Haddok, or codlynge,
and pike hem clene, and skrape hem, and wassh hem clene, and parboyle
hem in good fressh broth of Turbot, haddok, Salmoñ, or pyk; and take
parcelly, and kut hit smale, and caste þere-to; and kut þe mawes in maner
of Tripes of peny brede, and cast al togidre in a potte, And lete boyle. And
whañ hit is y-boyled ynowe, that þey be al tendre, caste þere-to saffroñ, Salt,
And a litel vergeous, pouder of Gynger, And serue hit forth fore a good potage.

Welkes boyled. ¶ Take welkes, and caste hem in colde water, And lete hem
boyle but a lituH; And caste hem oute of the vesseH, And pike hem oute of
the sheH, and pike awey the horñ of hem, and wassh hem and rubbe hem weH
in colde water and salt, in two or thre waters; And serue hem colde, And caste
vppoñ hem leves of parcelly ywet in vinegre, And sauce to hem is vynegre.

Milkemete. ¶ [2] Take faire mylke and floure, and draue hem þorgh a
streynour, and sette hem ouer the fire, and lete hem boyle awhile; And theñ
take hem vppe, and lete hem kele awhile/ And þeñ take rawe yolkes of eyreñ
and drawe hem thorgh a streynour, and caste thereto a lituH salt, And set it
ouer the fire til hit be soñ-what thik, And lete hit noȝt fully boyle, and stere
it right well euermore. And put it in a dissh al abrode, And serue it forth
fore a gode potage in one maner; And theñ take Sugur a good quantite,
And caste there-to, and serue it forth.

Chared coneys,[3] or chardwardoñ. ¶ Take a quarter of clarefied hony, iij.
vnces of pouder peper, and putte bothe to-gidre; theñ toke 30 coynes
& x wardones, and pare hem, and drawe oute þe corkes [4] at eyther ende, and

---

[1] fol. 27b.   [2] fol. 28.   [3] Char de coynes, quince marmalade?   [4] ? cokes, or cores.

seth hem in goode wort til þey be soft. then bray hem in a morter; if they ben thik, putte a lituH wyne to hem, and drawe hem thorgh a streynour; And þen put þe hony and þat to-gidre, then sette al oñ the fire, and lete seth awhile til hit wex thikke, but sterre it weH with ij. sturrers for sitting to; And þen take it downe, and put þere-to a quarter of añ vnce of pouder ginger, And so moche of galingale, And so moche of pouder CaneH, And lete it cole; then put hit in a box, And strawe pouder ginger and caneH there-oñ: And hit is comfortable for a mannys body, And namely[1] fore the Stomak. And if thou lust to make it white, leue the hony, And take so mocH sugur, or take part of þe one and part of þe oþer/ Also in this forme thou may make chard wardoñ.

[1] specially.

ASHMOLE MS. 1439. SAUCES.

CONTENTS.

[1]**Sauces pur diuerse viaundes. Chaudoun.**—Take gysers, and lyuers, and hert' of Swanne; and if þe guttys ben fat', slyt' them,[2] and caste þem þer-to, and boile þem in faire watre: and þanne take þem up, and hew þem smal, and thanne caste þem in-to þe same broþe, (but strayne hit þurgh a straynour firste); and caste þer-to poudre peper, canel, and vynegre, and salt', and lete boile. And þanne take the blode of the Swanne, and freysshe broþ, and brede, and draw þem þurwe a straynour, and cast' þer-to; and lete boile to-gedre. And þenne take poudre of' gyngere, whanne hit' is al-moste y-now, & put' þer-to, and serue forth.[3]

Sauce alepeuere.—Take fayre broun brede, toste hit, and stepe it' in vinegre, and drawe it' þurwe a straynour; and put' þer-to garleke smal y-stampyd, poudre piper, salt, & serue forth.

Sauce galentyne.—Take faire crusteȝ of' broun brede, stepe þem in vinegre, and put' þer-to poudre canel, and lete it' stepe þer-wyþ til it be broun; and þanne drawe it þurwe a straynour .ij. tymes or .iij., and þanne

---

[1] lf. 36.   [2] clence thaym, added after them in different ink.
[3] with the swan, added in different ink.

put þer[to] poudre piper and salte: & lete it be sumwhat stondynge, and not to þynne, & serue forth.

Sauce gingyuer.—Take white brede, stepe it wiþ vynegre, and draw it .ij. or .iij. tymes þurȝ a straynour; and thanne put þer-to [1] poudre gingere, and serue forþe.

Sauce for a gos.—Take percelye, grapis, clowes of garleke, and salte, and put it in þe goos, and lete roste. And whanne þe goos is y-now, schake out þat is wiþ-in, and put al in a mortre, and do þer-to .iij. harde ȝolkes of egges; and grynd al to-gedre, and tempre it vp wiþ verious, and caste it upon the goos in a faire chargeour, & so serue it forth.

Sauce camelyne.—[2]Take faire brede, and cut it, and toste it; and take vynegre and wyne, and stepe hit þer-in, and draw it þurwe a straynour wiþ poudre canel, and draw it .ij. or .iij. tymes, til it be smothe. And þanne take poudre ginger, sugre, and poudre of clowes, and cast þer-to. And loke þat it stonde wil by clowes, & by sugre; and þanne put þer-to a litil safroune, and salt, and serue hit forþ þicke y-nowe.

Sauce rous.—Take brede, and broyl it vpon þe colous, and make it broune, and ley hit in vynegre, and lete it stepe; and þanne take piper, canel and notemyggeȝ, and a fewe of clowes, and cast it to-gedre in-to a mortre; and take þe brede out of þe vynegre, and bray þer-wyþ. And whanne it is y-brayd y-now, tempre it wyth wyne and vinegre, and draw it þurgh a straynour as þou woldiste galyntyne.

Sauce for stokefysshe.—Take faire broþe of elys, oþer of pyke, or els of freysshe Samon, and strayne it þurwe a straynour: and take faire percely, and hewe it smal, and put þe broþe and þe percele iu-to a faire erþyn vessel; and put þer-to poudre gingere, and a litil verious, & lete boile to-gedre. And þanne take faire sode stockefysche, and ley it in faire hote watre: and whanne þou wilt serue it forþe, take þe fysshe fro þe watre, and ley it in a clene disshe; & cast þe sauce al hote þer-on, and serue it forth.

Sauce for stokfysshe in an-other maner.—Take curnylles of walnotys, and clouys of garleke, and piper, brede, and salt, and caste al in a morter; and grynde it smal, & tempre it up wiþ þe same broþe þat þe fysshe was sode in, and serue it forþe.

[3]**Sauce for peiouns.**—Take percely, oynouns, garleke, and salt, and mynce smal the percely and þe oynouns, and gryndle þe garleke, and temper it wiþ vynegre y-now: and mynce þe rostid peiouns and cast the sauce þer-on a-boute, and serue it forth.

---

[1] *salt*, added in different ink.   [2] lf. 36 bk.   [3] lf. 37.   Heading in margin.

Sauce for shulder of moton.—Take p*er*cely, and oynons, and mynce þem and þe rostyde shulder of Moton; and take vynegre, and poudre gingere, salt, and cast' a-pon þe mynced shulder, and ete hym so.

Sauce vert.—Take p*er*cely, myntes, diteyne, peletre, a foil or .ij. of' cost-marye, a cloue of garleke.   And take faire brede, and stepe it with vynegre and pip*er*, and salt'; and grynde al this to-gedre, and tempre it vp wiþ wynegre, or wiþ cisel, and serue it' forþe.

Surelle.—Take Surel, wasche hit, grynde it', put' a litil salt', þer-to, and strayne hit', and s*er*ue *forth.*

Sauce p*er*cely.—Take p*er*cely, and grynde hit' wiþ vynegre & a litel brede and salt', and strayne it' þurgh a straynour, and serue it' forþe.

Sauce gauncile.—Take floure and cowe mylke, safroune wel y-grounde, garleke,[1] and put in-to a faire litel pot'; and seþe it' ouer þe fire, and s*er*ue it' forthe.[2]

Pip*er* for feel and for venys*oun*.—Take brede, and frye it' in grece, draw it vp wiþ broþe and vinegre : caste þer-to poudre pip*er*, and salt, sette on þe fire, boile it', and melle it' forþe.

White sauce for capons y-sode.—Take almoundis y-blaunchid, and grynde þem al to douste; tempre it' up wiþ verious and poudre of gingere, and melle it' forþe.

Black sauce for capou*n*s y-rostyde.—Take þe Lyuer of' capouns, and roste hit wel; take anyse, and grynde parysgingere, and canel, and a litil [3]cruste of' brede, and grynde hit' weH aH to-gedre; tempre hit up wiþ verious, and þe grece of the capon, þanne boile it' and serue forþe.

Sauce newe for malardis.—Take brede, and blode y-boilid, and grynde it to-gedere, and draw þurw a cloþ withe vynegre; do þer-to poudre gyngere, and pip*er*, and þe grece of the malarde; salt' it' and boile, and melle it forthe.

---

[1] *peper, salt,* added in different iuk.   [2] *with the goos,* added.   [3] lf. 37 bk.

LAUD MS. 553 (BODLEIAN LIBRARY).

CONTENTS.

LAUD MS. 553 (BODLEIAN LIBRARY).

[1]**Peynreguson.**—Nym resons & do out ye stones, and bray it in a morter with pepir & gingiuer, & salt and wastel bred; tempre hit with wyn, boille hit, dresse hit forth.

Amendement of salt mete.—Tak a fare lynne clout / & do therynne a disshful of ote-mele, byne hit, & hange it in thy pot doun to ye boteme. Set it from ye fuyr & let hit kele / suththe set hit aȝen to ye fuyr / & drawe out thy clout & that is goude.

For to make amydon.—Nym whete at midsomer / & salt, & do it in a faire vessel / do water therto, that thy whete be yheled / let it stonde ix days & ix nyȝt, & eueryeday whess wel thy whete / & at ye ix days ende bray hit wel in a morter / & drie hit toȝenst ye sonne / do it in a faire vessel / & kouere hit fort, thou wil it note.

Teste de cure.—Nym rys, whas hem / drie hem / & bray hem al to doust in a morter, & amydon therwith: tempre it vp with almand mylk / cast therto poudur and safron / & sugur / nym luys, turbot, and elys / & gobete hem in mosselys, & sauge & perceli / mak coffyns of thi past / do thy fissh therynne; cast aboue goud poudur & sugur; kerue it, bake it, and ȝif hit forth.

Sweteblanche.—Nym chikons or hennes, skald hem, drawe hem in morselys, & seth hem with good beofe. nym ȝolkes of eyren ysoden hard / & almande mylk, and grind to-gedere / nym ye floures of ye rede vyne, & salt, & bray al in a morter: boille hit / nym thy chikons or thy heñ, ondo hem in disshes, do thy sewe aboue / & also myȝt thou do fissh days with lyuere of turbut or of other manere fissh with almand mylke.

[2][**Ryschewys close?**].—Nym flour and eyren, & kned to-gedere / nym figus, resons, & dates, & do out ye stonys, & blauchid almandis, & goud poudur,

---

[1] lf. 5.　　　　　　　　　　[2] lf. 5b.: see p. 55.

& bray to-gedere / make coffyns of ye lengthe of a spanne / do thy farsour therynne, in euerych cake his porcioṅ / plic hem & boille hem in water / & suththe roste hem on a gridel & ȝif forth.

Bukenade.[1]—Nym fressh flessh, what it euere be. Seth hit *with* goud beof, cast therto mynsed oynons & good spiceric, & lie hit with eyren, & ȝif hit forth.

Cyuele.—Nym almandes, Sug*ur* & salt, & payn de mayn, & bray hem in a morter / do therto eyren, fric hit in oylle or in grese, cast theron sug*ur*, & ȝif hit forth.

Caudele.—Nym eyren, & sweng wel to-gedere / chauf ale & do therto / lie it with amydoṅ, do therto a porcioṅ of sug*ur*, or a p*er*ty of hony, & a p*er*ti of safroṅ; boille hit, & ȝif hit forth.

Saug saras*er*.[2]—Tak Almandes, fryo hem in oille, & bray hem, tempre hem *with* almand mylke & red wyn, & ye thrudde p*er*ty shal be sug*ur* / & if hit be noȝt thikke ynow, lie it w*ith* amydoṅ or w*ith* flour de rys; colo*ur* hit w*ith* alkinet, boille hit, dresse it, florissh hit aboue with pomme-garnet, and ȝif forth.

Rape.—Nym luyss or tenge, or oth*er* manere fissh / frye hit in oille de olyue; ny*m* crostes of whyt bred, resons, & canele, bray hit, tempre it vp w*ith* good wyn, drawe it thorw a colou*ur* / let hit be al ycoloured w*ith* canele, boille hit, cast therto clous, maces, and quibibes, do thi fissh in thi disshes, & thi rape aboue, messe hit, & ȝif forth.

[3]**Egredouces.**—Tak luyȝs or tenges, kerf hem in mosselis, fri hem in oille: ny*m* vynegre / & ye thrudde p*er*ty sug*ur*, mynce oynons, & boille smal, & clous, maces, & qibibus, & dresse hit forth.

Figee.—Nym figes, & boille hem in wyn, & bray hem in a morter with lied bred; tempre hit vp w*ith* goud wyn / boille it / do therto good spicere, & hole resons / dresse hit / florisshe it a-boue with pomme-garnetes.

Pomesmoille.—Nym rys & bray hem in a morter, tempre hem vp with almande milke, boille hem: nym appelis & kerue hem as small as douste, cast hem yn after ye boillyng, & sug*ur*: colo*ur* hit w*ith* safroñ, cast therto goud poudre, & ȝif hit forth.

Rys moilles.—Nym rys, bray hem, tempre vp w*ith*' almand mylke: boill hem, cast therto sug*ur* / & salt hit, & dresse hit forth.

Apple moys.—Nym appeles, seth hem, let hem kele, frete hem thorwe an her syue: cast it on a pot / & on a fless day cast therto goud fat broth of bef,

---

[1] MS. *Dukenade.*   [2] *i.e.* Sauce Sarrasine.   [3] lf. 6.

& white grese, sug*ur* & safro*w*), & on fissh days almand m*y*lke, & oille de
oliue, & sug*ur*, & safro*w*) : boille hit, messe hit, cast aboue good poudre, &
*j*if forth.

Soupes dorrees.—N*y*m oynons, mynce he*m*, frie he*m* in oille de olyue :
ny*m* oyno*n*s, boille he*m* w*ith* wyn, tost whit bred, & do it in dishes / and
cast almand mylke thero*w*), & *y*e wyn & *y*e oynons aboue, & gif hit forth.

[1]**Peys de almayne.**—N*y*m white peson & boille hem / & thanne tak he*m*
*v*p, & wash he*m* clene in cold wat*er*, fort that *y*e holys go of : do he*m* in a
clene pot / do water the*r*to th*a*t hit be a-wese / let he*m* sethe *v*ppo*w*) colys /
that the*r* be no lye / coue*r*e thi pot / that the*r* go no breth out / whenne
hit beth *y*sode, do he*m* in a mort*er* & br*a*y hem smal, tempre hem *v*p with
alma*n*de milke, & with flo*ur* de rys, do th*er*to safro*ñ* & salt, & boille hit
& dresse hit forth.

Tauorsay.—N*y*m *y*e hed of *y*e codlyng & *y*e liu*ere*, & pike out *y*e bones /
cast the*r*to goud poudre of piper & gyngin*er*, and gif forth.

Haddoke in Cyuee.—Sh*a*l be *y*opened & *y*wasshe clene / & *y*sode &
*y*rosted on a gridel ; grind pep*er* & saffro*w*), bred & ale / mynce oynons, fri
he*m* in ale, & do th*er*to, and salt : boille hit, do th*y*n haddok in plat*er*es, &
thi ciuey aboue, & *j*if forth.

Chauudo*w*) of fissh.—N*y*m *y*e liu*ere* & *y*e poke. Seth hit, hakke hit smal /
gri*n*d pep*er* & safron, bred & ale, tempre hit with *y*e broth / boille hit, do
salt th*er*to, & messe hit forth.

Mortrowes of fissh.—Tak *y*e rowys of fissh / & *y*e liu*ere*, seth hit, hakke
hit, grind pep*er*, bred & ale, tempre hit w*ith* *y*e broth : do salt th*er*to, boille
hit, & messe hit forth.

Blaumang*er* of fissh.—N*y*m a pond of ris, seth he*m* fort hit berste, let
he*m* kele : cast th*er*to mylk of two pond of almandes / n*y*m *y*e perch oth*er*
*y*e loppest*er*e or dric haddok, tese the*r*to, and boille hit / cast th*er*to sug*ur*,
& *j*if forth.

Potage of ris.—N*y*m *y*e ris, whess he*m* clene, seth he*m* fort hit breke :
let hem kele, do the*r*to almand mylke, oth*er* of kyn,[2] colo*ur* it w*ith* safro*w*),
salt hit, & *j*if forth.

Numbles.—Sh*a*ll be *y*whess clene in wat*er* & salt, & *y*sode in water / n*y*m
[*Cetera desunt*].

[1] lf. 6*b*.   [2] *i.e.* kine : *cow milk.*

RECIPES FROM DOUCE MS. 55,

Ab. 1450 AD.

CONTENTS.

¶ **Oyle Soppes. Ca**pitulum **lxiiij.**—Take and buille mylke, and take yolkes of eyren tryed fro the white, and draw hem; then cast to the milke and hete it, butt lete it nat buille, & ¹styrre it weH tiH it be summe-whate thikke: then cast ther-to sugre and salte, and cutt feyre paynemayne in soppes, & cast the soppes there-on, & serue it forth in maner of potage.

¶ **Capon en Counfyt. ¶ Ca**pitulum **cij.**—Take fressH broth, and wyn, & persely, & saverey, and a liteH sauge, and lete buille to-gedrys: and crome ther-to herde ²yolkes of eyren tyH it be weH thykke, and kest ther-to pouudre of gyngeuere y-nogH, & vertious, and salt, and saffron; and take a good rosted capon, & ley hym in a chargeur, & ryse the legges and the wynges, butt [set] ham nott fro the body; and kest on the capon the licour aH hotte, & serue it forth.

¶ **Cokentrice. ¶ Ca**pitulum **ciij.**—Scalde a capon clen, & smyte hem in-to the wast oueretwarde, and scaude a pygge, and draw hym, & smyte hym in the same maner; and then sewe the forthyr parte of the capon and the hyndyr parte of the pygge to-gedrys, and the forther parte of the pygge ³and the hynder parte of the capon to-gedyr: then draw the whyte & the yolkes of eyren, and cast ther-to, and svette of a schepe, and saffron, & salt, and pouudre of gyngeuere, and grated brede; and medle aH to-gedre with thyn

---

¹ lf. 34b. ² lf. 47b. ³ lf. 48.

honde, and putt it in the cokentrice, and putt it on a spite, and roste hem ; and endore hem with yolkes of eyrow, and pouudre of gyngeuere, and saffrow, & ioissħ of persely or malves, & draw hem, and endore hem aħ abowte in euery perty of hym).

¶ **Crane roste. Ca**pitulu**m c.vij.**—Take a crane, and cutt hym in the rofe of the mouth, and lete him blede to deth : and cast a-wey the blode, and schalde hym, & draw hym vndyr the wynge or att the vent, & folde vpp hys legges att the kneys vndir the thye ; & cutt of the wyngys next iunte the body,[1] and lete hym haue hys heuede & hys necke on ; saue take awey the wesyng, [2]and wynde the necke a-boute the spyte, and bynde hit, & putt the bille in the body and the golett ; and reyse the wynges and the legges as of a gose ; and yiff þou schalt sauce hym, mynce hym fyrst, and sauce hym withe pouudre of pepyr, and gyngeuere & mustarde, vynegre & salt, and serue hym forth.

¶ **Fesaunt rost. Ca**pitulu**m cviij.**—Lete a fesaunt blede in the mouth, and lete hym blede to deth ; & pulle hym, and draw hym, & kutt a-wey the necke by the body, & the legges by the kne, & perbuille hym, & larde hym, and putt the knese in the vent : and rost hym, & reise hym vpp, hys legges & hys wynges, [3]as off an henne ; & no sauce butt salt.

Herow rost. ¶ **Ca**pitulu**m c.x.**—Take an herow, & lete hym blode in the mouth as an crane, & scalde hym & draw hym att the vent as a crane ; and cutt awey the boow of the necke, & folde the necke a-boute the [4]spite, and putt the hede yune att the golet as a crane ; & breke awey the boow fro the kne to the fote, and lete the skyn be stille, and cutt the wyng att the Joynte next the body, and putt hem on a spite : and bynde hys legges to the spyte with the skynne of the legges, & lete rost, & reyse the legges and the wynges as of a crane, and sauce hym with vynegre, and mustard, and pouudre of gyngeuere, & sett hym forth.

¶ **Bitore roste. Ca**pitulu**m cxj.** — Slee a bytour in the mouth as an herow, & draw hym as an henne, and fold vppe hys legges as a crane ; & lete the wynges be on, & take the boow of the [5]necke aħ awey as of an herow : & putt the hedde in the golet or in the shuldre, and rost hym ; and ryse the legges & the wynges as þou dost of an heron, & no sauce butt salt : & sett hym forth.

Egrett rost. Capitulu**m cxij.**—Breke an egrettes nekke, or cut the rofe

[1] *i.e.* cut off the wings at the joint next to the body.
[2] lf. 50.   [3] lf. 50*b*.   [4] lf. 51.   [5] lf. 51*b*.

of hys mouth, as of a crane, & scalde hym, and draw hym as an henne; &
cutt of hys wynges by the body, and the heued & the necke by the body,
& folde hys legges as a bitore, & rost hym : & no sauce butt salt.

¶ **Plouer rost.** ¶ Ca*pitulu*m **Cxix.**—Breke the skulle of a plouere, &
pull hym drye, and draw hym as a chike, and cutte the legges and the
wynges by the body, and the heued and necke aH-so, & roste hym, and reyse
the legges and wynges as an henne : and no sauce butt salt.

¶ **Snyte rost.** ¶ Ca*pitulu*m **Cxx.**—Slee a snyte as a plouere, & lete hys
necke be hole saue the [1] wesyng; and lete hys heuede be on, and putt it in
the schuldre, and folde vppe his legges as a crane, & cutt his wynges and
roste hym, & reyse hys legges and wynges as an henne ; & no sauce butt salt.

[2] ¶ **Sturgeon buille ou turbutt.** ¶ Ca*pitulu*m **Cxlvj.** Draw a turbutt
or a sturgeon, and chyn hym, & cutt them in brode pecis; and buille
hem in water and salt y-nogh, and serue hym forth colde, a pece or too in
a dissh with vert sauce : and cast persely leves wette in vynegre on hym.

¶ **Charlete.** ¶ Ca*pitulu*m **Clxxviij.** — Seth melke yn a pott and cast
ther-to salt and saffron ; & hew feyre buttes of calues or of porke smaH, and
cast ther-to : and draw the white & yolkes of eyren, and cast to the licour
when it builleth, and a liteH ale, and stirre it tiH it crudde. and yiffe þou
wilt haue it forced, hete milke scaldyng hoote, and cast ther-to rawe yolkes
of eyren and poudre of gyngeuere, and sugre & clowes & maces, & lete natt
fully buille ; and press the cruddes in feyre [3] lenyn cloth, & lessh it, & ley
too or thre lesshes in a dissh : & cast the farsyng ther-on, & serue it
forth hote.

[1] lf 53b.   [2] lf. 60b.   [3] lf. 76.

GLOSSARY AND INDEX.

[The following works are referred to :—*Forme of Cury* ; *Liber Cure Cocorum* ; Ancient Cookeries in WARNER, *Antiquitates Culinariæ* (1791); NAPIER, *Noble Boke of Cookry* (1882); R. HOLME, *Academy of Armory* (1678); COTGRAVE, *French Dict.* (1611); GODEFROY, *Dict. de l'Anc. Langue Franc.*; MURRAY, *Eng. Dict.* (1885, etc.). The thick type shews Recipes that are in this volume ; italics shew recipes in the Banquets, but if in inverted commas, the recipe is quoted from another Cookery. The spelling of the other Cookeries has been corrected, where needful.]

A-boue, *adv.*, 14, 17 ; A-bouen, 29 ; A-bouyn, 14, 21, 35, 54 ; A-boue, *prep.*, 54 ; A-bouyn, 54. Above.

Aboujte, *adv.*, 73 ; A-bowte. 21, 29, 31 ; Abought, *prep.*, 78 ; A-bowte, 31, 54. About ; round.

Abowe, *vb.t.*, 79. Bow ; bend.

A-brode, *adv.*, Caste al a-brode, holdyn a-brode, 7, 92. Abroad ; about; stretched out.

Abyndoun, *sb.*, 20. See *Amidoun.*

A-chatry, 67. Acatery ; provisions bought.

Acord, *sb.*, Be hys owne acord, of itself, 17.

A-cordant, *adj.*, 50. Accordant; in accordance.

A-doun, *adv.*, 17, 54 ; Adown, 7. Down.

A-force, *vb.t.*, with Sugre or hony, 55, with spices, 29 ; A-force, *pp.*, 3 ; A-forse, 17. Afforce ; season, make substantial. This is the Fr. *enforcer*, see *Porcelle farce enforce*, on page 58. The word *enforcer* is still used of a person growing fat : and *force* is applied in England for fattening animals ; see HALLIWELL. Compare next word ; pork and oatmeal being used to the Gruel.

A-forcyd, *pp.* 1, Charlet a. ryally, 17 ; Doucettes a., 55 ; Chawettys a-forsed, 46 ; Kyde a-Forsyde, 41 ; Gruelle a-forsydde, 6.

Aftyrward, 21, Afterward.

Ale, *sb.*, 11, 13, 16, 86, Stale Ale, 12, 96, New ale, 10 ; Sethe Fygys in Ale, 43 ; Ale draft, 19, Ale dregs, or bottoms ; Ale yeest, 96, Ale jest, 44, Ale yeast.

Alegre, *sb.*, 28. Alegar; ale vinegar.

Alkenade, *sb.*, 29, 30, 31, 48 ; Alkinet, 113. Alkanet.

Al to-broke, 85, Alle to-broke, 44 ; Al to-choppe, 41, Alle to-choppe, 20, 34, Alle to-choppyd, 41 ; Alle to-falle, 32. Quite broken, chopped, etc.

Allemaundys, *sb.*, 10 ; Alman, 18 ; Almande mylke, 30, 112 ; Almandys, 1 ; Caudell de Almondes, 96, Cawdelle de Almaunde, 16, see F. of C. 87, "*Cawdel of Almaund mylk*"; Almaunde mylke, 11, 14, 21, 26 ; Almaundis, 56 ; Almaundys, 9, 13, 15, 16, Fride Creme of A., 7, 91, see F. of C., No. 85, "*Creme of Almaundes,*" WARNER, p. 69, "*Crem of almonde mylk*"; Almondes, 88, 90, 91, Froyte de almondes, 91, Froyde almoundys, 7, Cheaut de

Almondes, 96, see NAPIER, p. 76, "*Hoot milk of a.,*" and "*Cold mylk of a.,*" also Douce MS. No. 160. "*Chaud let dalmaundes.*" Almonds.

Almaunden, *adj.*, 17. Almond; of almonds: there should be no comma after it.

Almaynne, Hagas de, 44, Hagas de almondes 84 ; Bruet of Almaynne, 19, Bruet of A. in lente. 19 ; Peys de Almayne, 114. These are possibly all German dishes, but *Allemagne* and *Almonds* got confounded, as in the first two recipes, which are 'the same dish, and have almonds in them.

Almonds, see *Allemaundys.*

Along, *adv.*, Datys y-taylid a-long, lengthwise, 27.

Aloes de Roo, 61; Allowes de Mutton, 83 ; Alows de Beef or de Motoun, 40 ; Alowys, 3. See WARNER, p. 74, "*Alaunder of moton*" and "*of beef*"; NAPIER, p. 29, "*Alander de moton,*" p. 30, "*Alander de beeff.*" COTGR., "*Aloyau de bœuf.* A short rib of beefe, or the fleshie end of the rib, diuided from the rest, and rosted." Compare a mutton-chop.

A-lye, *vb.t.*, 13, 17, 19. Allay; mix : Fr. *Allayer*, COTGR. See *Ly.*

Amendement of salt mete, 112.

Amidons, *sb.*, 16 ; For to make Amydon, 112 ; Amyndons, 22 ; Amyndoun, 28. Fr. *Amidon,* Wheat flour, steeped, strained, and dried in the sun : see L.C.C., p. 7, NAPIER, p. 101.

A-morwe, 33, 37. Amorrow; next morning.

An, *conj.*, passim. And.

Aneward, *adv.*, 34. Onward; on it.

Aneys, *sb.*, 53 ; in comfyte, 32 ; Auys in comfyte, 8, 10, 28. Anise.

Apoñ, *prep.*, 92. Upon.

Appeles, *sb.*, 113 ; Appelis, 113 ; Appelys, 16, 20 ; Appil, 38 ; Apple mose, 2, or Apple muse, 20 ; Apple moys, 113 ; see WARNER, II. 17, 35, *Prompt. Parv.*, p. 13, "*Apulmos,*" "*Appulmos,*" NAPIER, p. 121, "*Appillmose*"; compare "*Mush,* Anything mashed," HALLIWELL. Apple

moyle, 30, Pomesmoille, 113, called "*Appulmoy*" in F. of C., No. 79, "*Pommes moiled,*" or "*molid*" in NAPIER, p. 119, and "*Pommys morles,*" in WARNER, p. 46, on which page there is also "*Rys* (Rice) *moyle,*" (called "*Resmolle*" in F. of C., 96). The *moyle,* or *morles,* is the French *Mol, Molle,* soft. Applys, 29, 30, 39.

Applade Ryalle, 30. So called from the apples in it : compare *Quynade.*

Appraylere, 39. See COTGR., "*Appareillé*; dressed, cooked, or seasoned, (as meat)." This dish is well spiced.

Arbolettys, 20, Fr. *Herbelettes,* Small herbs ; see F. of C., No. 172, "*Erbolates.*" The dish is spelt *Arbelettys* in A. See *Herbelade.*

AsmaH, 95. As small.

A-to, 5, 22, 40. In two.

Auence, *sb.*, 5 ; Auens, 69. Avens ; Bennet.

A-wese, 114, A-wash. See Overwose, and note 4 on p. 86.

Aȝen, *adv.*, 53, Again : Aȝenward, *adv.*, 54. Once more.

Bacon, see *Bakon.*

Bake Mete, 54 ; Bake Mete Ryalle, 55 ; Bake Metis, 47. Baked Meat.

Baken, *vb.*, 54. Bake.

Bakke, *sb.*, 41. Back.

Bakon, *sb.*, 6 ; Bakoun, 32. Bacon.

Bakyn mete, 33. Baked meat.

Balloke brothe, 10, 89. See F. of C., No. 109, WARNER, p. 68, NAPIER, p. 86. This broth is called "*Balowryly broth*" in WARNER, p. 49.

Banquets, 57, 58, 59, 60, 61, 62, 63, 67, 68. See Forewords.

Barbel, 104 ; BarbeH boyled, 104.

Barlyche, *sb.*, 37. Barley.

Bastard, *sb.*, 37. A sweet Spanish Wine. See Ord. & Reg., p. 473.

Bastard, *adj.*, 13, 21, 22.

Basyn, *sb.*, 34. Basin.

Bater, *sb.*, 54, 73; Batur, 73; Bature, 15, 38, 54 ; Baturys, 39. Batter.

Baude, *vb.t.*, 76, 105 ; Bawde, 18, 70. Cut in thin slices ; Fr. *barder.*

Be, *prep.*, 18, 23, 26. By.

Beef y-Stywyd, **6**, Stwed Beeff, **72** ; Bef, 34, Stekys of venson or bef, **40**; Beff, 1, 5 ; Beofe, 112.

Be-helyd, *pp.*, 37. Beheled ; covered.

Be-hynde, *prep.*, 14. Behind.

Ben, *vb.*, 19, 26, 27. Been ; be.

Benecodde, *sb.*, 48 ; Bene koddys, 43. Bean-cod.

Beof, *sb.*, 113 ; Beofe, 112. Beef.

Berde, *sb.*, 39. Beard ; brim.

Bere, *sb.*, 49. Bear.

Berme, *sb.*, 44, 52, 73, 90. Barm ; yeast.

Betayñ, *sb.*, 69. Betony.

Bete, *sb.*, 5 ; Betus, 69. Beet : Beets.

Bete, *rb.,t.* b. to-gedere (in cooking), 39. Beat.

Beterre, *adj.*, 33. Better.

Be-twene, *prep.*, 39 ; Be-twyn, 39, 54. Between.

Bey, *vb.*, 27. Be.

Birdys, Smal, 1, 55 ; Bryddys, 9 ; Smal Byrdys, 52, Smale Byrdys y-stwyde, 9.

Bitore roste. 116 ; Bytor rosted, 79. Bittern : Fr. *Butor.* See *Bytor.*

Bittern, see *Bitore.*

Bladys, *sb.*, of Percely, 35 ; Barlyche & Percely, 37. Blades.

Blake, *adj.*, with Blode, 38 ; Blak sugur, 91, Blake sugre, 7, 28, 51. Black.

Blamang, 21, (Flesh), Blamanger, **85**, (Flesh), see Douce MS., No. 26. WARNER, II. No. 14 and No. 33, and p. 75, L.C.C. p. 9, F. of C., No. 36 and No. 192, NAPIER, p. 102, "*B. of flesche*" ; **Blamanger of Fysshe, 23, 114**, see L.C.C. p. 19, NAPIER, p. 111, WARNER, p. 46 ; see also p. 55, " Blaumanger to potage ;" Blamangere, 2. Blancmange ; Blancmanger.

Blanche, *adj.*, B. almondes, 90. Blanched.

Blanche, *vb.t.*, 20 ; Blaunche, 19 ; Blawnche, 7, 9. Blanch : whiten.

Blanche Porrey, 90 ; made of the white of leeks : see DUCANGE, "*Porrecta*, Jusculum ex poris confectum," (also *Porrata.*) See *Pereye.*

Blandesore, 68 ; Blandissorye, 9 ; **Blaunde Sorre, 84** ; Blaundysorye,

21 ; Blaundyssorye, 2. See WARNER, p. 55, "*Blaundesore to potage*," NAPIER, p. 35, "*Bland sorre*," p. 105, "*Blank de Sirre*" ; F. of C., No. 37, "*Blank Dessorre*," 193, "*Blank Desire*"; WARNER, II. 29, "*Blank surry*," p. 47, *Blank de Sure*, and p. 49, "*Blank de Syry*"; L.C.C., p. 12, "*Blonk desore.*" With regard to *Blaundesorre*, see WARNER, p. 75. It is made with *Blaunche Mortreves*, by setting leches of that dish in syrup made of wine and spices. The latter part of the word seems to indicate the saffron or sorrel colour. Fr. "*Soré*, Reeked, made red," COTGR.

Blank powder, 15 ; Blanke pouder, 15, 19 ; Blaunche powder, 27, 37 ; Blawnche powder, 11, 24. See COTGR., "*Pouldre blanche*, a powder compounded of Ginger, Cinnamon, and Nutmegs ; in use among Cookes."

Blaunche perry, 33, Blaunche Perreye, 32, Blawnche Perrye, 14 ; Blaunche de ferry, 27 ; Blaunche brawen, 34, Blaunche brawne, 71, See Douce MS., No. 49.

Blaunchid, *adj.*, 10, 38 ; Blawnchyd, 21. Blanched.

Blaunderellys, 59.

Blode, *sb.*, 8 ; late blode, let blood, 52 ; lete blode, 78.

Bokenade, Vele, kede, or henne in, 13 ; Autre Vele in b., 13 ; see F. of C., N. 118, WARNER, No. 52, NAPIER, p. 25, (Veal) ; Bukenade, 113, and Buknade, 85, (two recipes,) see F. of C., No. 17, "*Bukkenade*," WARNER, II. No. 45, Douce MS., No. 76 and No. 77, (Various meats) ; L.C.C., p. 12, and NAPIER, p. 105, (Fat Pork) ; see also WARNER, p. 54, "*Bukenade to potage.*"

Bolas, 24 ; Lorey de Boolas, 25 ; Bolasse, 24. Bullace.

Boll, *sb.*, 74 ; Bolle of tre, 7, Boll of tre, 92, Bowl of wood ; Treen bolle, 16, 95 ; Bolle, 20.

Bonte, *sb.*, Crees bonte *or* bunte, 38, Linen sieve : compare Crescloth, in HALLIWELL.

Bonys, *sb.*, 6, 55. Bones.

Borage, 5, 8 ; Burage, 92.

Bruet of Almaynne, 19, see WARNER II. 31, F. of C., 47, "*Brewet of Almony,*" WARNER, p. 55, "*Blaunche bruet of Almayn,*" and pp. 55, 77, "*Browet of Almayne,*" L.C.C., p. 11, "*Brewet de almonde,*" NAPIER, p. 105, "*Bruet de almonds*"; "*Allemagne*" apparently getting perverted to "Almonds": **Bruet of Almaynne in lente,** 19; **Bruette Sareson,** 19; **Honnys in b.,** 18, see NAPIER, p. 114; **Oystrys in b.,** 23; **Walkys in b.,** 23: **Tenche in b.,** 23; **Chykonys in b.,** 23, see L.C.C., p. 22; **Muskelys in b.,** 24, see F. of C., No. 122; **B. saake,** 27, see WARNER, p. 78, "*Browet seeke*"; *Bruet Mon amy,* 68; see NAPIER, p. 32. This is boiled cream, boiled again with brayed curds, honey, and butter: thickened with yolks of egg, and leched. **Brwet,** 21. See COTGR., "*Brouët:* Potage, or broth; also, any liquor, podge, or sauce, of the thicknesse, or consistence of that whereof our pruine-tarts are made." NAPIER, p. 34, has also "*Eles in Bruet,*" as also WARNER, pp. 68, 85.

Bryndons, 15, and **Bryndonys.** It seems as if this were *Bryndous,* as it is glossed *bryneeus* in margin of A., and the form *brendouse* (more likely *u* than *n*) occurs there, and is glossed *lozenges*: but it is not the dish called "*Brymeus*" in F. of C., though that is probably the same word, and ought to be printed "*Brynieus.*"

Bryse, *vb.t.,* 6. Bruise.

Bryth, *adj.,* 12. Bright; glowing in colour.

Bukenade, 113, see Bokenade.

Bullace, see *Bolas.*

Buttes of Porke, 53, 54, 76; **Buttys** of Vele, 14, 48, of Calf or of Porke, 17, 85, Porke, 44. Butts, buttocks.

Butter, *sb.,* 73; **Buttur,** 83. See Boter.

Buttry, *adj.,* 75. Buttery; soft as butter.

By-clippe, *vb.t.* 48. Beclip.

Bynde vppe flat with flowre of rys, Bynd vppe with Flour of Rys, oþer

with whetyn floure, 33. Make stiff: see MURRAY, Bind, 10.

Byne, *vb.t.,* 112. Bind; tie.

Bytor rosted, 79, see Douce MS., No. 111. NAPIER, p. 62, "*Bittur Rost.*" Bittern.

Bytyng, *adj.,* of Pepir, 40. Biting; hot, stinging.

Bywese, 24: compare *Wese* in Douce MS., Recipe 174. *Skaldyd bywese* seems to mean "just a-wash," or hardly covered. Compare *ouer-weryd,* on p. 25, which is used in same sense, and see *A-wese.*

Caas, *sb.,* in caas, 96. In case.

Cabbage, see next.

Cabochis, 69, Caboges, 6, 33; see WARNER, pp. 52, 75, Douce MS., No. 173. This is the French *Caboche,* Head, which is still used in the Channel Islands for Cabbage.

Cacche, *vb.int.,* 26. Catch; stick: still used in this signification in cookery, of meat, etc., when burnt to the pan.

Cakys, *sb.,* 15. Cakes.

Calf, 17; Calfes fete, 37; **Caluys fete,** 25; **Calvis,** 85.

Canel, *sb.,* 6, 7, 8, 9, 13; **Canele,** 113; **Caneħ,** 92, 95, **Floure of Caneħ,** 71; **Canelle,** 12, 13, 14, 20. Fr. *Cannelle,* Cinnamon.

Canvas, *sb.,* 20, 27, 41; **Canneuas,** 39, Canvas (for straining).

Capon, 2; Capons stwed, 72; **Capon en Counfyt, 115,** see WARNER, p. 56; **Capoun in Consewe.** 18, see WARNER, II. 6, and F. of C., No. 22, "*Capons in Concy,*" and see *Consewe,* below; **Capoun in Salome,** 33; **Capoun or gos farced,** 41, **Goce or Capoun farced,** 81, see Douce MS., No. 36; **Capons of hie grece,** 67, **Capoun de haut grece,** 57, *i.e.* crammed; **Capoune broþe,** 31; **Capounys,** 21.

Carpeis of Venesoũ, 68.

Carpys, *sb.,* 21. Carps.

Cas, *sb.,* 25. Case.

Cast, *vb.t.,* 25; **Caste,** 12, 25; **Caste** vppe out of a potte, 34.

Caudel Ferry departed with a bla-manger, 31; **Caudeħ Fery,** 91,

Chyne, *sb.*, 102, Chine, back : Chyne bōn, 103, Chine-bone.

Chyne, *vb.t.*, 102, 104. Chine, chop.

Chyrioun, 2 ; **Chyryoun, 29**, see F. of C., No. 58, *Chyryse*, WARNER, p. 47 ; Chyryis, 29. Cherries.

Cinnamon, see *Canel.*

Ciprys, Cyprys, Vyaund de, 21, 28. Cyprus.

Cincy, 114, see Cyncy.

Clarey, *sb.*, 93 ; Clareye, 35 ; Clarre, 93 ; Clerye, 35. Clarry ; aromatic wine. See note in WARNER, p. 90.

Clarifi, *vb.t.*, 35. Clarify.

Clarifiyd, *adj.*, hony, 12, 15, 22, 35 ; Claryfiyd Boter, 53. Clarified.

Clees, 102, Claws.

Clene, *adv.*, c. chargeaunt, 30 ; c. rennyng, 31. Clean ; quite.

Cleucy, *vb.int.*, 21. Cleave ; stick.

Cleuyng, *sb.*, 42. Cleaving ; sticking.

Close, *vb.t.*, 45, 46.

Cloþe, *sb.*, 17, 19. Cloth.

Cloues, *sb.*, 80, 82 ; Cloue, Clouys of garleke, 110 ; Clous, 113 ; Clowes, 6, 10, 13, 15, 91, Pouder of Clowes, 97 ; Clowys, 8, 9, 10, 13, 35. Cloves : Fr. *clou.*

Clowte, *sb.*, 37. Clout ; cloth.

Clowty, *adj.*, 53. Clotty.

Clowtys, *sb.*, 47. Clouts, clots (of cream).

Codelynge, Trype of Turbut or of, 18; Codlynd, 11 ; **Haddok or codlyng,** 104, see Douce MS., No. 144, "*Haddok on codlyng buille*"; Codlyng, 2, 10, 14 ; Codlyngis, 16. Codling.

Codling, see *Codelynge.*

Coffyn, *sb.*, 74, 93, Coffyns, 73 ; Cofyn, Cofynne, 47 ; Cofyns, 45, 55 ; Cofynnys, 53. Coffin ; crust of a pie.

Cokentrice, 115 ; **Cokyntryce, 40**; Cokyntryche, 62. See WARNER, p. 66, "*Cokagrys*," F. of C., No. 175, *Cocagres* ; which form is made up of *Cock*, and *Grys* or *Gris*, pig, the animals which jointly make up the dish.

Cole, *vb.t.*, 107. Cool.

Coleys, 10. See WARNER, II. 11,

"*Colys*," also p. 80, "*Colys of flessh*"; L.C.C., p. 20, "*Kolys*"; NAPIER, p. 112, "*Colles.*" Fr. "*Coulis* : A cullis, or broth of boiled meat strained ; fit for a sicke, or weake bodie," COTGR.

Colonur, 113. Cullender.

Coloure, *vb.t.*, 7. Colour.

Colpons, *sb.*, 89. Coupons ; slices.

Colouryd Sew without fyre, 20 ; see NAPIER, p. 38.

Colous, *sb.*, 109. Colys, 17, 29, 54, 114. Coals.

Colys, *sb.*, 69. Coles : cabbages.

Comad, *sb.*, 56 ; Comade, 42, 46, 48, 50, 51, 55, 56 ; Commade, 48, 54. Mixture. The word is used in F. of C., 113 ; and is spelt Commode in A.

Come to-gederys, 45. Unite ; come to one consistence.

Comfyte, *sb.*, Anys in c., Anise preserved in sugar, 8, 10, 32 ; Brawn in comfyte, 34 : see WARNER, p. 59, "*Bor in counfett*," and p. 79, "*Boor in confith*" ; Datys in comfyte, 63 ; Sugre in comfyte, 32, where A. reads "Sugre of confitens."

Commelyche, *adj.*, 34. Comely, seemly.

Compost Potage, 59, see L.C.C., p. 18.

Composte, Perys en, 12, 87 ; see NAPIER, p. 100, Douce MS., No. 57. See also COTGR. : "*Composte* : a pickled, or winter Sallet of hearbes, fruits or flowers, condited in vinegar, salt, sugar or sweet wine."

Confeccions, 88, Confections ; preserves.

Congere, *sb.*, 14 ; *Congre*, 59 ; see NAPIER, p. 73, "*Congur.*" Congereel.

Consewe, Capoun in, 18. This seems the same as *Capon in Concis*, see F. of C., 22, WARNER, II. 6, L.C.C., p. 24, "*Capons in Conisye.*" NAPIER, p. 116, "*Capon in couns.*" *Concis*, again, seems to be the same word as *Ganse* or *Gauncely*, and no *Gauncely* is mentioned in either of the above.

Coney, see next.

Conyng, 80, see NAPIER, p. 64, Douce MS., No. 116, "*Cony rost.*" **Conyng, Mawlard, in gely or in cyuey, 14,**

Conyng, hen, or Mallard, 80, see Douce MS., No. 68, "*Cony, gelyn, ou malard en oyle,*" NAPIER, p. 79, "*Cony or malard in cery;*" Conyng in Gravey, 80, Conyngys in graueye, 18, see WARNER, II. 10, p. 58, and p. 78, F. of C., No. 26, L.C.C., p. 8, Douce MS., No. 66, NAPIER, p. 101; Conyngys in cyvveye, 20, see F. of C., No. 25, L.C.C., p. 20, NAPIER, p. 112, WARNER, p. 59, and p. 78; Conyng or hen in clene broth, 80, ("*clere broth*" in Douce MS., No. 67), see WARNER, p. 59, F. of C., No. 66, which both read "*Conynges in clere broth*"; Cony; O. Fr., *Connin*. HOLME, Armory, II. vii. 132, says—"A cony is a rabbit after the first year; the animal being a rabbit till the end of the first year."

CopuH, *sb.*, 67. Couple.

Corances, Corauns. Currants. See *Rasonys*.

Core, *sb.*, 51; Corys, 24, 30.

Corkes, *sb.*, 106. Cokes, Cores.

Costardys, *sb.*, 47. Costards: (apples).

Cost'-marye, 110, herb.

Cours, Course, *sb.*, 49. Layer.

Cowche, *rb.*, 44. Couch; lay.

Cowe Mylke, 29, 110.

Coynes, 106, Quinces.

Crabbe or Lobster boiled, 102, see Douce MS., No. 134, Napier, p. 70; *Crabbe au Creveys*, 59; Crabbys, 28.

Crane, rosted, 78, 116, see L.C.C., p. 35, NAPIER, p. 61.

Crayfish, see *Creuez*.

Crees, 38. Compare "*Crescloth*, Fine linen cloth," HALLIWELL.

Cream, see next.

Crem de Coloure, 20; Creme, 2, 8, 10, Fride C. of Almaundys, 7, 91, see Douce MS., No. 12, WARNER, p. 69, "*Crem of Almonde mylk*," NAPIER, p. 42. "*Creme of Almonds*"; C. Boylede, 8, 92, see WARNER, pp. 69, 82, Douce MS., No. 13, NAPIER, p. 32, "*Creme boyle*;" C. Bastarde, 33; *Creme Moundy*, 62: *Creme Vine* 69, ? Cream with wine over it.

Creme, *vb.t.*, 93. Crimme; crumble, see *Kreme*.

Creuez, *sb.*, 49; Creucys, 59. See HOLME, *Armory*, II. xiv. 338, "*Crevice*, or *Crefish*," (crayfish); O.F. *Crevice*, Mod. Fr. *Ecrevisse*. It includes Lobsters.

Crodde, *sb.*, 17; Croddes, 36, 43, 73; Croddys, 36, 56; Cruddes, 86; Cruddis, Cruddys, 53. Curd.

Crodde, *vb. int.*, 17; Croddith, 92; Crudde, 86, 92. Curd; curdle.

Cromez, *sb.*, 53; Cromys, 33, 52. Crumbs.

Cromyd Marow, 55. Crumbed (crumbled) marrow.

Croppe of netle, 69. Young top.

Crostes, 113, see Cruste.

Crouste, *vb.int.*, 32. Crust over.

Crowne, *sb.*, 52. Crown.

Cruddes, see *Crodde*.

Crustade, 50, 55, Custarde, 74, see Douce MS., No. 22, WARNER, p. 65, "*Crustade*," L.C.C., p. 40, F. of C., No. 154, "*Crustardes of Flessh*," F. of C., No.156, "*Crustardes of Fysshe*;" Crustade lumbard, 51, Custard lumbarde, 74, see NAPIER, p. 53, "*Custad lombard*," Douce MS., No. 23; Crustade Ryal, 55, 68; C. gentyle, 55; NAPIER, p. 54, has also a "*Custad opyne*," *i.e.* open. FLORIO, 1659 ed., "*Crostata*, the crust or coffin of a pie, a pastie, a custard, a tart, any kind of crusty meat, any pie or pastie-crust, any meat drest upon tostes or crusts."

Cruste, *sb.*, 53; Crustys of whyte brede, 30; Cruste Rolle, 46.

Cryspez, 44, Cryspes, 93, see F. of C., No. 162, "*Cryspes*," No. 163, "*Cryspels*," Douce MS., No. 61, "*Crispes*," WARNER, II. No. 26, "*Cryppys*"; Cryspis, 3. COTGR., "*Crepez*, ou *Crepets*: Fritters; also, Wafers." Mod. Fr. *Crépe*.

Culpe, *rb.t.*, 48. Cut in thick slices: Fr. *Couper*.

Curlewe rosted, 79, see Douce MS., No. 113; Curlewys, 57.

Curnylles, 109, Kernels.

Custard, see *Crustade*.

Cyprys, Cyprus, see *Vyand*.

Cytte, *vb.t.*, 5. Cut.

Cyuele, 113.

Cyuey, cyrey, 49; Conyng, Maw-lard, in gely or in cyuey, 14, see NAPIER, p. 79, "*Cony or malard in cery*," WARNER II. No. 51, "*Mallard in cyuey*"; Harys in Cyueye, 18, Tenche in c., 23, see NAPIER, p. 80, Conyngys in cyueye, 20. Mod. Fr. *Civet* or *Civé.* Stew with chives.

Dace, 20.

Darioles, 53, Dariolles, 75; Daryoles, 47, 55, 56; see Douce MS., No. 71, L.C.C., p. 38, "*Darials*," F. of C., No. 183, "*Daryols*," NAPIER, p. 56, "*Daryolites*," WARNER, p. 66, "*Daryalys*." See COTGR., "*Darioles*, Small pasties filled with flesh, hearbes, and spices, mingled and mixed to-gether."

Dates, *sb.*, 33, 88, 94; Datis, 24, 53; Datys, 12, 15, 16, 19, *D. in comfyte*, 63.

Defaute, *sb.*, of def., 22, in def., 29; in defawte, 20, for d., 41. Default.

Degre, *sb.*, 36. Degree; pitch (of colour).

Del, Dele, *sb.*, 21, to del jolkys of eyron, 21; A gode dele Salt, 15, *i.e.* of Salt. Deal; portion.

Departe, *rb.t.*, 21; *Gely Departed*, 69, compare the Recipe on p. 31; Departyd, 31. Depart; part into shares; split.

Dewte, *vb.t.*, 43.

Deye, *sb.*, 36, 37, 56. Dairy-maid: see CHAUCER.

Deye, *rb.*, 52. Die.

Dise, *rb.t.*, 69. Dice; cut into Dice.

Disshful, 112.

Dissoñ, *sb.*, 67. Dozen.

Diteyne, 110. Dittany.

Diting, *sb.*, 105. Dighting; prepara-tion.

Do, *rb.t.*, do away, 10; Do aboue, put above, 112; Do it in a faire vessel, Put it in, 112; Do þer-to, Add thereto, 13, 14, 110, 112; Do medle, Make meddle, or mix, 82; Don, 10, Done, do.

Doble, *vb.t.*, 39. Double; fold over.

Doderellys, 61, Dotterels.

Dogħ, 73, Dough: see *Dow.*

Doke, 64, Duck.

Dore, *rb.t.*, 38, 40. Glaze; compare next word, and *Endore.*

Dorre, Soppes, 90, Soupes dorrees, 114, Soupes Dorroy, 11, Soupes dorye, 11; *i.e.* Sops endored, or glazed with almond milk. Dorry, *sb.*, 11. See *Endore.*

Doucete, *adj.*, 33; Doweet, 7, 29, 30. Fr. *Doucet*, sweetish.

Doucetȝ, 50; Doucettes, 55, D. a-forcyd, 55; Doucetys, 64; Douccttys 4; *Doweet Ryal*, 62, Dowcetys, 55: "*Doucet*; A lytell flawne," PALS-GRAVE. Cheesecake.

Douun, *adv.*, 7. Down.

Doust, *sb.*, 112; Douste, 110, 113. Dust.

Dow, *sb.*, 42, 43, stronge Dow, 49. Dough.

Draf, *sb.*, 22; of Almaundys, 16. Draff; refuse.

Dragge, *sb.*, 11. Dredge.

Draw, *vb.t.*, 7, 8, Draw vp, 7, Strain; Draw þorw straynowre, 5, 8, 9, Draw uppe þorw strayn., 20; draue, 106.

Drawe, *vb.t.*, 9. Draw; eviscerate.

Drawyd, *adj.*, 5. Drawn (through strainer).

Drawyn grwel, 10, see Douce MS., No. 33: A. reads here "*Browne gruelle.*" Drawyn Eyroun, 42, 44. Drawn (through strainer).

Dregge, *sb.*, 99; Dragge, 11. Dredge.

Dresse, *rb.t.*, d. forth, 13, yn, 14; Dressyst yn, 15. Dress; serve in to table.

Dressing knyfe, 93: see *Dressoure knyf.*

Dressoure, *sb.*, 24, 28, 30, 31, 34, Dresser: Dressoure knyf, 53, Dresser knife, apparently knife for trimming meat for the table; called *Dressing knyfe* in Douce MS., and above.

Dropey, 2; Chykons in dropeye, 30; see F. of C., No. 19, "*Drepee*," which is the recipe for the sauce.

Dropping, *sb.*, 77, 99. Dripping.

Drow in Sonne, 38, Dry in sun.

Fars, *sb.*, 45. Farce; stuffing.

Faste, *adv.*, 27. Fast; tight.

Fastyng dayis, 17.

Fauntempere, 19; spelt Faintempere on page 2.

Fayre, *adj.*, see *Faire*.

Fecche, *vb.t.*, 36. Fetch.

Felettes of Porke endored, 82, F. in galentyne, 82; see Fylettes.

Fere, *sb.*, in fere, together, 20.

Fere, *adj.*, 83. Fair: moderate sized. See Faire.

Fesaunt Rost, 116, Fesaunte rosted, 78; see NAPIER, p. 60.

Feþer, *sb.*, 31, 53. Feather.

Fey, *sb.*, 101. Liver; Anglo-Fr. *Feie*.

Fig, see *Figus*, *Fyggs*.

Figee, 113; Fygey, 94, Fygeye, 24; see WARNER, p. 46, F. of C., No. 89, NAPIER, p. 119, "*Figge*," Douce MS., No. 162, "*Figee*." The dish is called "*Fyguade*" in L.C.C., p. 42. A "*Fyge to potage*," is also given in WARNER, p. 67. The "*Fygey*" in WARNER seems to be from *Figé*, thickened, see COTGR., "*Laict figé*," as there are no figs in it; at the same time the figs thicken it, and *Figuade* would be the more likely form from *Figue*.

Figus, 112. Figs.

Fillet, see *Felettes*, *Fylettes*.

Firmanty, 105: see *Furmenty*.

Fissh, Blaumanger of, 114, Blamanger of Fyshe, 23; Chauudon of fissh, 114; Mortrewes of Fysshe, 14, Mortrowes of fissh, 114; Iuschelle of F., 16; Gelye de F., 26; Potage on a Fysdaye, 29; Fyssday 9; Potage on fysshday, 15; Fysshcday, 11, 30. Fish.

Flake Water, 21, should probably be "slake," *i.e.* warm.

Flampoyntes bake, 53; Flampoyntys, 4; see F. of C., No. 113, No. 184, "*Flaumpeyns*," WARNER, p. 66, "*Flaumpoyntes*"; Flampayn, 60; Flaumpoyne, 60. *Flaumpoynte* is *Flan pointé*, and is so called from the small points of pastry with which the open Flawn was stuck, and made bristly.

Flat, *adj.*, bind up f., 33; scrue in flatte, 33; sette out almost flatte, 33. The word here refers to the stiffness, or thickness, of a semi-fluid; see especially Recipe cxxix. p. 29.

Flathons, 51, Flathonys, 73; see Douce MS., No. 16, "*Flathonys*," L.C.C., p. 39, "*Flaunes*;" Flathouns in lente, 56, see WARNER, p. 48, "*Flownys in Lente*." COTGR., "*Flans*, Flawnes, Custards, Egge-pies." LITTRÉ, "*Flan*. Tarte faite avec de la crème fouettée, des œufs et de la farine." The word is derived from the low Latin *Fladonem*; compare O.H.G. *Flado*, Mod. G. *Fladen*. They were open tarts.

Flawns, see *Flathons*.

Fle, *vb.t.*, 10, 18. Flea: flay.

Flesh, Tartus of, 74; Tartes de chare, 47, 52; Fless day, 113; Flesshe day, 30; Mortrewys de Fleyssh, 14; Fleysshe, 1, 10, Rapeye of F., 25. "F[le]ysshe" in Recipe cxix. p. 28, should be "Fysshe," as A. also reads.

Florche, *vb.t.*, 30; Florisshe, 113; Floryssche, 47. Flourish; garnish.

Flos campy flour, 31. Flower for ornamenting dish.

Floundres boiled, 102, see Douce MS., No. 136.

Flour, *sb.*, 38; Floure Rys, 38; Whetyn floure, 33; Flowre of whete, 46, Whete Flowre, 38, Flowre of Amidons, 16, F. of Canelle, 15, F. of rys, 6, 15, 16, 18, 19, 20, 29.

Flowre, *vb.t.*, 26. Flour.

Flowres, *sb.*, 23; Flowrys, 20, 29, F. of hawþorn, 29; Flowþerys, 20. Flowers.

Foiles of parcelly, 102. See *Foyle*.

Forced with milke and rawe yolkes of eyren, 117. See *A-forcyd*.

Fore, *prep.*, 106. For.

Forlonge wey, or ij, 91; Forlongwey, 7; A. reads here "a furlonge Way or ij," while the Douce MS. has "Forlange." This apparently means the time one would take to that distance.

Fors, *sb.*, It is no fors, 33. Force; matter of importance: a French Idiom, see COTGR., *Force*.

tyne, 8, see NAPIER, p. 89, F. of C., Nos. 28, 117, WARNER, p. 58, L.C.C., p. 31 : Galyntyne, 109, O.F. *Galentine.* For the Recipe for *Galentine* see Sauces.

Galingale, *sb.*, 107 ; Galyngale, 13, 15, 34, 54. See COTGR., " *Galingal.* The Aromaticall root of the rush called Cypresse, and English Galingale."

Galon, *sb.*, A gode g., 22 ; Galouns, 12, 22. Gallon.

Gape, *vb.int.*, (of boiled muscles opening), 90.

Garbage, 9, 72, see Douce MS., No. 83, NAPIER, p. 78 ; Garbagys, 9. Giblets.

Garleke, *sb.*, 23, 110 ; cloue, 110, Clouys of garleke, clowes of g., Cloves of garlic, 109.

Garlic, see *Garleke.*

Gauncely, 2 ; Elys in Gauncelye, 22 ; Hennys in G., 23. See " *Janse, jance, gance,* sorte de sauce ;" GODEFROY. It would almost appear to be properly a sauce for goose ; compare " *Gunces,* Anseres silvestres ;" DUCANGE. It is also spelt GaunceH, as in Douce MS. : for the sauce see *Sauces.*

Gaylede, 22.

Gele of peson, 95, Gelye de Fysshe, 26, see Douce MS., No. 175, F. of C., No. 101, WARNER, p. 72, II. No. 36 (Fish or Flesh) ; Gely (calves foot), 86, see Douce MS., No. 174 ; Gelye de chare, 25, see F. of C., No. 102, " *Gele of Flessh,*" NAPIER, p. 42, " *Gilly of fleshe,*" WARNER, p. 44, and p. 61 ; *Gele Potage,* 68. Fr. *Gelée.* Jelly.

Geloferys, *sb.*, 19 ; Gelofres, 15 ; Gelofre3, 48 ; Gelofrys, 21. Gilliflowers.

Gelyne in dubbatte, 13, Gelyne endobat, 80, see Douce MS., No. 69, and *Dubbate* : Gelyne in brothe, 81, see Douce MS., No. 89, see also recipes under *Hen.* Fr. *Gelin,* Hen.

Gilliflower, see *Geloferys.*

Ginger, see *Gyngere.*

Gobet, *sb.*, 31, 55 ; Gobettys, 6, 13, 18, 23, 55. Gobbet ; lump.

Gobet, *vb.t.*, 54 ; Gobete, 112. Gobbet ; cut into gobbets.

Gobouns, *sb.*, 10. Gobbets.

Goce, *sb.*, 81, Goose. See *Goos.*

Goions fryid, 60. Fried gudgeons.

Golet, *sb.*, & Golett, 116. Gullet.

Goos in hogepotte, 18, see WARNER, p. 57, p. 84, and II. No. 22, F. of C., No. 31, L.C.C., p. 32 ; Goce or Capon farced, 81, Capoun or gos farced, 41, see Douce MS., No. 36 ; Gos, 2 ; Gees, 8 ; Wilde gese, 76. Goose.

Graspeys, 59 ; Royal Fish, as Sturgeon or Whale, but applied also to other fish.

Grate, *vb.t.*, 6.

Gratid, *adj.*, brede, 16, 21 ; gratyd, 14. Grated.

Grauey, Oystres en 13, 100 ; Whyte pesyn in g., 33 ; Conyngys in graueye, 18 ; Grauy, 1 ; Oystrys in g. bastard, 13. Gravy.

Graynys, *sb.*, 28 (? as next) ; of parise, 6, parys, 34, Perys, 27, Grains of Paradise ; of Pome-garnad, 29.

Grease, see *Grece.*

Grece, *sb.*, 7, 8, 14, 34, 45 ; Whyte gr., 29 ; Gres, 43. Grease.

Gredelle, *sb.*, 40 ; Grydelle, 21. Girdle (for cooking).

Gredyl, *vb.t.*, vp broun, 40. Girdle ; cook on girdle.

Gredire, *sb.*, 102, 103 ; Gredreñ, 100 ; Gredryñ, 102, 103 ; Gredyre, 36. Gridiron.

Grene, *adj.*, 15, 20 ; Grene chese, 48. Green.

Gret, *adj.*, a gret dele, 12, Gret Roysouns, 15, Grete roysonys, 33, Great Raisins, *i.e.* not Currants ; Grete pyes, 76 ; Gretter, 15, Greater.

Gridel, 114, see *Gredyl.*

Groundyn, *adj.*, 38, Ground ; brayed.

GrowelH, 70 ; Growelle Force, 70, Gruelle a-forsydde, 6, see Douce MS., No. 32, L.C.C., p. 47, " *Gruel of fors,*" F. of C., No. 3, " *Grewel forced,*" WARNER, p. 51, " *Growel of force,*" NAPIER, p. 88, " *Gruelle enforced* ;" L.C.C., p. 20, has also " *Gruel of Porke* ;" Drawyn grwel, 10, see

Douce MS., No. 33 ; Grwele, 10 ; Grwelle, 1. Gruel.

Gruel, see *Growell.*

Grynd, *vb.t.*, 12 ; Grynde, 9. Grind.

Guisseh, 87 ; see *Iuschelle.*

Gullys, 62, 63. Gulls.

Gurnard, *sb.*, 25 ; G. rosted or boyled, 103, 104, see Douce MS., No. 141, NAPIER, p. 74 ; Gornard, 14 ; *Gurnyd broylid with a syryppe,* 62.

Gutte, *sb.*, of purpays, 42, ? the pouch : Guttys, 108. Gut.

Gyngaudre, 15, Gyngautrey, 94 ; see Douce MS., No. 161, WARNER, p. 70, "*Gyngawtre,*" F. of C., No. 94, "*Gyngawdry.*"

Gyngerbrede, 35 ; Gyngere brede, 3. Gingerbread.

Gyngere, *sb.*, 10, 11, 17, 25, 32 ; Whyte Gyngere, 21 ; Gyngeuere, 115 ; Gyngiuer, 114. Ginger.

Gysers, *sb.*, 72, 76, 108 ; Gysour, 41 ; Gysowrys, 9. Gizzard. O.F. *Gezier.*

Hacke, *vb.*, 14, 18 ; Hak, 76 ; Hakke, 13, 14, 18, 23. Hack ; hew.

Haddok, *sb.*, 10, 11, 16 ; Haddok or Codlyng, 104, see Douce MS., No. 143 ; Haddoke in Cyuee, 114, see NAPIER, p. 72. Haddock.

Hagas de Almaynne, 44, Hagas de almondes, 84, see NAPIER, p. 43, "*Hagges of Almayne,*" Douce MS., No. 21. "*Hagys dalmaygne*" ; Hagase, 3 ; Hagws of a schepe, 39, see L.C.C., p. 52. Haggis.

Hak, *vb.t.*, 76. Hack.

Hake, *sb.*, 16.

Hakkyd, *pp.*, 32. See Hacke.

Halful, 55, Half-full.

Halfyndele, 20 ; Halvyndele, 41. Half-deal, or part.

Halybutte, 60, Halibut.

Ham, *pron.*, 37. Them.

Handfulle, *sb.*, 28. Handful.

Handys, *sb.*, 14 ; Hond, 16 ; Hondys, 15, 35. Hand, hands.

Hanoney, 43, 84. See also Douce MS., No. 24. Apparently *Oignoné* ; see also *Oignonade,* in LITTRÉ, a dish with many onions in it, as this dish has.

Hard, *vb.t.*, 56, Harde, 54 ; Harde, *vb.int.*, 47 ; Hardyd, p. 50. Make hard.

Hard, *adv.*, sethe hard, 12. Fast ; sharply.

Hardid, *adj.*, 56. Harded ; hardened (in oven).

Hare, *sb.*, 19, Hare in Wortes, 69 ; Harys in Cyueye, 18, see WARNER, II. 8, L.C.C., p. 21, NAPIER, p. 113 ; WARNER has also "*Haris in Talbotays,*" II. No. 9 (see this Work, p. 19), and "*Hares or conynges in seue,*" p. 78, see L.C.C., p. 21.

Haselle, *sb.*, leuys, 31 : Spete of h., 39. Hazel.

Hawþorn, Flowrys of, 29 ; Hawthorun, 20. See *Spyneye.*

Hasselet, *sb.*, 97 ; Hastelette, 106. Harslet : Douce MS., " Haslet." "*Hastelet,* dimin. de *haste,* viande rôtie."—GODEFROY.

Hed, *sb.*, 9, 16 ; Hedys, 16, 42. Head.

Hef, *vb.*, 53. Heave ; lift.

Hegh, *adj.*, 75. High.

Held, *vb.*, 39. Throw ; cast.

Hele, *vb.t.*, 27, 47, 73. Cover.

Helyd, *p.p.*, 52. Covered.

Hem, *pron.*, 14, 15, 19, 34, 40. Them : 18, 19, 40. Him.

Hen, *sb.*, 14 ; Conyng or hen in clene broth, 80, see Douce MS., No. 67 ; Conyng, hen, or Mallard, 80, see Douce MS., No. 68 ; Vele, kede, or henne in Bokenade, 13 ; Hennys in bruette, 18, see WARNER, II. 7, NAPIER, p. 114, L.C.C., p. 22, and p. 49 ("*Henne in brothe*") ; Henuys in Gauncelye, 23, see L.C.C., p. 24, NAPIER, p. 116 ; Henne, 13 ; Hennys, 19, 21. See *Gelyne.*

Her, *sb.*, Her syue, Hair sieve, 113.

Herbelade, 54, Herbe-blade, 76 ; see NAPIER, p. 58, "*Hayrblad opyn,*" (i.e. open, with no top crust,) Douce MS., No. 184. So called from the herbs in the cakes. See DUCANGE, "*Herbolasto,*" a cake stuffed with herbs.

Herbs, see *Erbis.*

Here, 24. The hairy appendage of the Mussel, called " Muskles Wool," in HOLME, Armory, II. xiv. 345 ; now called the Byssus.

Heroñ rosted, 78, H. rost, 116, see
L.C.C., p. 35, NAPIER, p. 62, Herous,
68 ; Heyroun, 62.

Heron-sewe, 68 ; Heron sewes, 61 ;
Heronsewys, 59. Hernshaw ; young
Heron.

Herte, sb., 41 ; Hertys, 8. Heart.

Hery of bonys, 14 ; Hairy with
bones.

Hete, sb., 22 : vb., 11 ; hete hote, 12.
Heat.

Heyroun, 62. Heron.

Hew, vb.t., 7, 17 ; Hewe, 6, 17.

Hogepotte, Goos in, 18 ; "Hochepot:
A hotch-pot, or Gallimaufrey."
—COTGR.

Hoglies, sb., 51 ; Howe, 37 ; Howhys,
25 ; Hojos of fele, 86. Hock.

Hol, adj., 19, 27 ; Hole pepir, 8, 9 ;
Hool, 55 ; Hoole, 12. Whole.

Hold coloure, keep colour, 25 ;
Holdyn, pp., 7.

Hole, vb.intr., 7, Hull ; lose the husks ;
Hoole, vb.tr., 33, Hull ; strip off hulls.

Holl, sb., 105 ; Holys, 7, 32, 114.
Hull ; husk.

Hondefull, sb., 72. Handful.

Honge, vb.intr., 36 ; hongy, 7. Hang.

Hony, 6, Clarifiyd h., 12, Hwyte
Hony, 29.

Horñ, 106, of Whelk.

Hote, adj., 10, 12. Hot.

H.q., 12. Hoc quære : like q.v.

Hure, hyre, adj., 13, 18. Her.

Hwyte, adj., Hony or Sugre, 29,
Sugre, 54. White.

Hy, adj., komyth on hy, boils up, 17.

Hym, pron., 18 ; Hyt, 35. Him : It.

Hyrchouns, 62. See Yrchons.

I-ete, 99, Eaten.

Isope, sb., 27 ; Isoppe, 74. Hyssop.

I-sothe, pp., 18. Sodden.

Ioissh 116, Juice.

Jollys of Samoun, 61, Salmon Jowls.

Ioutes, 5 ; Iouutes, 1. See NAPIER,
p. 108 (Almond), L.C.C., p. 15,
"Jouts dalmond," F. of C., No. 88,
(Almond), WARNER, p. 67, "Jowtes

of Almand Mylke ;" F. of C., No.
73, "Frenche Owtes ;" F. of C., No.
5, "Eowtes of Flessh," WARNER, p.
52, "Joutes on flesh day." p. 80,
"Jowtes of flessh" ; WARNER, p. 80,
"Jowtes of fysshe" ; L.C.C., p. 47,
48, "Joutes," (Vegetables). Iust seems
equivalent to Jus, Juice, see COTGR.,
and is spelt Joust in WARNER, p. 89 ;
and see DUCANGE, "Jutta, potionem
confectum ex lacte spissiorem."

Ioynte, sb., 116.

Iuce, sb., 92 : Ius, 15, 31, 40, 41,
45 ; Juse, 21. Juice.

Iunte, vb.t., 116. Joint.

Iuschelle of Fysshe, 16, Iusshell, 95
(Fish) ; Iussell, 95 ; see WARNER,
p. 86, "Jussel of fysshe." Douce
MS., No. 166, "Guissell" (Fish) ; see
also WARNER, p. 82, "Jussel of flessh."
NAPIER, p. 26, "Juselle sengle,"
(flesh), p. 87 and p. 104, "Jusselle"
(Flesh), L.C.C., p. 11 (Flesh), WAR-
NER, 11. No.21 (Flesh), and WARNER,
p. 82, F. of C., No. 44, "Jusshell
enforced." "Jussel, jus, potion," GODE-
FROY : Juscellum is late Latin for soup.
See Guissell.

Kake, sb., of dow, 43 ; 85. Cake.

Kaste, vb., 52 ; Kest, 115. Cast :
throw.

Kede : Vele, kede, or henne in Bokenade, 13, 85, see Douce MS., Nos. 76,
77 ; Kede rosted, 81, see NAPIER, p.
65 ; Keed 85 ; Kyde a-Forsyde, 41.

Kele, vb.int., 7, 12, 13, 24 ; Kelid, 38.

Kelyng, sb., 94, 96. Keeling.
HOLME, II. xiv. 334, says it is the
common Cod, but it seems identified
with Codling elsewhere. FLORIO,
1659 ed., see Eng.-Ital. part, trans-
lates it by Merluzzo, which he says
is the Haddock-fish, or according to
others the Sea-whiting.

Kerf, vb., 38 ; Kerue, 22, 36, 112.
Carve : cut.

Kerve, vb.t., in a morter, 70, Bray.

Keuere, vb.t., 45, 52 ; Kouere. 112 ;
Kyuer, 43 ; Kyuere, 46, 50. Cover :
see Ceuere.

Kid, see Kede.

on fische dais"; Lesyngys, Lesyng}, 44. Lozenges.

Let lory, 17, Lethe lory, 85, see F. of C., No. 81 ; Lete lardys, 3, Letlardes, 92, Lette lardes, 35, see WARNER, p. 63, "*Leche lardys*," NAPIER, p. 87, p. 106, "*Ledlardes*," L.C.C., p. 13, "*Lede lardes*," F. of C. No. 68, "*Lete Lardes*." Fr. *Lait*, Milk : the "Let lardes" seem originally to have been "Let lardé," or "Larded milk," and to have been changed to the substantive *lardes* or *lardys*, and become "Milk lards," and the *Let* even got changed into *Leche*, as above, the larded milk being cut into Leches. HOLME also says that *Leach* is "a king of jelly, made of cream, ising-glass, sugar and almonds, with other compounds."

Lete, *vb.*, see Lat.

Leuer, *sb.*, 16, 41 ; Lyuer, 16 ; Lyuerys, 9, 16. Liver.

Leuys of percely, 7, of borage, 8. Leaves.

Leuyth, 40, Remaineth.

Ley, *vb.t.*, 109. Lay.

Ley, Leye, *sb.*, 32. Lie ; Lees of wine.

Ling, see *Lenge*.

Litel, *adj.*, 16 ; A litil an a litil, 17 ; Littel, 16 ; Litul, Litu॥, 71 ; Lytel, 24 ; Lytelle, 53 ; Lytil, 15, 16, 17 ; Lytylle, 18. Little.

Liver, see *Leuer*.

Loach, see *Loches*.

Lobster, see *Lopster*.

Loches, Lochys, 24, Loaches: Menese or loche boiled, 104, see Douce MS., No. 148.

Lof, *sb.*, 6. Loaf.

Loft, Oñ, Aloft, 78.

Longe Fretoure, 43, L. Frutours, 73, 68, see *Fretoure* ; Lange wortys de chare, 5, see Douce MS., No. 1 ; Lange Wortes de Pesoun, 5, 89, see Douce MS., No. 2.

Longebeff, *sb.*, 5. "*Lange de bœuf.* Ox-tongue, rough or small Buglosse," COTGR. : A. reads here "longedebef."

Lopster, *sb.*, 102, Crabbe or Lopster boiled, 102, see WARNER, p. 47 ;

Lopstere, 24 ; Loppestere, 114. Lobster.

Lorey de Boolas, 25 : "Lora, Potionis mellitæ genus," DUCANGE. There is honey in the Bullace.

Lozenges, see *Lesenges*.

Luce, *sb.*,39,42,57; Luys,112; Luyss, 113 ; Luy}s, 113. Full-grown Pike.

Lust, *vb.*, 41 ; Luste, 55. List; like.

Luys, Luyss, see *Luce*.

Ly, *vb.t.*, 15, 19 ; Lye, 13. Allay ; mix. See *A-lye*.

Lycour, *sb.*, 6, 11 ; Lycoure, 12, 26; Lycowre,11,13; Lykoure,12. Liquor.

Lyer, *sb.*, 20 ; of Brode cromys with wyne, 33. Liour ; mixture : spelt "lyre" in F. of C., p. 28.

Lyid, *pp.*, 13. Allayed.

Lykey, *vb.*, 31. Like ; please.

Lynne clout, 112, Linen clout.

Lynen cloþe, 9, 34.

Lyode Soppes, 11. ? Allayed, steeped sops.

Lyte, *adj.*, 17. Little.

Lyuerys, 9 ; see *Leuer*.

Ly}t, *adj.*, 17. Light ; small.

Mace, *vb.t.*, 35. Make.

Maces, *sb.*, 6, 10, 15 ; Mace}, 46; Macys, 8. Mace ; the spice.

Malasade, 83, see Douce MS., No. 10, and *Meselade* ; Malesade, 84.

Mallard : Conyng, heñ, or Mallard, 80, called "*Cony, yelyn, ou malard en oyle*," in Douce MS., No. 68 ; Mawlard, 8, 12, 63, Conyng, M. in gely or in cyuey, 14, the same Recipe as above ; WARNER, II. No. 51, and p. 62, 85.

Malmens bastard, 93, Malmenye Furne}, 48. See *Mammenye*.

Malvis, *sb.*, 69 ; Malwys, 5, 15. Mallows.

Mammenye bastarde, 22 ; Maumenye Ryalle, 22 ; Mawmene, 88 ; see Douce MS., No. 167, NAPIER, p. 118, "*Mammony*," WARNER, II. No. 30, "*Mammene*," p. 76, "*Marmene*," F. of C., No. 20, "*Mawmenee*," No. 194, "*Mawmenny*," L.C.C. p. 26, "*Momene*" : WARNER has also on p. 55, "*Maw-*

mene to potage," (a soup). The word
is apparently derived from the Fr.
malmener, the meat being teased
small. Compare *Malmenye*, above.

Mange moleyn, 36. Possibly named
after a person; see *Rys Moleynȝ*
on page 59 : both have Rice as
ingredient.

Manged brede, 83, Manchet bread ;
Douce MS. " Maynche ": see *Mengyd
Flowre,* and *Paynemain.*

Mannys, 97, Man's.

Marbyl coloure, 34. Marble colour :
variegated.

Marbylle, *adj.*, **29,** Marbly ; A.
reading " marbely."

Marew, *sb.*, **56 ;** Marow, **40, 44 :**
Marw, 6 ; Marwe, 6, 8, 51 ; Mary, 9
(but A. reads here " meribonys," in
place of " mary, brothe,") 74, 84 ;
Marye, 32 ; Merow, 44, Merw, 9,
Marrow.

Maribonys, 55, Marw-bonys, **55,**
Mary-bones, 70, Marybonys, 5, Mery-
bonys, 5, 6, 46. Marrowbones.

Marling; Fryid Marlyng, **59,** Merlyng soþe, 61. Whiting : Fr. *Merlan.*

Marrow, see *Marew.*

Mawe, *sb.*, **38, 39 ;** Mawes, **18, 106 ;**
Mawys, 18, 38. Maw ; stomach.

Mawmeny, 68, see *Mammenye.*

Medel, *vb.t.*, **73 ;** Medle, **75 ;** Med-
ylde togidre, 73. Meddle : mix.

Melle, *vb.t* , **24, 30.** Mell ; mix.

Mence, *vb.t.*, **41.** Mince.

Menese or loche boiled, 104, see
Douce MS., No. 148; Menyse, 104.
Minnows.

Meng, *vb.t.*, **46 ;** Menge, **17.** Mix :
mingle.

Mengyd Flowre, 43, Manchet flour,
compare Manged brede, Meyned flour :
Douce MS. reads " Mayned flour."

Meselade, 42 ; Meslade, 43. ? *Meslade,*
mixture : spelt Malesade in Douce
MS. and in A. See *Malasade.*

Messe, *vb.t.*, **30, 114 ;** Messe forth,
11, 114. Mess ; portion.

Metys, 35, Meats.

Meyned floure, 83 : flour for Painde-
main, or Manchet bread, see *Mengyd
Flowre.*

Mighti, *adj.*, **71.** Mighty : strong.

Milk, see Let.

Milkemete, 106 ; Milke Rostys, 40,
called *Mylke Rostyd,* on page 3, see
NAPIER, p. 109, WARNER. II. No.
25, L.C.C., p. 17 ; Mylke of almaundys, 6, 7, 13.

Millet boyled, 104, see Douce MS.,
No. 147, Mullet. Fr. *mulet.*

Millewell, *sb.*, **96 ;** Milwel, **43, 48 ;**
Milwelle, 48 ; Mulwyl taylys, 61 ;
Mylwell, 16. Mulvell : said to be
Haddock. See, however, HOLME,
Armory, II. xiv. 334, where he says :
" The *Keling* or common Cod, is
called the *Welwell* in Western parts
of England." In the *Eng. It.* part
of FLORIO, ed. 1659, the Melwel also
is identified with the Keeling ; also
in COTGR. (see "*Merlus*"), and is there
said to be a small kind of Cod, of
which Stockfish was made. See
Keeling.

Mince, *vb.*, see *Myce, Mynce.*

Minnows, see *Menese.*

Molberys, 28, Mulberries.

Molde to-gederys, 35. Mould, or
roll, together.

More, *adv.*, **19.**

Morreye, A rede, 28 ; Murrey, 19 ;
Murreye, 28 ; see F. of C., No. 38,
"*Morree,*" WARNER, p. 48, "*Morrey,*"
11. No. 37, "*Murrey,*" p. 84, "*Murre*"
and p. 56, "*Murre to potage*" (a soup).
It is so called from the mulberry, or
dark red colour of the dish, and in
the recipe in WARNER, 11. No. 37,
mulberries are used to colour it :
sometimes wine or saffron is used.
It. *Mora,* mulberry : "*Morèllo,* the
murreyor black-berry colour," FLORIO;
"*Morèe:* A kind of murrey, or darke-
red colour," COTGR. ; "Moratum :
Potionis genus ex vino et moris
dilutis confectæ," DUCANGE ; also
Moretum.

Morter, *sb.*, **11, 27, 28 ;** Mortere, **28,**
35, 53 ; Mortre, 109. Mortar for
braying.

Mortrewes of Fysshe, 14, 114, Mortrewes of Pesyñ, 90, see Douce MS.,
No. 82, NAPIER, p. 111, WARNER,
p. 86, F. of C., No. 125, L.C.C.,

p. 19 ; **Mortreus de Chare, 70,** Mortrewys de Fleyssh, 14, see Douce MS., No. 81, WARNER, p. 75, NAPIER, p. 102, L.C.C., p. 9 ; **Whyte Mortrewes, 19** (Hens), White Mortrewys of Porke, 28, see F. of C., 45, "*Mortrews*," and WARNER, II. No. 5, "*Morterelys*," F. of C., No. 46, "*Mortrews blank*," NAPIER, p. 106, WARNER, p. 62, L.C.C., p. 13, "*Blanchyd mortrews*," all made from Hens and Pork. Italian *Mortarello*, a Mortar, FLORIO: in DUCANGE "Mortariolum" is applied to a dish prepared from bits of meat, and there are also the forms "Mortairol," and (in LITTRÉ) "Mortayrol": see *Mortadello*, "A large sausage," in LITTRÉ. Modern *Mortress*, A dish of pounded meat: the *ll* being liquid in the French would give the form Mortrews.

Morwe, Morrow, see *A-morwe*.

Mosselle, *sb.*, 42 ; Mosselles, 83, Mossellys, 30, 112. Morsel.

Motley, *adj.*, 36.

Moton, *sb.*, 8, 9 ; Motoun, 9 ; **Alows de Beef or de m.,** 40, 83 ; **Trype de m.,** 7, 82, see Douce MS., No. 4 ; Brest de mottoñ in sauce, 85, see Douce MS., No. 86 ; Stwed Muttoñ, 72 ; Mutoun, 8 : see *Mutton*.

Mountance, *sb.*, 42. Amount.

Mow, *vb.*, 38. May.

Mowntayne, *sb.*, 84. Compare *Mountance*, above.

Muscules in broth, 90, see Douce MS., No. 78, NAPIER, p. 78 ; M. in shelle, 90, see Douce MS., No. 79, NAPIER, p. 78 ; Muskelys in bruette, 24, see F. of C., No. 122 ; WARNER, p. 68, has also "*Musculs in sewe*": Musculis, 90 ; Muskele, 24. Mussel.

Mussel, see Muscules.

Muttoñ, Stwed, 72 (Stewed); **Tripe de M.,** 82, see Douce MS., No. 4 ; Allowes de M., 83, see Douce MS., No. 17.

Myce, *vb.t.*, 71, 76, 99. Mince. Fr. *micer, michier*.

Myced, *adj.*, and *pp.*, 72, 75 ; Mysed, 74. Minced.

Myddel, *sb.*, 42 ; Myddelle, 52. Middle.

Myghty, *adj.*, 12. Mighty ; strong : (Broth).

Myid brede, 39, 49. Crumbed bread : Fr. *Mie*, crumb ; see L.C.C., p. 8, "Myed," p. 11, "Myud."

Myleȝ in Rapeye, 46.

Mylt, *vb.t.*, 51 ; Mylte, 86. Melt.

Myltes, *sb.*, 70 ; Myltys, 8. Milts ; spleens.

Mynce, *vb.t.*, 16, 29, 110, Mince : Mynced, *adj.*, 15, 16, 76 ; Myncyd, 14, Minced. See *Myce*.

Myntes, 110. Mints ; the herb.

Mythty, Myȝthty, *adj.*, m. wyne, 22. Mighty ; strong.

Myȝt, Myȝth, *vb.*, 27. Might.

Namely, *adv.*, 41, 107. Especially.

Nape, *vb.t.*, 102, 105.

Navel, 14.

Nedyl, *sb.*, 40. Needle.

Neme, *vb.t.*, 6, 22 ; Nym, 14, 21, 23, 30, 39 ; Nyme, 23, 30, 32. Nim ; take.

Neres, *sb.*, 70 ; Nerys, 8. Ears : A. reads here "eris."

Nese Bekys, 45, see "*Nysebek*," F. of C., No. 173.

Nesshi, *adj.*, 75 ; Neyshe, 6 ; Neyssche, 48, 53 ; Neyssho, 24, 27 ; Nessher, 94. Nesh ; soft.

Nombles of Veneson, 70, Nomblys of þe venyson, 10, see Douce MS., No. 39, F. of C., No. 13, and No. 54, WARNER, p. 53, and II. No. 12 ; see also NAPIER, p. 103, and L.C.C., p. 10, (any) ; NAPIER, p. 90, "*Nombles of fische*." Numbles, p. 114, is imperfect. Umbles. O.F. *Nombles*; compare Late Lat. *Numbulus*, for Lat. *Lumbulus*.

Non, *adj.*, 35. None ; no.

Notemyggeȝ, 109. Nutmegs.

Noteye, 31. So called from the nuts in it.

Nowne, 73. Oven.

Nowt, *adv.*, 6, 8, 11 ; Noȝt, 7, 8, 16. Not.

Numbles, see *Nombles*.

Nutmegs, see *Notemyggeȝ*.

Oatmeal, see Otemele.
Obleies, *sb.*, 73; Oblye, 46. Oble;
thin cake. Cotgr., "*Oublie*: A wafer
cake ; such a one especially as is
sweetened only with honie ; also, the
thinne past that serves for the bot-
tomes of Tartes, and March-panes."
See Ducange, *Oblata.* There are
the forms *Oblée* and *Oblie*, and the
original sense of the word is *conse-
crated wafer*, as an offering.
Of, *adv.*, 8; *prep.*, 27, 42. Off.
Oil, see *Oyle*.
Oille de oliue, 114. Olive oil. See
Oyle.
On, *adj.*, 36, 53, One; *prep.*, 5, 40.
In.
Ondo, *vb.t.*, 17. Undo.
Oneȝ, *adv.*, 44; Onys, 6, 7, 18, 45.
Once.
Onions, see *Oynons*.
Ope, *vb.t.*, 18. Cut open.
Or that, Till that, Till, 55.
Orage, *sb.*, 5. Orach. Ang.-Fr.
Orache, Fr. *Arroches*, see Cotgr.:
Lat. *Atriplex*, see Mowat, *Alph.*,
p. 22.
Otemele, *sb.*, 6, 10; Ote-mele, 42.
Oatmeal.
Oþer, *conj.*, 21, 22, 34. Or.
Ouer-cast, *vb.t.*, 49; Ouer-caste, 48.
Turn over.
Ouere-couer, *vb.t.*, 85. Cover over.
Ovenne, *sb.*, 53; Ovyn, 47, 48, 54;
Ovynne, 50. Oven.
Ouer eve, 20 ; Ouernyȝth, 33, Over
night.
Ouer-renne, *vb.int.*, 36, 37. Overrun,
run over.
Ouerþwart, *adv.*, 40 ; Oucretwarde,
115. Across.
Ouer-wewyd, *pp.*, 25. Compare
"*Biwered*, covered," Halliwell :
wewyd is glossed "wasshe," *i.e.*
washed, in A.
Ouer-wose, 86. Washed over; com-
pare A-wese. Douce MS. reads
"wese."
Owrys, *sb.*, 7, 37. Hours.
Oyle, *sb.*, 12, O. of Olyff, 30 ;
O. soppes, 96, 115, O. soppys, 12,
see Napier, p. 81. Oil.

Oynons, *sb.*, 6, 110; Oynonys, 5, 8,
9, 10 ; Oynouns, 109 ; Oynenons, 14.
Onions.
Oystres en grauey, 13, 100, see
Douce MS., No. 65, F. of C., No.
121 ; Oystrys in g. bastard, 13 ; O.
in bruette, 23, see L.C.C., p. 53,
Warner, p.47 ; O. in cevey, 100, see
Douce MS., No. 184, F. of C., No. 123.

Paast, *sb.*, 74, 97, 105 ; Paaste, 98 ;
Paste : see *Past.*
Pacience, *sb.*, 69. Patience (the
herb) : Snakeweed, a kind of dock.
Pancake, 46.
Panche, *sb.*, 82, panches, 94 ;
Pannches, 94. Paunch.
Panne, *sb.*, 42, 43, for frying; Erthen
pannys, 54.
Panteryse, 59.
Papyns, 9. Cotgr., "*Papin*; Pap
for children."
Parboyle, *vb.t.*, 6, 8, 12, 13, 41 ; Par-
boyled, 100 ; Parboylid, 13. Parboil.
Parboylinggo, *adj.*, 84, That is being
parboiled.
Parcelly *sb.*, 72, 81 ; Parcely, 72 ;
Parcill, 81. Parsley. See *Perceli*.
Parchement, 46.
Pare, *sb.*, 30. Paring ; peel : A.
also thus.
Pare, *vb.t.*, 7, 12, 16, 24, 27, 30, 34,
47, 51, 71, Pare ; peel (fruit and meat);
Pare in ij. or in iij., 87, cut in two
or three.
Pareȝ, Pyeȝ de, 53, Pies of Parys, 75,
see Napier, p. 58, Douce MS., No.
72 ; Parysgingere, 110. Paris.
Paris, see *Pareȝ*.
Parsley; see *Parcelly* and *Perceli*.
Parte, *vb.t.*, 20, Part; divide.
Partrich rosted, 78, see Napier, p. 61,
Douce MS., No. 109 ; P. stwed, 78,
Pertrich stewyde, 9, see Napier, p.
95, Douce MS., No. 28 ; Pertriches,
19 ; Pertryche, 1. Partridge.
Party, *sb.*, 20, 27, 40 ; Partye, 29,
40 ; Parti, 40. Part.
Partye, 46, Party coloured.
Past, *sb.*, 45, 51 ; Paste, 39, 41, 98 ;
Paast, 74, 75. See *Paast.*

Pastelade, 59. *Pystelade chaud*, 62, *P. fryid*, 62, *Petelade Fryid*, 62. Pastelet, ? Pasty : it may be a pounded dish.

Payne Puffe, 61, 68 ; Payn pur-dew, 42, P. purdeuȝ, 83 ; see Douce MS., No. 7, NAPIER, p. 46, "*Payn par-dieu* ;" **Peynregusoū**, 112, see F. of C., No. 67, "*Payn Ragon* ;" there is also "*Payn Fondew*" in F. of C., No. 59. "Payn purdew" may be compared with "Payn Fondew," the bread being lost or covered in what is poured on it, and possibly *dissolved* in the "Payn Fondew." In NAPIER the bread is smothered in Batter, here apparently in butter. See also LITTRÉ. "*Pain*, 10. *Pain perdu*, nom donné en cuisine provinciale, à la brioche frite." For "Payn Puffe," see *Pety Pernantes*.

Paynemain, *sb.*, 8, 11, 52 ; Payne-maynne, 11 ; Paynemaynnys, 11 ; Paynmain, 83 ; A Paynmain, *i.e.* a loaf of the bread, 90; Paynmaū, 83. "Floure of payndemayn" is mentioned in L.C.C., p. 40. Painmain is apparently the same as Manchet bread (see **Payn purdeuz** on p. 83), and its full form seems *Pain Manchet* or *Pain de Manchet*. Manchet is possibly "Manchet," or "Manchot," and refers to the short curtailed character of Roll bread. Note the round sops of the "paynemaynnys" in Recipe xxix, on p. 11. The gradual curtailing of the word is shewn on comparison of "Manged brede," at p. 83, and "Mengyd Flowre" on p. 43, with "Meyned flour" and "Maynch brede" in the Douce MS. O.F. *Pain demaine*, Latin "Panem dominicum," is generally given as derivation.

Peacock, see *Pecok*.

Pear, see *Pere*.

Peceȝ, *sb.*, Pecys, 6, 7, 8, 12. Pieces.

Pecher, Pechir, *sb.*, 39. Pitcher.

Pecok rosted, 79, see Douce MS., No. 128 ; Pokokkys, 58.

Peions, 67, *Peions rosted*, 68, Sauce for peiouds, 109 ; Pyionys, 58, Pigeons. For "*Pegions stewed*," see NAPIER, p. 107, F. of C., No. 48, L.C.C., p. 14.

Pele, *sb.*, 51 ; Pelys, 50. Baker's Peel.

Pele, *vb.t.*, 8, Pyle, 8 ; Pylle, 12, 26. Peel ; skin.

Peletre, 110, Pellitory.

Pelettys, Pellettys, *sb.*, 31, 34, 39. Pellets.

Peny brede, 7, 18, 97, 106, Penny's breadth. In first example read "they" (=the) "peny brede."

Pepir, *sb.*, 10, 15, 55 ; Pepyr, 8, 10; Perpir, 40 ; Piper, 109. Pepper.

Pepyn, *sb.*, 32. Apparently Fr. *Pépin*, the seed of fruit, COTGR. : it seems applied to the germinating part of the pease.

Perase, 22, Fryid Gyngere perase, ? Ginger parings, or "pares."

Perceli, *sb.*, 6 ; Percely, 5, 7, 10, 15, Percile, 21. Fr. *Persil*, Parsley. See *Parcelly*.

Perche boiled, 102, see Douce MS., No. 135, NAPIER, p. 75 ; Perchys, 21, 26. Perch.

Pere Wardones, Peer Wardons, 88, Pere Wardonys, 12, Warden Pears, see *Wardons* ; Peris in Syrippe, 87, 58, 59 ; P. en composte, 12, 87, see Douce MS., No. 57, and F. of C. has "*Peeres in confyt*," No. 132 ; Perys, 24, 25, 37, 54. Pear.

Pereye, *sb.*, 32 ; Perre (Pease), 83, see Douce MS., No. 9, Blaunche Perreye (Pease), 32, see WARNER, p. 85, "*Perre*" (Pease), F. of C., No. 70, "*Perrey of Peson*," WARNER, p. 66, "*Porre of Peson*," L.C.C., p. 44, "*Porry of white Pese*" ; Blawnche Perrye (Leeks), 14, Blanche porrey (Leeks), 90, see Douce MS., No. 84, L.C.C., p. 44, "*Blaunchyl porray*," WARNER, pp. 51, 85, (Leeks). There is also a "*Porrey Chapeleyn*" in WARNER, p. 49, made up of Onions, Olive oil, and Almond milk, boiled together. See DUCANGE, "*Porrecta*, Jusculum ex poris confectum," also *Porrata*. It would almost appear as if *Purée* (= *Purata*, strained,) and *Porrée* (= *Porrata*) got confused.

Pesone, Longe Wortes de, 89, Lange wortes de Pesoun, 5, see Douce MS., No. 2 ; Pesyn, *sb.*, 5, 32, Whyte

P. in Grauey, 33; Peys de almayne, 114. Pease.

Pestel, *sb.*, 6. Pestle.

Pestelle, Siryppe pur vn, 40, see NAPIER, p. 46, "*Pestelles of pork endored.*" Pestel is still used for a leg of pork.

Pesyñ, Mortrewes of, 90, see Douce MS., No. 82; Fr. *poisson*, fish.

Petelade, see *Pastelade.*

Pety Pernauntes, 51, 74 (2 recipes), Pety Pernollys, 50. These seem to be the same dishes, with different spelling, but representing possibly the same word; as the recipe on page 50 is the same as that on page 74. The dish is identified with Payn Puff in F. of C., No. 196, and is glossed "Petypanel a marchpayne", in Leland's *Collectanea*, VI., page 6; this would give a hint of the origin of the word, which is equivalent to the Italian "*Panello,* any little loaf, bun, roul, or manchet," FLORIO; the Paffs being like little loaves, or buns. There is also the Italian *Panella,* with same signification. See F. of C., Nos. 195, 196, "*Pety Pernaunt,*" Douce MS., Nos. 8 and 58. The dish is spelt "Pety perneux," in the Banquets on pages 58,59 of this book.

Peuard, Brawne in, 71, Braun en Peuerade, 11, 12, the same dish: see Douce MS., No. 47, F. of C., No. 135, WARNER, p. 79, "*Boor in pererarde, or Boor in egredouce,*" Recipes for the Sauce are given in F. of C., No. 135, "*Pevorat for Veel and Venyson,*" and in WARNER, p. 64, "*Perrate sauce.*" It is the French *Poivrade,* sauce made with pepper: see *Piper.*

Pewter dysshe, 26, 42.

Peynregusoñ, 112.

Peys de almayne, 114, Pease and almond milk.

Pheasant, see *Fesaunt.*

Pie, see *Crustade.*

Pies of Parys, 75, Pye3 de pare3, 53, see Douce MS., No. 72, NAPIER, p. 58, Paris Pies; Gretepyes, 76. See *Crustade.*

Pigeon, see *Peions.*

Pigge or chikeñ in Sauge, 72, see

WARNER, p. 56, "*Pygges in sauge*"; Pigge Farced, 82, Pygge y-farsyd, 40, see Douce MS.,No.37. Apparently sucking pigs.

Pike en galentyne, 101 (2 Recipes), see NAPIER, p. 79, Douce MS., No. 75, No. 151; Pike boyled, 101, see Douce MS., No. 131; Pike in brase, 101, see Douce MS., No. 73, NAPIER, p. 34, "*Pyk in Braisselle,*" p. 79, "*Pik in Brasy,*" WARNER, p. 86, "*Pik or tenche in Brasyle*"; there is also "*Pyk in sauce,*" in NAPIER, p. 96.

Pikkyll pour le Mallard,77, see Douce MS., No. 19, Pickle: L.C.C., p. 31, has "*Pyknlle,*" (Capons).

Piper for feel and for venysoun, 110, see F. of C., No. 135. Poivrade, Pepper Sauce. See *Peuard.*

Pipes, *sb.*, 70; Pypis, 8. Bronchial tubes: ? lungs, generally.

Plais, *sb.*, 103, Plaise boiled, 103, see Douce MS., No. 140; Plays, 26, 103, 105; Playse, 103. Plaice.

Plante, *vb.t.*, 25, 27; Plonte, 98. Plant.

Platere, *sb.*, 17, 27, 41, 114. Platter.

Platte, *adj.*, 44.

Plie, *vb.t.*, 113. Ply; fold.

Plom, *vb.t.*, 76. Plump, into a pot.

Plouer, 79, Plouer rost, 117, see NAPIER, p. 64.

Pocerounce, 3; Pokerounce, 41.

Poche, Eyron en, 24. Poached eggs; see *Eggys.*

Poddyng, 41, see *Puddyng.*

Poke, 114. See *Pouche.*

Pokokkys, 58. Peacocks.

Polettys, 38. Pullets.

Pome dorreng, 58, see WARNER, p. 58, "*Pondorroge*": the "orroge" is apparently *orange,* the Pommes being coloured yellow. Pome dorres, 38, *Pomez endoryd,* 63, WARNER, p. 89, "*Pomes Dorre,*" II. No. 42, "*Pomme dorry,*" F. of C., No. 174, "*Pomme dorryes,*" L.C.C., p. 37, "*Powme dorrys.*" So called from the *Pommes,* or Rissoles, being endored, or glazed, with yolk of egg. Pomesmoille, 113, see WARNER, p. 46, "*Pommys morles,*" i.e. "Pommes molles," or crushed apples. Pommes. 1 ; **Poumes, 14** ; Pomys, 62 ; Pommys, 15 ; see NAPIER, p. 120. Pompe, 31 ; **Pompys, 34** ; **Pumpes,** 31. All the above are variations of the French *pomme*, applied to globular lumps of minced meat : compare "*Pome di sdegno*, a kind of made dish, that Cooks make round as apples."—FLORIO. In A. the "pompys," on page 31, are called "pepyngis," or pippins.

Pome-garnade, *sb.*, 28 ; Pome-garned, 30 ; Pome-garne}, 38, applied here to Rissoles, in the same way as the *Pommes* above. Pomegranate.

Pomppe, *sb.*, 24, Pulp : A. reads here " Pappe."

Pond, *sb.*, 114. Pound.

Poper, 63.

Porcelle farce enforce, 58, ? Sucking Pig stuffed and made rich : Porcellys, 58.

Porcyon, *sb.*, 9, 10, 18, 25 ; Porcyoun, 11, 18. Portion.

Pore, *vb.t.*, 16, 26. Pour.

Porke, 6, 14, 19, etc.

Porpeys, Sturgeon pour, 105, see NAPIER, p. 53, " *Porpas, sturgion or turbut*," (baked) ; Firmenty with, p. 105, Furmenty wit*h* purpaysse, 17, see Douce MS., No. 171, F. of C., No. 69, and No. 116, NAPIER, p. 86, WARNER, p. 66 ; Puddyng of p., 42 ; F. of C., No. 108, has " *Porpeys in broth*." Porpoise.

Porpoise, see *Porpeys*.

Porrey, Blanche, 90, see *Pereye*.

Poshote, *sb.*, 15, 36 ; Poshotte, 36. Posset.

Possenet, *sb.*, 23, 72. Posnet ; small pot. " A little brasse pot or posnet, *Een koper potken ofte ketelken*."—1660, HEXHAM.

Potage, 33, 8, 10, 11, 16 ; P. on a fysshday, 15, 29 ; P. colde, 30 ; P. of Roysons, 30 ; P. de egges, 94, called in Douce MS., No. 100, "*Pocched egges*"; P. of ris, 114; *Brode canelle Potage, i.e.*, Whole Cinnamon Soup, 59; *Compost Potage*, p. 59 ; WARNER, p. 51, has " *Potage de frumenty*," and " *Potage of rys*," at p. 46.

Poteil, *sb.*, 94 ; Potelle, 22 ; Pottel, 73. Pottle ; two quarts.

Poterous, 93, Potrous, 53 ; see F. of C., 177, "*Potews*," which is probably its right form, like Mortrews, the termination representing the liquid *l* : see DUCANGE, *Potellus*, O. Fr. *Potel*. The dish was made in pots, which were afterwards broken, but in this volume coffins of paste are used. Compare "*Sachus*" in F. of C., No. 178, made in bags (O. Fr. *sachel*), and see *Bourreys*.

Pouche, *sb.*, 101, 102 ; Powche, 103 ; Pouuche, 101 ; Poke, 114. Poche, stomach of fish.

Pouder, Recipe Cj., p. 24, powdered spice generally ; Poudre, 113, Poudur, 112, *?* pepper ; Pouder Canelle, 20, 38, Poudre canel, 109; Powder Canel, 11, P. of Canelle, 20 ; Pouder of Clowes, 97 ; Poudre of clowes, 109 ; Pouder of gyngere, 7, 19, Poudre of gyngere, 108, Poudre ginger, 109, Pouþer Gyngere, 19, Powder Gyngere, 8, 9, 10, of Gyngere, 20 ; Poudre piper, 109, Powder Pepyr, 10, 11, 14 ; Pouudre, 116 ; Clowys powþer, 14 ; Pouder Marchaunt, Pulverized spices, 25.

Powajes, 27 : ? meaning. A. reads "powares."

Powder, see *Pouder*.

Powderd, *adj.*, 14 ; Poudrid, 91. Powdered ; salted.

Powdryng of beef, Salting of beef, 69 ; this probably ought to read, "a nijt powdryng of beef," with no comma there.

Pownche, *sb.*, 7. Paunch.

Powre, *vb.t.*, 87. Pour.

Poynant, *adj.*, 33 ; Poynaunt, 6 ; P. & dowcet, 7, 33. Poignant ; piquant with vinegar.

Poynte with Venegre, 29. Point, make acid : Fr. *poindre*.

Prenade, 91, in Douce MS., No. 105, "*Brewes*": possibly this ought to read " Prouade," and is a perversion.

Prik, *sb.*, 82. Prick ; pin, skewer.

Prik, *vb.t.*, 82, skewer ; Prycke, 36, Prick ; stick.

Primrose, see *Prymerose.*

Prune3, 51, 52.   Prunes.

Prymerose, 25, 29, see NAPIER, p. 56, "*Prymerolle.*"   Primrose.

Puddyng of Purpaysse, 42 ; Poddyng of Capoun necke, 41 ; *Puddyng de Swan necke*, 61.

Pul, *vb.t.*, P. dry, 79, Pull dry, 78, 79, Pluck clean ; Pulle, 9.

Pulcynyes farce3, 58, *Pulsons farce*, 61, (misprinted Pulsous), Fr. *Poussin* ; chicken.

Pullayñ, 67, Pullets.

Pured buttur, 103, Clarified butter.

Pygge y-farysd, 40 ; *Pygge in sage*, 59, 63, see WARNER, p. 56; Pyggys, 25.

Pyk, *sb.*, 106 ; Pyke, 16 ; Pykys, 26, 30.   Pike (the fish), see *Pike.*

Pyke, *vb.t.*, 10.   Pick : see *Pike.*

Pyle, *vb.t.*, 8.   Peel.

Pylt, *vb.t.*, 21.   Put.

Pyn, *sb.*, 7 ; Pynne, 11.   Pin.

Pynade, 34, see WARNER, p. 49, "*Pynade,*" F. of C., No. 51, "*Pynnonade.*" *Pynenade in paste*, 60, possibly ought also to be *Pynenade.* The dish is named from the Pines, or "Pynotys" in it : the other recipes read "pynes."

Pynes, *sb.*, 95, 97 ; Pyne3, 24, Pyne3 and clowys, 53 ; Pynys, 15, 16, 22, 75, 91, 94 ; in this last case the Douce MS. reads "pepyr pynes," or whole pepper, but all the examples may not mean pepper, as the seeds of fir pines seem to have been used.

Pynotys, 34 : ? Pine nuts or cones.

Pypis, see *Pipes.*

Pystelade, see *Pastelade.*

Quantite, *sb.*, 5, 6.   Quantity.

Quart, *sb.*, 35 ; Quarte, 101.

Quarter, *sb.*, 106 ; Quartercñ of pouder caneH, 101.   Quart.

Quarter, *sb.*, Fore q., 8 ; Quarterys, 6, 31, 49.

Quarter, *vb.t.*, 18.   Cut in quarters.

Quayle rosted, 79, see Douce MS., No. 115, NAPIER, p. 61.

Quayle, *vb.int.*, 27.   Curdle.   Fr. *cailler.*

Quibibes, *sb.*, 6, 37, 113 ; Quybibes, 19, 20, 21 ; Quybibe3, 24, 46 ; Quybibys, 15 ; Quybybis, 13.   Cubebs.

Quince, see *Quynces.*

Quyk, *adj.*, 99.   Quick ; alive.

Quynade, 27, see "*Connat,*" in F. of C., No. 18. So called from being made of Quinces : compare *Applade.*

Quynces, 27, 51 ; Q. or Wardones in paast, 97, 51, Quyncis, 51 ; *Quyncys in comfyte*, 58, *i.e.*, preserved Quinces ; Charde-quynce, 12, 13 ; Chared coneys, or chardwardoñ, 106 ; *Quynes bakyn*, 69.

Quyschons, 40 : compare Cushion of Bacon.

Quystis scune, 8, see NAPIER, p. 44, "*Quystis*" : ? "stune," not *scune.* Cushats, wood-pigeons : A.S. *cusceote.*

Rabbit, see next, and *Conyng.*

Rabette rosted, 81, see Douce MS., No. 117, NAPIER, p. 64.

Raisins, see *Rasonys.*

Rales, 69.   Rails ; Landrails.

Ransched, *pp.*, 39.   Rinsed.

Rape, 113, Rapeye, 30, 48, (Fish), see Douce MS., No. 164, "*Rapes,*" NAPIER, p. 118, "*Rape of Fisshe*" ; Rapes, 95, Rapeye, 16, (two Recipes), 28, 43 (Fruit), see F. of C., No. 83, L.C.C., p. 16, NAPIER, p. 109, "*Rape,*" WARNER, p. 49, "*Rapee,*" and H. No. 49, "*Rapy*" ; Rapeye of Fleysshe, 25, see WARNER, p. 45.

Rasinges, Rasons, 88.   Shavings, parings.

Rasonys, *sb.*, 23 ; Raysonys, 30, 52, of Coraunce, 14 ; Raysounys, 51 ; Reysons of coraunce, 75 ; Potage of Roysons, 30, Roysons of Corauns, 16 ; Roysouns Coraunce, 22 ; Roysonys, 16, 22, 28, of coraunce, 13, 31, of Corauns, 15, 29 ; Currants. Grete Reysons, 97, G. Reysynges, 75, Gret Roysonys, 47, Raisins, in modern usage.

Rastons, 52, 98, see Douce MS., No. 63, "*Rastonurs.*" "*Raston* : A fashion of round, and high Tart,

made of butter, egges, and cheese."
A. spells this "Rascons," and glosses
it as "rascoris," and the word might
be "Rastouurs," above.
Ray boiled 103, see Douce MS., No.
145, "*Rygh buille.*"
Raynolle}, 42 ; Raynollys, 3; see
WARNER, p. 81, "*Rayneeles.*" "*Ray-
molles de blanc de chapon.* The
brawne of a Capon, Raisins of the
Sunne, and marrow shred all to-
gether, then made into little cakes or
leaues, and fryed with seame or Hogs
sewet, and serued vp with sugar
strewed on them."—COTGR.
Red Wyne, 10, 26 ; R. Rosys, 24 ;
Rede Rose, 29, R. vyne, 112.
Reke,*vb.t.*,29. Reek; heat over coals.
Remenaunt, *sb.*, 12. Remnant.
Renge, *sb.*, 38. Ring Strainer.
Renne, *vb.int.*, 11, 26, 44. Ronne,
pp. 44. Run.
Rennyng, *adj.*,44 ; Rennyng, 6, 9, 15,
19 ; Rennynge,94. Running; fluid.
Rennyn, *vb.inf.*, 25. Run.
Rew, *sb.*, 53. Row.
Re}ge, *sb.*, 11. The Ray : see *Ray.*
Ris, *sb.*, 114; Rys, 22, see NAPIER,
p. 82, p. 108, L.C.C., p. 16 ; Rys
moilles, 113, see WARNER, p. 46;
Potage of ris, 114, see WARNER, p.
46 ; *Rys Moleyn},* 59 ; WARNER, pp.
62, 74, has also "*Rys Lumbarde*" ;
Rys, 12, 14 ; Flowre of rys, 13.
Risschewes, de frute, 97, Risshewes,
93 (Fruit), Ryschewys in lente, 43,
(Fruit and Fish), R. close et Frye},
45, R. close, 112, (Fruit), see Douce
MS., No. 88, F. of C., No. 182 ; Rissh-
shewes, 98 ; Risshewes de Mary,
85, Ryschewys of marow, 44, see
Douce MS., No. 87; L.C.C., p. 39,
WARNER, p. 65 (Flesh). Now Ris-
sole : see COTG., "*Rissolle* : A Iewes
eare ; or Mushrome thats fashioned
likea Demie-circle,and grows cleaning
to trees ; also, a small and delicate
minced Pie, made of that fashion."
Roche, *sb.*, 20, Breme or Roche boiled,
102, see Douce MS., No. 138 ; Rochys,
21. Roach.
Roddys ende, 52. Rod's end.
Rolle, Cruste, 46.

Roppis, *sb.*, 39. Ropes ; guts. See
HOLME, II. vii. 132, "Sheeps Belly,
or Intrals,the puddings called strings,
or Rope."
Rose, Rede, 29 ; Red Rosys, 24.
Roseye, 24. So called from being
made of Roses ; see WARNER, II.
No. 41, and No. 47, F. of C., No. 52:
WARNER, No. 47, has no roses in it.
Roste, *vb.t.*, 12, 14, Roste him on a
gredire, 103. Roast.
Rosty, *vb.int.*, 15. Roast.
Rove of the mouthe, 78. Roof.
Rowys, 114. Roe of fish.
Ruchet, 60, see NAPIER, p. 74,
"*Gurnard or Rochet.*" Comp. Fr.
Rochau. Rock-Fish, and see FLORIO,
"*Roccate,* the Cook-fish, or Sea-
thrush."
Ruschewys, 45, see *Risschewes.*
Ryal, *adj.*, 40; Ryalle, 21, 22 ;
Ryaly, 2, Ryally, 17. Royal : Roy-
ally. The Cookeries also say "fit
for a lord " ; in same sense.
Rybbys, *sb.*, 6, 8, 10, 26. Ribs.
Ryght, *adv.*, 5 ; Ryth wyl, 20,
Rythte smal, 37 ; Ry}t fatte, 35,
Ry}th smal, 46 ; Ry}th, 6, 8.
Rynsche, *vb.t.*, 24. Rinse ; splash.
Ry}t, see *Ryght.*

Saake, Bruette, 27, Sake, 2; see
WARNER, p. 78, "*Browet seeke.*"
Sad or flatte, 92. Douce MS., and.
Saf, *vb.t.*, 39. Save.
Saferon, *sb.*, 70 ; Saferoun, 43 ;
Safron, 5, 9 ; Safroun, 6, 10, 13, 15,
26 ; Sapheron, 70. Saffron.
Saffron, see *Saferon.*
Safroun, *vb t.*, 32, 49. Saffron.
Salmon fressh boiled, 102, see Douce
MS., No. 132 ; Samon roste in
Sauce, 102, see Douce MS., No. 169,
NAPIER, p. 97 : Salmond, 102 ;
Samond, 100 ; Samoun, 16.
Salome, Capoun in, 33 ; Salomene, 21 ;
Soupes of Salomere, 35.
Salt, *vb.t.*, 32, 41.
Samaca, 59, *Frutoure Samata,* 62 ;
see NAPIER, p. 45, "*Samartard.*"

The first example should be *Samata*. The Fritter is made of Flour, Curds, Eggs, Cream, and Grease, and is served with sugar on it.

Sardeyne₃, 24.

Sareson, Bruette, 19 ; Saug saras*er*, 113, Sauke Sarsoun, 30. Fr. *Sarrasine* ; Saracen.

Sauces ; Sauce alepeuere, 108, Sauce oylepeu*er*, 77, see NAPIER, p. 77, "*S. aliper*," Douce MS., No. 94, "*Saunce alpeuere*" ; Sauce camelyne, 109, Sauce gamelyne, 77, see Douce MS., No. 92, "*Saunce camelyn*," NAPIER, p. 48, "*Sauce c. for quaylle*," F. of C., No. 144, "*Sause camelyne*," L.C.C., p. 30 ; Sauce Galentyne, 77, 108, see Douce MS., No. 98, NAPIER, p. 77, F. of C., No. 138, L.C.C., p. 30, WARNER, p. 64 ; Sauce gauncile, 110, Sauce sermstele, 77, (called "*S. gauncell*," in Douce MS., No. 93), see L.C.C., p. 29, WARNER, p. 65, "*Gaunsell for gese*" (see *Gauncely*) ; Sauce gynger, 77, Sauce gingyu*er*, 109, see Douce MS., No. 96, NAPIER, p. 77, F. of C., No. 139, WARNER, p. 64, L.C.C., p. 52 ; Sauce for a gos, 109 ; Sauce newe for malardis, 110, see L.C.C., p. 27, and Black sauce, below ; Sauce for peiou*n*s, 109 ; Sauce percely, 110 ; Sauce rous, 109, Fr. *Rousse*, ruddy ; Saug saras*er*, 113 ; Sauke Sarsoun, 30, see F. of C., No. 84, "*Saurse Sarzyne*," or Saracen ; Sauce sermstele, see *S. gauncile* ; Sauce Sorell, 77, Surelle, 110, Fr. *Surelle*, Sorrel ; Sauce for shulder of moton, 110 ; Sauce for stokefysshe (two Recipes), 109 ; Sauce Verte, 77, 110, Green Sauce, see Douce MS., No. 95, NAPIER, p. 77, F. of C., No. 140, WARNER, p. 64 ; Black sauce for Capou*n*s y-rostyde, 110, see F. of C., No. 137, WARNER, p. 64, on which page is "Black Sauce for Mallard" (for which also see F. of C., No. 141); White sauce for capon*s* y-sode, 110, see F. of C., No. 136, L.C.C., p. 28, WARNER, p. 64 : F. of C. No. 30, has also "*Sause madame*." See *Pikkyl* and *Piper*, in Glossary.

Sauereye, *sb.*, 18. Savory.

Sauge, 28, Sauoge, 41, compare "*Suegeat*," in F. of C., No. 161 ; Pigge or chiken in Sauge, 72 ; Sawge, 2, 6, 8, 10, 17, 20, 28. The herb Sage.

Sauke Sarsoun, 30, see Sauces.

Saunderys, *sb.*, 12, 15, 16, 21 ; Sawnderys, 8, 12, 13. Saunders.

Saused, *pp.*, 72. Soused ; salted.

Saweere, *sb.*, 22, 42. Saucer.

Sayn, *vb.int.*, 33. Say.

Scalde, *vb.t.*, S. with hey *or* strawe, 99, 100 ; Skalde, 18, 32. Scald.

Schake out, 109, Shake out.

Schale, *vb.t.*, 13. Shell.

Schap, *sb.*, 53. Shape.

Scharpe, *adj.*, 38. Sharp.

Schene, *vb.t.*, 23. Skin ; shell : A. reads *Shene*.

Schepe, *sb.*, 40. Sheep.

Schere, *vb.t.*, 40 ; Shere, 11. Shear ; slice.

Schevres, *sb.*, 40. Shivers ; thin strips.

Schoche, *vb.t.*, 101 ; Skoche, 101. Scotch ; notch.

Schoppe, *vb.t.*, 9. Chop.

Schorge, *vb.int.*, 42. Scorch.

Schort & þikke, 52.

Schouyl, *sb.*, 53. Shovel.

Schrede, *vb.t.*, 8, 10, 29 ; Screde, 30. Shred.

Schrympe, *sb.*, 42, Shrimp ; see *Shrympes*.

Schul, *vb.*, 30, Shall ; Schuld, 19, Should ; Schuldyst, 45, Shouldest.

Schulle, *sb.*, 24, 42 ; Schullys, 23. Shell. A. reads "schyllys."

Sculle, *sb.*, 80 ; Skoll, 79. Scull.

Sefe, *sb.*, 20 ; Seve, 32 ; Her syue, Hair sieve, 113.

Self, *adj.*, 19, 23 ; Selue, 32 ; Sylf, 14. Self ; same : compare Selfsame.

Senglere, Teste de, enarme₃, 57, Boars head and tusks ; *Blanke singuler leche*, 69. Fr. *Sanglier*, Wild boar.

Serge, *vb.t.*, 20, Sift : spelt *Sarge* in A.

Serue forth (to table), 6, 10, etc. ; Seruyst in, 6.

Seruyce, *sb.*, 34. Service.

Sesyn, *vb.t.*, 19 ; S. vp, 10, 12. Season.

Sethe, *vb.t.*, 6, 12 ; Seþin, *pp.*, 32 ; Sith, 90 : Seth, *vb.int.*, 99. Seethe. *Sethe* in Recipe vj, p. 6, is *sette* in A.

Sew, *sb.*, 18 ; Colouryd S. wit*h*out fyre, 20, see NAPIER, p. 38 ; Sew trappe, 54, so called from the pans or *Trappes* in which it is made. These are solids. See *lumbarde*, 58. Sewe, 9, 17, 20, 99. Broth. MAYHEW & SKEAT derive Sew from A.S. *séaw*, but it is suspiciously like the French Ciué, or Siué, see COTGR.; compare "Harus in a sewe," L.C.C., p. 21, Hares or Conynges in sewe, WARNER, p. 78, where it represents Ciué. At the same time Mr. Mayhew does not think it possible. *Ciué*, however, is used for a liquid without onions, upon page 49 : see *Errata*.

Sewet, *sb.*, 41. Suet : see *Suet*.

Shrympes, 103. Shrimps.

Sirip, *sb.*, 12, 40 ; Sirippe, 15 ; Siryppe p*ur* un pestelle, 40 ; Syrip, 11 ; Syrippe, 3, 15, 21, Peris in syrippe, 87 ; Wardonys in syryp, 7 ; Syryppe, 13, 21. Syrup.

Sith, *vb.t.*, 90. Seethe.

Sitting to, 107. Sticking.

Skalde, *vb.t.*, 18, 32 ; Skaldyd, 24 ; Skladdyd, 25. Scald : see *Scalde*. On p. 32, ? read "skalde hem" [wi*t*h hey].

Skaldyng hote, 17.

Skeme, *vb.t.*, 7. Skim.

Sket, *sb.*, 102. Scotch : Douce MS. has *skoch*.

Skilfully thik, 101, Skylfully þikke, 8, Reasonably, nicely thick.

Skluce, *sb.*, 25. Viscous compound.

Skoll, *sb.*, 79. Skull.

Skore, *vb.t.*, 25 ; Skoure, 45. Scour.

Skrape, *vb.t.*, 18. Scrape.

Skym, *vb.t.*, 22. Skim : see *Skeme*.

Skymer, *sb.*, 44 ; Skymoure, 17, 54. Skimmer.

Skyn, *sb.*, 11 ; Skynne, 26 ; Skynnys, 26. Skin.

Slake, *adj.*, 21 (*Flake* is printed here). Slack ; lukewarm : *warm* in A.

Sle, *vb.t.*, 78, 79. Slay.

Slepyr, *adj.*, 23. Slippery ; greasy. A. reads " sliper."

Smal, *adj.*, 10 ; Smaller or grett*er*, 15.

Smoth, *adj.*, 77. Smooth.

Smyte, *vb.t.*, 6, 13. Smite ; chop.

Snyte, 80 ; Snyte rost, 117 ; see Douce MS., No. 120, L.C.C., p. 35, " *Wodcok, snyȝt, and curlue*," NAPIER, p. 65, "*Snyt rost*"; Snytys, 58.

Sode, *adj.*, 42. Sodden.

Soft, *adv.*, 22, Softe, 17, Softly ; Sofftere and sofftere, 17.

Soke, *vb.t.*, S. out, 25. Soak out ; let soak out.

Sokingly, *adv.*, boile s., 72. Soakingly ; thoroughly : still used thus.

Sole, boiled, rost, or fryed, 103, see Douce MS., No. 141 ; NAPIER, p. 71, has "*Sole in brase*."

Soperys, *sb.*, 46, 55. Suppers.

Soppes Dorre, 90, Soupes dorrees, 114, Soupes dorye, 11, S. dorroy, 11, see Douce MS., No. 51, F. of C., No. 82, WARNER, p. 46, L.C.C., p. 14, NAPIER, p. 107 ; Lyode Soppes, 11 ; S. Jamberlayne, 11, Soppes pour Chamberleyne, 90, see Douce MS., No. 52, " *Soupes Chamberlayn*"; Oyle Soppys, 12, 96, see Douce MS., No. 158 ; Soupes of Salomere, 35 ; see also NAPIER, p. 51, and F. of C., No. 129, " *Soupes in galentyne*"; Soppis, 1, 52. COTGR. : " *Soupe* : A sop, or peece of bread in broth : also pottage, or broth (wherein there is store of sops, or sippets)." Soup is still served thus in France.

Sorcell rosted 79, see Douce MS., No. 118, " *Sarcelle rost*," NAPIER, p. 64 ; Teal.

Sore Sengle, 25. This looks like " Single Sore," compare " *Jussell sengle*," in NAPIER, p. 26 : see, however, COTGR., " *Soringue* : Eele sauce made of fried Onions, and toas-bread steeped in Pease broth, then strayned with wine, vinegar, Cinnamon, Ginger, and other spices, all put into a pot

with the Ecles cut into peeces, and
(after a little seasoning with saffron
and salt) throughly boyled." **Elys
in Sorre**, 89, see Douce MS., No. 25.
The Fr. *soré* means reeked or made
red, as the saffron would do. Compare *Blaundesore*.

Sotelte, *sb.*, 57, 58, 59, 60, 61, 62,
63, 67, 68, 69. Subtlety, or device
to deck the Table: see Forewords.

Sothe, *pp.*, 37, 46: **Soþin**, 6, 46,
Sothyn, 7, 9, 11. Sod; sodden.

Soundes, *sb.*, 96; **Soundys**, 26. Cod
Sounds, or swimming bladders.

Soups, see *Soppes*.

Sowsyd, *adj.*, 12. Soused; pickled.

Spaulde de Motoun, 59, **Spawdys de
Motonn**, 63. Spaud; shoulder.

Spaune, *sb.*, 14, **Spawne**, 90. Spawn.

Spete, *sb.*, 8, 15, 38, Spete of haselle,
39. Spit.

Spete, *vb.t.*, 38; ben spetid, 38. Spit;
put on spit.

Spicere, *sb.*, 113; Spicerie, 113;
Spicerye, 30; Spycery, 19, 28, 35.

Splat, *adj.*, 101. Split.

Splat, *vb.t.*, 105; Splatte, 104. Split.

Splentes, *sb.*, 73. Splints.

Spone, *sb.*, 41. Spoon.

Sprynge, *vb.t.*, 31. Springe; sprinkle.

Spycis, 28. Spices.

Spyneye, 20, see WARNER, II. No. 46,
F. of C., No. 57: so named
from O.Fr. *Espine*, Hawthorn. See
Hawþorn.

Stampe, *vb.t.*, 6, 7, 16, 38, 77. Stamp;
grind.

Stekys of venson or bef, 40.

Stept, 77, Steeped.

Ster, *vb.t.*, 46; Stere, 8, 9, 14, 26;
Sture, 26; Styre, 23. Stir. A.
reads "styue" (stew), in Recipe xiiij,
page 8.

Stipe, 16: see readings at end of
Forewords.

Stockfish, see next.

Stokfissh, 89, S. in sauce, 100, see
Douce MS., No. 31; Stokfysshe, 10;
Stokkefysshe, 26. Stockfish. See
COTGR.: "*Merlus*, *ou Merluz*: A
Mellwell, or Keeling, a kind of small
Cod, whereof stockfish is made."

Modern French *Merluche*, Haddock.
Stockfish seems to have been made
of all sorts of Cod, and even of
Porpoise.

Stonde, *vb.int.*, 88, 109. Stand; be
stiff.

Stonding, *adj.*, 95; Stondyng, 16,
95; Stondynge, 16, 109. Standing;
stiff.

Storgeoun, *sb.*, 13; Storioun, 57;
Storion in brothe, 13; see *Sturgeon*.

Straw, *vb.t.*, 23; S. on, 15; Strawe
Canel a-boue, 16. Strew.

Strawberye, 29; Strawberys, 29;
Stawberye, 2; Streberies, 75.

Strayne, *vb.t.*, 6, 8, 11. Strain
through strainer.

Straynour, *sb.*, 6, 11; Straynoure,
6, 10, 11, 41; Straynourys ende, 44;
Straynowr, 5, 6; Straynowre, 5, 10;
Strainwoure, 16. Strainer.

Strek, *vb.t.*, 95. Strike.

Strype, *vb.t.*, 27. Strip.

Stew, see *Stwed*.

Stuff, Stuffe, *adj.*, 71. Stiff.

Stuffe, *vb.t.*, 32, 40, 41; Stuffyst,
40. Stuff with forcemeat.

Stulfur, *sb.*, 76. Stuff for stuffing.

Sture, see *Stere*.

Sturgeon boiled, 104, see WARNER, p.
47, NAPIER, p. 71; Sturgeon buille
ou turbutt, 117; Storion in brothe,
13, Sturgeoñ in broth, 104, see
Douce MS., No. 80; Sturgeoñ pour
porpeys, 105, see Douce MS., No.
181, "*Sturgeon ou purpays ou turbut
furnie}*," NAPIER, p. 53, "*Porpas,
sturgion, or turbut*"; Storioun leche,
37.

Sturmye, 26.

Stwed Beef, 72, see Douce MS., No.
3; Stwed Muttoñ, 72; Capons
Stwed, 72; Partrich stwed, 78,
Pertrich stewyde, 9; Smale Birdys
y-stwyde, 9. Stewed.

Styke, *vb.t.*, 31. Stick.

Styre, see *Stere*.

Sucking Pig, see *Porcelle*.

Suet, *sb.*, 76; Svette, 115; Swet,
40; Swette, 40; Sewet, 41.

Sugre, *sb.*, 11, Whyte s., 7, Blake s.,
7, Whyte oþer blake, 51; S. of Ali-

saunder, 39, Alysaundre, 50, from Alexandria ; S. of Siprys, 16, Sugur of Cipris, 95, from Cyprus ; Sugre in confyte, 32, ? comfits, A. "Sugre of confitens" ; Sugre water, 7 ; Sugour water, 85, Sugur water, 91 ; Sugur, 85, White s. or blak, 73. Murray's Dict. gives Black Sugar as Liquorice, but ? unrefined sugar.

Sumdele, *adv.*, 21, 49. Somedeal ; somewhat.

Suththe, *adv.*, 112, 113. Afterward.

Swañ rosted, 78, see Douce MS., No. 106, "*Cignet roste.*"

Sware, *adj.*, 36, Square : see also L.C.C., p. 45.

Swenge, *vb.t.*, 40, 55. Swing; mix.

Swerde, *sb.*, 6, 14. Sward ; rind.

Sweteblanche, 112.

Swyne, *sb.*, 8, 70 ; Swynys grece, 41. Swine ; pig.

Swythe, *adv.*, 39. Quickly.

Syfte, *vb.t.*, 38. Sift.

Sylf, see *Self.*

Synamoun, *sb.*, 34. Cinnamon.

Synewes, *sb.*, 53 ; Syneys, 37 ; ȝynes, 37. Sinews.

Syngnettys, 57. Cignets.

Syrip, *sb.*, 11 ; Syrippe, 15, 21 ; Wardonys in syryp, 7. See *Sirip.*

Syrup, see *Sirip, Syrip.*

Syue, *sb.*, 113. Sieve.

Syȝth, *sb.*, 32. Sight; quantity.

Take, *pp.*, 52.

Talbottys, 19. See WARNER, II., No. 9, "*Haris in talbotays,*" F. of C., No. 23, "*Hares in talbotes.*"

Talow, *sb.*, 39 ; Talour, 39. Tallow; fat.

Tannye, 26. Compare Fr. "*Tanné,* Tawnie."—COTGR. The dish is of that colour.

Tansey, 86, Tansye, 45, see Douce MS., No. 176, L.C.C., p. 50, "*Tansy cake.*" So called from the Tansy in it.

Tart de Fruyte, 98, see Douce MS.,

No. 101 ; **Tartes of Frute in lente,** 48 ; **Tartus,** 75 (Cheese), **Tartes de chare,** 47, 52, **Tartus of Flesh,** 74, see· Douce MS., No. 45, "*Tartes de chare,*" NAPIER, p. 52, F. of C., No. 168, "*Tartes of Flesh*" ; **Tartes of Fysche,** 47, see F. of C., No. 170, WARNER, p. 48, "*Tartys of Fysch owt of Lente*" ; *Graunt tartez,* 58, **Grete pyes,** 76.

Tauorsay, 114.

Tayleȝ, 27, **Taylys,** 2, **Taylours,** 94, **Tayloures,** 15, **Taylowres,** 1 ; see Douce MS., No. 104. See COTGR., "*Taillis*: A Hachee ; or made dish of Creuises, the flesh of Capons, Chickens, or Veale, bread, wine, salt, veriuyce, and spices ; also a kind of gellie," as the dish is here.

Taylid Datys, 55. Cut Dates.

Temper, *vb.t.*, 10, 19, 20 ; Tempere, 9, 11 ; Temperyd, 12, 20. Mix.

Tenche in bruette, 23, ; T. in cyueye, 23, see F. of C., No. 120, NAPIER, p. 80 ; T. in Sawce, 23, see NAPIER, p. 117, L.C.C., p. 25, "*Tenche in graue*" ; **Tenche in brase,** 105, see NAPIER, p. 71, WARNER, p. 86, Douce MS., No. 150 ; **Another diting of a tenche,** 105 ; Tenchys, 26, 30.

Tendure, *adj.*, 105. Tender.

Tese, *vb.t.*, 10, with a pyn, 21, 43, 114. Tease ; shred small.

Tesid, *adj.*, 89 ; Tesyd, 22. Teased ; shred small.

Teste de cure, 112.

Þan, *adv.*, 6, 7 ; Þanne, 6, 7, 10, 24 ; Þenne, 9, 10, 24. Then.

Þe, *pron.*, 6. Thee.

Þer-an, 29, Thereon ; Þer-yn, 18, 20, 47, Þer-ynne, 7 ; Þer-on, 6, 11, 20, 29 ; Þer-to, 6, 18, 29 ; Theruc-owt, 36, throughout ; Þer-vppe, 30, 49, Thereon ; Þer-vppe-on, 18, 49, Upon it ; Þer-with, 29.

Þes, *adj.*, 34. These.

They, *art.*, The, 7 : see Note 3.

Thikke, *vb.int.*, 91. Thicken.

Þinne, *adj.*, 12 ; Þynne, 109. Thin.

Þombe, *sb.*, 21. Thumb.

Þorgh, *prep.*, 101 ; Þorw, 5, 6, 9, 22 ;

þorwe, 12, 22, 47 ; þurgh, 108, 109 ; þurwe, 108 ; þurӡ, 109. Through.

þowsand, *adj.*, 43. This is a curious mistake on the part of the transcriber and should be "a dozen": he took the "dd.," as Douce MS. has it, for twice five hundred. See "dd." on page 67.

þrifti Mylke of Almaundys, 31, þrifty M., 56 ; þryfty, 34. Not too strong.

Thrawe, *vb.t.*, 101. Throw.

þridde, *adj.*, 49 ; Thrudde, 113 ; þryd, 49 ; þrydde, 30, 50. Third.

Throte-boH, *sb.*, 79, Adam's Apple ; top of windpipe.

þrowe þorw straynour, 8.

þryis, *adv.*, 11. Thrice.

þwerte, *adv.*, 31. Thwart; athwart.

To, *adv.*, 6, 11, 22. Too. In Recipe xj, p. 7, A. reads "do hem to-gedir," and "to" has the same meaning : dele note 7.

To, *adj.*, 7, 14, 21. Two.

To-geder, *adv.*, 38, 40 ; To-gedere, 7, 21 ; To-gederys, 5, 13, 38, 55. Together.

Tolle, *vb.t.*, 40. See *Toyle*.

Toste, *vb.t.*, 11, 30. Toast.

Tostes, *sb.*, 12. Toasts.

Tow, *adj.*, 49. Tough.

Towres, 46.

Toyle, *vb.t.*, 16, 24, 54 ; Tolle, 40. Rub : *Twille* in Douce MS. : see *Trull*.

Toӡenst, *prep.*, 112. Against; in.

Trappe, Sew, 54. Compare *Trape*, pan or dish : the Pudding, a kind of Yorkshire, is made in two pans.

Trayne rost, 97, 60 ; see Douce MS., No. 157 ; Treyne. 7. Train : so called from its length.

Tre, *sb.*, BoH of tre, *i.e.* wood, 92. See *Treen*.

Treen, *adj.*, 13 ; T. dyssche, 53 ; T. bolle, 16. Wooden ; spelt "Treyn" in Douce MS.

Trenchours, Trenchourys, 41. Trenchers ; slices. Fr. *Trencheoir*, COTGR.

Tripe de Muttoñ, 82, Trype de Motoun, 7, see Douce MS., No. 4 ; T. of Turbut or of Codelynge, 18,

T. de Turbut, 106, see Douce MS., No. 170.

Troundeӡ, *sb.*, 42. Round slice ; compare *Trundle*, HALLIWELL.

Troute, boyled, 102, see Douce MS., No. 133, NAPIER, p. 69 ; Troutys, 20 ; Trowtys, 21.

TruH, *vb.t.*, 76, 95. Troll, trowl ; twist : Douce MS. *Twille*.

Trusse, *vb.t.*, for roasting, 81.

Tryе, *vb.t.*, 42 ; Tryid, *pp.*, 27. Try ; pick, pull. Fr. *Trier*.

Tryude, *pp.*, 74. This seems to mean broken up, or rubbed up in the sugar : but Recipe xx, page 51, reads "y-tryid ӡolkys," *i.e.*, separated from the white.

Turbot. Turbut, 16, 18 ; T. boyled, 105, see NAPIER, p. 73 ; T. roste ensauce, 106, see Douce MS., No. 168, NAPIER, p. 96 ; Tripe of Turbut, see *Tripe*.

Twyis, *adv.*, 11. Twice.

Tylle, *adv.*, 12. Till.

Tyne, *sb.*, 49, 50 ; Tyneӡ of batter, 49. Compare Tine of a fork ; spike.

Vanne, *vb.t.*, 70. Fan.

Veal, see *Vele*.

Vele, kede, or henne in Bokenade, 13, Autre Vele in bokenade, 13, see F. of C., No. 118 ; Vele rosted, 81, see Douce MS., No. 123 ; Piper for feel and for venysoun, 110.

Venegre, *sb.*, 7, 10 ; Vynegre, 8, 10, 72, 109 ; Winegre, 110. Vinegar.

Venison, see next.

Venisoñ or bef, Stekys of, 40 ; Venyson w*ith* Furmenty, 6, Furmenty with v., 70, see Douce MS., No. 180 ; V. in Broth, 10, 70, 63, see Douce MS., No. 38 ; Nombles, or Nomblys of V., 70, 10, see Douce MS., No. 39, F. of C., No. 54, WARNER, p. 53, and II. No. 12 ; V. y-bake, 51, 73, see Douce MS., No. 40 ; Venysoun, 1, 10, 49, V. rosted, 81, see Douce MS., No. 124, NAPIER, p. 66 ; *Veny-soun Roste*, 64, has "in syrup" added to it, in A.

Verge sauce, 102, 104, Vert Sauce.

Vergeous, *sb.*, 72; Verious, 7, 8, 9; 109; Veriows, 13; Vertious, 115, Veryous, 18, 20. " *Verjuice* is the juice of Crabs, or sour apples"; HOLME, III. iii. 85.

Vergyussauce, 103, 104. Verjuice-sauce.

Vernage, *sb.*, 22; Vernage pime꜀, 28. " *Vernaccia*, a kinde of strong wine like malmesie or muskadine, or bastard wine;" FLORIO, 1598. The 1659 ed. says, "A kind of winter-wine." Compare It. Vernaccia, a severe winter: see MAYHEW & SKEAT.

Vessclle, *sb.*, 17, 20; Wessell, 91. Vessel; Fr. *Vaisselle*.

Viaundbruse, a Potage, 67; *Viaund Ryal*, 57; *Viaunt Ardant* (probably brought in with flaming spirits), 61; **Vyaund de cyprys bastarde, 21, Vyaund de ciprys Ryalle, 21, Vyaunde de cyprys in lente, 28,** see NAPIER, p. 102, F. of C., Nos. 97, 98, WARNER, pp. 58, 76, L.C.C., p. 8; **Vyande Ryalle, 32,** see F. of C., No. 98, WARNER, p. 76; **Vyand leche, 36, 37, 38,** see NAPIER, p. 41, " *Cold leshe viand* "; **Vyaunde Furne꜀ sau꜀ noum, de chare,** (two Recipes), 49; *Vyand Goderygye*, 63; *Vyand Motlegh*, 63. Fr. *Viande*, Meat.

Vinegar, see *Venegre*.

Umbles, see *Nombles*.

Vnce, *sb.*, 107; Vnces, 106. Ounce.

Vnneth, *adv.*, 84, 85; Vnneþe, 38, 43, 44; Scarcely.

Vnderneiþ, *prep.*, 105; Vnder-nethe, 7. Underneath.

Vn-pullud, 99, Unshred.

Vntrusse, *vb.t.*, 41. Entruss on spit.

Votrelle꜀, 69, is probably the Dish mentioned in NAPIER, p. 44, as " Votose "; the liquid *ll* would give *Votreirs*, and possibly *Voteirs*; after *Mortrews*. *Votose* is made up of Gobbets of Marrow, cut Dates, sugar, powdered Ginger, Saffron, Salt, which is put between leaves of paste, closed, baked, and then cut in pieces two inches square: it is also called *Votese*.

Urchins, see *Yrchons*.

Vyū, *sb.*, 104; Vynnes, 106, Fin.

Vyolet, *sb.*, 5, 29; Vyolette, 23, 29. Violet.

Waffres, 39; Waffrys, 39, 63. Wafers.

Walkys in bruette, 23; Walkys, 60; Welkes boyled, 106, see Douce MS., No. 164, NAPIER, p. 74; Wylkys, 60.

Walnotys, 109. Walnuts.

War, *adj.*, 38. Ware: aware.

Wardons, 87, Wardones, 106; Wardonys in Syryp, 7, see WARNER, p. 72; Quyncis or Wardouns in past, 51; Chardewardon, 12; Chare de Wardone, 88. Warden Pears. " A Warden is like a Quince, but brown and spotted; of them there are several sorts."— HOLME, *Armory*, II. iii. 47.

Ware, *vb.int.*, 42.

Warme hot, 8.

Washe, *vb.t.*, 5; Wassche, 5; Wasshe, 10; Waysshe, 25; Whas, 112; Whess, 112, 114; Wasshen, *pp.*, 84; Wasshem, 18, 20, 23, Wash 'em.

Wast, *vb.*, 25. Waste.

Wastel, *sb.*, 22; Wastel bred, 112, Wastilbrede, 28, Wastylbrede, 28, Wastel bread: bread made of fine flour: Anglo-Fr. *Wastel, Gastel*, Fr. *Gasteau, Gâteau.*

Water, *sb.*, 13; Watere, 42; Watre, 109.

Watteryd, *adj.*, 26. Watered; soaked, to get the salt out.

Way, *sb.*, 73. Whey.

Wesing, *sb.*, 80; Wesyng, 116, 117. Weasand.

Wessell, *sb.*, 91. Vessel.

Wete, *sb.*, 105. Wheat.

Wete, *vb.t.*, 11, 48, 105; *adj.*, 48. Wet.

Wexe, *vb.int.*, 8, 17, W. hard, 35, Wexyth, 35. Wax; grow.

Whan, *conj.*, 18. When.

Wheder, *adj.*, 33, Whether; whichever.

Whele, *conj.*, 23. While.

Whelks, see *Walkys*.

Whete, *sb.*, 6, 15; Wete, 105. Wheat.

Wheþer-euer, 131. Whither ever, Wherever.

Whetyn floure, 33. Wheaten flour.

Whey, *sb.*, 56; Way, 73.

White of egges, 74, 75; **Whyte Mortrewes**, 19, 28 (Pork), see NAPIER, p. 106, WARNER, p. 62, L.C.C., p. 13, F. of C., No. 46; **W. pesyn in grauey**, 33; Whyte of eyroun, 11, 14, W. of lekys, 14, W. brede, 11, 30, W. sugre, 7, 8. For White Sauces, see *Sauces:* see also *Wyn.*

Whyle, A gret, 26, A long time; A good whylys, 42.

Wine, see *Wyn.*

With-owte, 48; With-ynne & with-owte, 47.

Wodecok, 80, see Douce MS., No. 121, NAPIER, p. 64, "*W. rost*," L.C.C., p. 35, "*W. snyzt, and Curlue.*"

Woldyst, 20, Wouldest.

Wole, *vb.int.*, 31; Wolle, 26; Wolt, 33. Will, Wilt.

Wollen, *adj.*, 32. Woollen.

Wombe, *sb.*, 39, of fish, Belly; 38, 39, of sheep, Maw, stomach; Wombe side vpward, 131.

Wort, *sb.*, 107, Unfermented beer.

Wortes de pesoun, Lange, 5, Longe W. de Pesone, 89 (Pease), see Douce MS., No. 2; Lange Wortys de chare, 5, see Douce MS., No. 1; Whyte wortes, 6; Hare in Wortes, 69; Buttered Wortes, 69, see NAPIER, p. 84, see also NAPIER, p. 82, "*Wortis.*"

Wryng, *vb.t.*, 29; Wryng þorw straynoure, *or* cloþe, 22, 28. Wring.

Wyl, *adv.*, 6, 7, 11, 20, 26; Wylle, 26. Well.

Wylkys, 60. Whelks.

Wyn, *sb.*, 20, Rede wyn, 20; Wyne, 7, 10, 20, Red wyne, 10, 26, Wyne crete (of Crete), 48, Swete Wyne, 22, 35, Whyte Wyne, 15, 35, Rochelle Wyne, 15. Wine.

Wyth, *prep.*, 13, With; Wyth-owte, 12.

Y-bake, 51, Y-baken, 54, Baked; Y-blaunchyd, 31, Blanched; Y-bontyd, 38, Bunted, sifted; Y-bounde with Floure of Rys, 39, Made stiff;

Y-boylid, 10, 18, Y-boylyd, 6; Y-braid, 48, Pounded; Y-broylid, 47; Y-choppid, 33, 46; Y-chowchyd, 26, Y-couched, laid; Y-clepid, 43; Y-closyd, 48, Closed (of a pie); Y-corven, 23, Cut; Y-coryd, 46, Cored; Y-cutte, 51; Y-dicyd, 22, Cut into dice; Y-draw, 6, 9, 10, 11, 15, 33, Y-drawe, 26, Drawn through strainer, see the verb *Draw;* Y-dressid, 8, 11, Dressed for table; Y-farsyd, 40, Stuffed; Y-fastenyd, 50; Y-gratyd, 15, 19; Y-grounde, 13, 18, 23, 110; Y-hackyd, 55; Y-harded, 99, Y-hardid, 52, Hardened; Y-heled, 112, Y-helid, 40, Y-helyd, 54, Covered; Y-hole, 22, this may be uncut, with the stones in; possibly *skinned*, Hulled; A. also reads thus: Y-kremyd, 40, Crimmed, crumbled; Y-kyt, 55, Cut; Y-leched, 86, Y-lechyd, 35, Leched, cut in strips; Y-like, 20, Alike; Y-mad, 6, 12, 51, made; Y-makyd, 49, Made; Y-mellid, 55, Y-mellyd, 28, 55, Mingled; Y-mengyd, 38, Menged, Mixed; Y-mynced, 6, 14, 18, Y-mynsyd, 13, Minced; Y-opened, 114; Y-pode. 29, ? Y-pared, pared (A. also reads thus): Y-pekid, 41, Y-pikyd, 37, Picked; Y-peyntid, 29, Painted; Y-pileyd, 37, Peeled; Y-rollyd, 48, Rolled; Y-rosted, 106, 114, Y-rostyd, 23, 38, Roasted; Y-schred, 49, Y-schredyd, 29. Y-scredde, 40, Shredded; Y-Skaldyd, 22, Scalded; Y-smete, 55, Smitten, chopped; Y-sode, 19, Y-sothe, 23, 37, 55, Sodden, boiled; Y-stekyd, 52, Y-stykyd, 35, Stuck; Y-strainyd, 17, Y-straynid, 55, Strained through strainer; Y-stwyde, 9, stewed; Y-swengyd, 25, Y-swonge, 35, 38, Swung, shaken, mixed; Y-take, 88, Taken; Y-tallyd, 27, Y-taylid, 27, 33, Cut, Fr. *Tailler;* Y-temperyd, 7, 17, 28, Mixed; Y-tryid, 11, 15, 36, 51, 52, Picked, separated, the last example apparently meaning "strained through strainer;" Y-wasche, 7, Y-wasshe, 23, 114, Washed; Y-wateryd, 43, Soaked; Y-wet, 102, 106, Y-wette, 52, Wet, steeped; Y-wreten, 21, Written; Y-wronge oute, 84, 91, Wrung out.

Yeest, 96, Yeast.

Y-fere, 18, Together.

Y-liche moche, 70, A like much, or quantity.

Ynouti, *adv.*, 75; Y-now, 5, 6, 8; Ynowe, 19, 35. Enough.

Yrchons, 3; Yrchouns, 38. 61, 62. Urchins; hedgehogs. See WARNER, p. 66, "*Urchonys.*" So called from being made bristly with Almonds.

Yreñ, *sb.*, 93. Iron.

Ys, 17, Is.

Yt, 15, 17, 35. It.

ȝelow, *adj.*, 20, 30. Yellow.

ȝere, *sb.*, 15, 29, 47. Year.

ȝest, *sb.*, 10, 44. Yeast.

ȝet, *pron.*, 31. It.

ȝif, *vb.t.*, 22, 29, 112. Give.

ȝif, *conj.*, 7, 9, 10, 11, 12, 30, 47. If.

ȝolkes of egges, 109; ȝolkys, 8, 9, 11, 12, 19, 29. Yolks.

ȝong, *adj.*, 54; ȝonge, 31. Young.

ȝynes, *sb.*, 37. Sinews.

STEPHEN AUSTIN AND SONS, PRINTERS, HERTFORD.

www.ingramcontent.com/pod-product-compliance
Lightning Source LLC
Chambersburg PA
CBHW020547270326
41927CB00006B/753